AUSTRALIAN
HERITAGE COOKING
FOR THE MICROWAVE

AUSTRALIAN HERITAGE COOKING
FOR THE MICROWAVE

general editor
MARIE McDONALD

Books For Pleasure

First published in 1991 by
Books for Pleasure
372 Eastern Valley Way
Willoughby NSW 2068, Australia

Reprinted in 1991

Produced by Weldon Russell Pty Ltd
4/52 Ourimbah Road
Mosman NSW 2088, Australia

A member of the Weldon International
Group of companies

National Library of Australia
Cataloguing in Publication data

Australian heritage cooking for the microwave.

  Includes index.
  ISBN 1 875202 35 8.

  1. Microwave cookery. I. McDonald, Marie.

641.5882

Publisher: Elaine Russell
Managing editor: Dawn Titmus
Project coordinators: Ariana Klepac, Jacquelin Hochmuth
Home economist consultant: Betty Dunleavy
Principal photographer: Rowan Fotheringham
Home economist, food and prop stylist: Carolyn Fienberg
Designer: Catherine Martin
Design assistant: Jean Meynert
Copy editor: Doreen Grézoux
Indexer: Glenda Downing
Illustrators: Vasanti Jansson, Jan Smith
Production: Jane Hazell

Typeset by Savage Type Pty Ltd, Brisbane, Australia
Separations by Scantrans, Singapore
Printed by Griffin Press, Netley, South Australia, Australia

A KEVIN WELDON PRODUCTION

MEASUREMENTS USED IN THIS BOOK

Standard Australian metric cups and spoons are used
to measure many of the ingredients for the recipes in
this book.

• All spoon and cup measures are level.
• The Australian metric cup holds 250 ml of liquid
ingredients, the half cup holds 125 ml and so on.
• The Australian metric tablespoon holds 20 ml of
liquid ingredients and the teaspoon 5 ml.

It should be noted that while the Australian tablespoon
is the equivalent of 4 (5 ml) teaspoons, a number of
other countries use a 15 ml (or 3 teaspoon) tablespoon.

Contents

Understanding Your Microwave Oven

There are five important points to understand about your microwave oven:

- It is easy to use
- It is completely safe
- Its versatility and potential are boundless
- Cooking is faster and more economical than traditional methods of cooking
- It is cool and clean

The microwave oven is considered by the converted to be as essential in the kitchen as a refrigerator, a freezer and a traditional oven. It is a very different method of cooking, but once you have become proficient you will wonder how you managed to cope without it.

One of the joys of microwave cooking is being able to have last-minute thoughts about your meal preparations. Desserts, for instance, can frequently be cooked while you are eating the main course.

Best of all, there will be a good deal less washing-up as many foods are cooked and served in the same dish. There is none of the sticking and congealing often associated with conventional cooking, making washing-up much easier.

Microwave energy does not affect the flavour of food. In fact, many foods cooked in the microwave oven taste better than when cooked conventionally and because of the nature and speed of microwave cooking, fewer nutrients and flavours are lost.

Many of the containers already in your kitchen are suitable for use in the microwave oven. (See Cooking Containers, page 16.)

READ YOUR INSTRUCTION MANUAL

Not all microwave ovens operate in exactly the same way, so the first rule when getting to know your oven is to read the manual. This book has been written for straight microwave ovens, not for combination or convection microwave ovens, though all the recipes are, of course, suitable for any microwave oven.

The recipes in this book have been tested in a standard 650 watt oven. Ovens with less power will need a little more time and those with more power less time. If in doubt, always be guided by your oven's instruction manual.

POWER LEVELS

The recipes in this book give the power level at which they should be cooked followed by the percentage of power, for example, HIGH (100%). Not all microwave ovens use the same terms for these power levels. A setting of 'LOW' on one oven might be called 'WARM' on another. To avoid confusion, be guided by the *percentage* given in the recipes in this book. For example, where one of these recipes calls for 50% power, choose the power level on your oven which is halfway between the lowest setting and the highest; for 30% power, choose a point one-third of the distance.

The following table provides a guide to the suggested variations in cooking time if you are using an oven other than a standard 650 watt oven. For example, if a vegetable recipe from this book takes 4 minutes to cook, it will need 20 seconds less in a 700 watt oven (that is, 5 less seconds per each of the 4 minutes), and 20 seconds more in a 600 watt oven.

ADJUSTMENT TO COOKING TIMES	
POWER	CHANGE OF TIMING PER MINUTE (+ OR −)
700 watt	− 5 seconds
650 watts	no change
600 watts	+ 5 seconds
550 watts	+ 10 seconds
500 watts	+ 20 seconds
450 watts	+ 30 seconds
400 watts	+ 40 seconds

POWER FLUCTUATIONS

If you are cooking at a time of peak demand, fluctuations in the power flow may occur. This means you will have to extend recommended cooking times for a recipe. Always set on the minimum time, check for 'doneness', and continue to cook until you are satisfied. You may need only a few seconds more.

When buying an oven most people pick the one that has features which appeal to them, but irrespective of your choice, the food will taste the same no matter which is chosen.

An essential factor to keep in mind when using a microwave oven is that it is better to undercook than overcook — even for a few seconds. Set the oven timer on the minimum time recommended for the recipe, test it, then if it isn't completely cooked, put it back for a few seconds (or minutes, if necessary) to complete cooking. Food overcooked in a microwave oven usually can't be revived!

Cooking with a microwave oven takes a little practice and you will have to rethink some of your customary cooking practices. Don't be disappointed if you have failures — it's part of the learning process.

TAKE IT SLOWLY

If you are a new microwave owner, don't be pressured by the family to cook the whole evening meal by microwave the day the oven arrives. It would almost certainly be a disaster. Start by cooking only one part of the meal — say, the vegetables, and gradually build up to all the menu, if you wish. Having everything come together at the right time takes a little practice but before long you'll be organising this without giving it a second thought.

You'll find that not all foods respond as well as you would like them to, but never overlook the fact that while this is so, there are few recipes that can't be cut short by the use of a microwave oven for at least a small part of their preparation.

HOW YOUR MICROWAVE OVEN WORKS

The energy used in microwave ovens is in the form of electromagnetic waves and is similar to the shortwave energy powering television sets, medical equipment and ultraviolet lamps. If you are puzzled about how 'waves' can cook, particularly in the absence of heat, carry out this simple experiment. Rub your hands together briskly. The heat you feel is caused by friction. This is similar to the effect that microwaves have when they come in contact with food. The waves cause the liquid or moisture molecules in the food to vibrate at an incredibly fast rate (2450 million times per second!).

Remembering that just rubbing your hands together generates some heat, it is easy to understand that the astonishingly fast rate of vibration of the moisture molecules in the food produces enough heat for cooking.

The waves themselves are not hot, they act on the moisture molecules in the food itself to generate heat for cooking. This means that the oven and the utensils used to hold the food do not become hot. An exception to this is a bowl of soup or any dish containing a very moist food or some liquid — after a certain length of time some heat will be transferred to the dish and it may become warm or even hot.

THE COOKING PROCESS

The microwaves are emitted from a magnetron (similar to the picture tube in a television set) into the oven. The waves are reflected by the metal walls, floor and ceiling of the oven, like light being reflected by a mirror, and bounce back and forth in an irregular pattern.

Some ovens use a turntable, others a stirrer fan to distribute the waves evenly so they enter the food from all angles. When cooking some foods it is recommended that they be raised from their usual position in the oven to attract more microwaves. The recipe will usually suggest 'elevating' the cooking container. This can be done by either using a microwave rack or simply an upturned microwave-safe cereal bowl or something similar under the cooking container.

Non-metal containers are used so that the waves pass through them and are not reflected away. On some occasions commercial products packaged in shallow metal trays — such as prepared meals — are heated, but not cooked, by

●

**For successful cakes use recipes
specially formulated for the microwave
and elevate the cooking pan on a
microwave-safe rack or bowl.**

●

microwave. (See Cooking Containers, page 16.)

The food absorbs the waves, but not in the way that we are sometimes told. Foods do *not* cook from the inside out, nor do microwaves constantly pass right through the food. In fact the waves penetrate only 2–4 cm (¾–1½ in) into food, depending on its density. The rest of the cooking is done by conduction or transfer of the heat through to the centre. Thus a beef roast *can* be cooked so that it is brown outside but still pleasantly pink, inside.

CONDITIONS THAT AFFECT COOKING TIMES

Foods taken straight from the refrigerator take longer to cook than the same types of food at room temperature.

Thick slices of particular foods take longer to cook than the same foods cut thinly, and a joint of meat such as a leg of lamb tends to cook more quickly at the thin or shank end than it does at the thicker end.

Foods can be arranged carefully in the oven to avoid over or undercooking. For example the thicker stalk ends of cauliflower or broccoli should be placed towards the outer edge of the cooking dish. The thinner end of a leg of lamb may be covered for part of the cooking time with a small piece of aluminium foil. Although this might seem a contradiction of the rule of 'no metal' for cooking in the microwave oven, the quantity of foil is very small compared with the size of the meat, so no harm is done and the thinner end is protected from overcooking.

SHAPE AND DENSITY

For the best results, food should be as uniform in shape as possible. However, more often than not, some parts are thicker than others, as with chicken or a leg of lamb. Parts that are thinner — wing tips, drumsticks, the ends of a joint, the tail ends of fish — should be covered with a small piece of aluminium foil to prevent overcooking or burning. (The foil should never touch the sides of the oven.)

Masking food with sauce is another effective shield and protects food from drying out.

ARE MICROWAVE OVENS SAFE?

The microwave oven has an excellent safety record. In the 15 years it has been in use in Australian kitchens, including restaurants, cooking schools and technical colleges, there is no record of injury to any microwave oven user.

All ovens sold in this country must meet the stringent safety standards of the electricity supply authorities in each state before they are allowed to be sold to either commercial or domestic users.

Microwave ovens have door-locking controls which ensure that the power is turned off automatically immediately the oven door is opened. If you feel that your microwave oven is not operating correctly, contact the manufacturer's service centre or the local electricity authority.

ADVANTAGES

There are a few things that the microwave oven doesn't do as well as a conventional oven but these are overshadowed by the host of outstanding advantages:

• Cooks with great speed. A roast will cook in less than half the time it would take in a conventional oven.

• Preheating is not necessary, so running costs are much less than for a conventional oven.

• Easier to clean as fat and spilt food do not bake onto the sides of the oven. Just wipe out with a damp cloth after each use. (Never use oven-cleaning sprays in a microwave oven — see page 19 for more information about cleaning a microwave oven.)

• Kitchen remains cool and comfortable as no heat is generated by the oven — only the food heats.

• Simple installation means the oven can be moved easily — take it to a holiday house or caravan and simply plug it in to the nearest power point.

• Food defrosts in a fraction of the time normally taken, giving freezer-to-table cookery a whole new dimension.

• Reheats food without spoiling. Food does not lose its original shape, flavour or nutrient value. This is a great advantage where family members eat at different times.

• You can use a wide variety of containers such as glass, china and a wide range of plastics as well as oven bags, cling wrap and paper. (See Cooking Containers, page 16.)

• Versatility: the microwave oven speeds up food preparation in many practical ways. It can soften butter or margarine in moments, melt chocolate and honey, dry fresh herbs in minutes and roast nuts.

• Ideal cooking method for children, the disabled and the blind because microwave ovens are at bench level, are safe and easy to use.

• Many cooking containers can be removed from the oven without wearing oven mitts.

COOKING CONTAINERS

It is now possible to buy a wide range of cookware made specifically for microwave use. Some are also suitable for lower-temperature use in conventional and convection ovens. Often it's a case of deciding between the cheaper container, possibly with a shorter lifespan, or one which is a good deal more expensive but which, with care, may last a lifetime — a decision that should be considered carefully before buying.

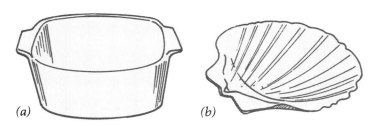

(a) Microwave-safe casserole, usually with lid.
(b) Scallop shell. Perfect for individual seafood starters.

CONTAINER SIZE

Container size may be an important factor in cooking certain foods by microwave.

• A single layer of food will cook more quickly in a wider, shallow container than the same amount placed into a smaller, deeper one in several layers.

• If a large container is used for a small quantity of food, ensure that the food is evenly spaced around the edge of the container for more efficient cooking.

• A tightly packed container does not allow the microwaves to enter as many surfaces of the food as one where each piece is separated slightly, resulting in longer and more even cooking.

NOTE The exception to these last two points occurs when a quantity of thinly cut and similarly textured vegetables are cooked in a bundle or 'parcel' enclosed in microwave-safe cling wrap. These vegetables, as explained in the chapter on vegetables, have the added benefit of concentrated steam to hasten their cooking and provide a more even build-up of heat.

• Larger, deeper containers are advisable for foods with more liquid, such as soups and stews. All food cooks more quickly at the outer edges of the container, so remember to stir regularly. The larger container lessens the possibility of boil-overs or spillage during handling.

CONTAINER SHAPE

The ideal container, one that receives the maximum, even amount of microwaves for absorption into the food, should be round, with straight sides and slightly rounded at the base edges. Ring-shaped containers allow microwaves to enter the container and food from the sides as well as the middle, providing more evenly cooked food in a shorter time. They are ideal for cakes, baked desserts, meatloaves, combination rice and pasta dishes and cut fruits and vegetables.

Narrow loaf pans are not as efficient as more compact types. The extremities receive the bulk of the microwaves and can cause overcooking. Strips of aluminium foil may be used to shield the corners or the whole end section for part of the cooking time to prevent this happening. The foil should be well secured, to ensure that it does not come into contact with the walls of the oven.

Square or rectangular containers would benefit from similar shielding at the corners.

Use deep, large, open-topped containers for any food likely to bubble up during cooking — rice, pasta, milk, liquids, jams and so on. When first cooking these foods, watch closely to assess suitable maximum quantities in future cooking. For jam and confectionery making, it is preferable to cook in smaller batches rather than risk dangerous and costly boil-overs.

THE RING MOULD

Because of the nature of microwave cooking, one of the most convenient containers is the ring or tube mould or pan. If you don't own a microwave-safe container of this kind, you can always 'make' one from one of your round microwave-safe casserole dishes by putting a greased, straight-sided glass in the centre to act as the tube. This works quite well for some cakes and puddings. However, the specially manufactured microwave variation would be a very worthwhile purchase. If you can manage it, buy two — one large enough for favourite family cakes and puddings and one smaller, but large enough to take your favourite

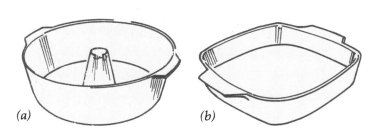

(a) Ring dish in microwave-safe plastic or glass. Ideal for cakes and puddings.
(b) Browning dish. For pan-frying or roasting.

meatloaf mixture. (Always check the cup volume of favourite recipes and compare the volume with the capacity of the available cookware.) Take into account that some cakes and puddings rise more when cooked by microwave. In some cases the rise may be only temporary, with the mixture subsiding a little before it is finally cooked; however, it must be taken into consideration if a spill-over is to be avoided.

BROWNING DISHES

Because of the speed of microwave cookery, special techniques are sometimes necessary to make food brown and appetising. Though rather expensive, browning dishes and grills provide the best means of achieving this aim and also represent one of the best investments you will make.

Usually made of glass ceramic (Crown Corning makes the best-known dishes), they have a special tin oxide coating on the bottom of the dish which absorbs microwave energy.

This is the only piece of equipment you can put, empty, into an oven while it is in operation. After a heating period of 5–8 minutes it will sear, brown and crisp the surface of the food while the rest is cooked by microwave energy.

This is ideal cookware for foods that would normally be grilled or fried such as sausages, chops, steak, hamburgers, toasted sandwiches, grilled fish or chicken. It is also used for browning roasts prior to cooking.

A browning dish becomes very hot and should be handled with oven-mitts. The heated dish should not be placed directly onto a kitchen bench that is not heatproof.

The dishes come in different types and sizes. They should never be covered with plastic wrap as it could melt and stick to the dish. The dish comes with its own lid, though when being used for a roast, it is advisable to cover meats with kitchen paper towel to prevent spattering — the lid would give the roast a braised result because of the steam trapped.

CONTAINERS WITH HANDLES

The most useful microwave containers are certainly those with handles. This is particularly so for new or inexperienced cooks and for the very young and the elderly. On some occasions the handles may remain reasonably cool, on others they may not. A quick touch will tell if oven-mitts are required. If you intend cooking large quantities of a casserole or similar food with a high liquid content, it is strongly recommended that a container with handles on either side be used. For these reasons Corning Ware, or similar quality containers are particularly useful for microwave use.

If you must use containers without handles, they are often easier to lift and carry when placed in the oven on a larger, shallow dish or plate.

Wide-necked jugs with large handles are ideal for many areas of microwave cooking. They are particularly suitable for sauces and custards where regular stirring is required. The purchase of several microwave-safe spoons or whisks for these occasions would be a very good investment.

MULTI-PURPOSE CONTAINERS

Though these, if of good quality, are more expensive than others, it is wise to consider how useful they could be, relative to your particular lifestyle. As finances allow, plan to build up a small collection of containers that are truly multi-purpose — suitable for direct conventional stove-top, convection and conventional oven, to withstand temperatures of 180-200°C and which are both freezer and dishwasher safe. Think of those occasions when a savoury dish or dessert has been cooked in the microwave and then the finishing touch is recommended — 'Brown lightly under a heated grill' — and you know or suspect the container you have used is not flameproof.

To be quite sure of your position with these special containers always check the manufacturer's guarantee. Limitations on use are usually stamped on the underside of these containers.

DISPOSABLE CONTAINERS

Apart from those used for packaged, frozen convenience foods, there are a few disposable containers available which are suitable for microwave cooking. These are manufactured from lightweight plastic, polyester-coated pressed paper and semi-rigid aluminium foil. Always use only as suggested in label instructions.

CHINA AND POTTERY

Do not use precious fine china in the microwave oven. Other china may be used if it is glazed and has no metal trim. Unglazed earthenware or pottery could absorb microwaves and should not be used. While many *glazed* pottery mugs are safe to use in the microwave oven, some become unnaturally hot when used, apparently because of the particular glaze involved. (See directions for testing container suitability on page 18.) If any items of china or pottery are cracked, it is possible that moisture has been absorbed during use or washing. Check these items for suitability also, as heating could cause a fracture where cracked.

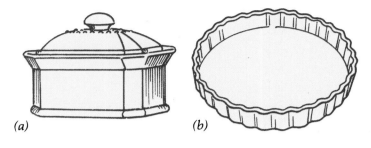

(a)   *(b)*

(a) Glazed china dish with lid. Large dishes of this type can be used as casseroles for cooking and serving.
(b) Glazed china flan dish. For pies with crumb or pastry bases.

CERAMIC

Utensils such as Corning Ware, or similar quality containers, may be used. Glass ceramic utensils can be used for microwaving and serving as well as on stove-tops and in conventional ovens.

GLASS

Crystal bowls or glasses must not be used in the microwave oven. Ovenware glass, such as Pyrex, (or similar quality containers), may be used as long as there is no metal trim. These are quite inexpensive, versatile and widely available. Use clear glass for pies, cakes and bread so you can check cooking progress by looking at the food through the base of the container. One should note, however, that for many cake and pudding recipes glass does not give as clean a 'turn-out' as some of the special plastic microwave containers.

WOOD, CANE AND STRAW

Though some short-term use of wood and cane containers for heating is sometimes recommended, it is felt that this should only be on rare occasions. Reports of damage to wooden bowls and cracking of cane or straw in baskets is not encouraging for regular use of these items. It is better to heat rolls, croissants and Danish pastries wrapped in kitchen paper or cloth napkins and then transfer them, still wrapped, to the bowl or basket for serving. If you decide to use these containers in the oven, check that wooden bowls have not been bonded with glue or coated with a special protective covering and that cane baskets have no metal binding.

PAPER

Since the advent of the microwave oven, paper towels have saved an inestimable amount of washing-up! There are many daily occasions when a paper towel can fill the role of container and napkin for hand-held savoury treats. It also plays a major role in absorbing fat and preventing spattering when cooking sausages or bacon.

COTTON AND LINEN

These pure fibres may be used to cover foods for reheating. Synthetic materials are not suitable. A damp serviette, for instance, will refresh stale bread, scones or muffins for quick reheating.

TO TEST IF CONTAINERS ARE MICROWAVE-SAFE

Cooking containers that are safe to use in the microwave oven are those that transmit microwaves, are non-porous, do not overheat and of course those that will not melt or warp.

If you are uncertain of the suitability of a container, whether it's one already in your possession or a recent acquisition, test it in the following way:
1. Place a cup filled with water in the dish, to be tested (in the case of the mug, place the cup separately, of course).
2. Set the timer for 1½ minutes and heat on HIGH (100%).
3. If the water is warm and the container cool, you may use the container for cooking by microwave. If the container is slightly warm around the edges, it may be used for short-term cooking or reheating. If the water is cool and the dish, plate or mug hot, do not use that item in the oven for any reason.

PLASTICS UNSUITABLE FOR USE IN THE MICROWAVE OVEN

Do not use plastic ware such as Melamine or Tupperware. Melamine becomes very hot and is unsafe to use. Tupperware is unsuitable for both long-term use, and for cooking foods that require lengthy cooking times in the microwave.

MICROWAVE OVEN ACCESSORIES

A good range of microwave oven accessories is available which in many ways makes life a little easier when cooking by microwave.

MICROWAVE SPOONS AND WHISKS

These are among the most economical purchases but also among the most used. It's very convenient to be able to leave a stirrer in a dish during cooking, particularly with frequently stirred sauces.

JUGS OR BOWLS WITH HANDLES

These have many uses and the handle adds stability during stirring. Look for a small microwave-

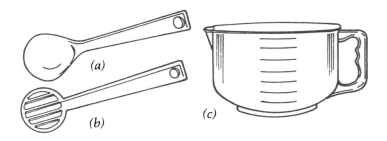

*(a) Plastic stirring spoon. (b) Plastic whisk.
(c) Clear plastic jug with handle. Can be used for measuring liquid ingredients or for mixing and cooking in the same container.*

safe plastic mug which comes with a lid — very handy for small quantities of vegetables, heating a single serve of soup or if you like a boiled egg for breakfast (wrapped in foil of course and immersed in water). It's just the right size and the handle keeps you safe from the boiling water.

A SET OF CUSTARD CUPS

These have many more uses other than cooking single serves of baked custard. Use them for melting butter, chocolate or copha, softening gelatine, poaching eggs, cooking baked apples and heating baby food.

MICROWAVE-SAFE FREEZER BAGS

These are great for cooking vegetables and they save on washing-up.

MICROWAVE-SAFE PLASTIC WRAP

This must be the ideal 'lid' for many microwaved foods. You can see what's happening inside and the steam contained will frequently speed up the cooking and keep valuable moisture trapped. Only plastic wrap recommended for use in microwaves should be used.

MICROWAVE RACKS

These are a valuable asset when it is desirable to keep food above moisture or fat which collects in a container during cooking. The racks can also be used to elevate dishes when required.

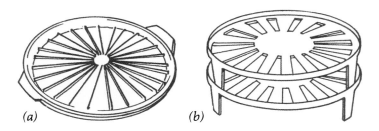

*(a) Roasting rack. Keeps meat roasts above the juices released by cooking.
(b) Two microwave racks stacked for heating separate dishes of food.*

KITCHEN PAPER TOWELS

These have many uses. They will cover food to stop spattering, or if you forget to cover, you'll use them to mop up the result! Use them as a 'plate' to hold a muffin for defrosting or heating. They are invaluable for soaking up unwanted fat when cooking bacon.

METAL IN THE MICROWAVE

The only metal suitable for use in the microwave oven is aluminium foil. Small pieces are used to shield sections of food to avoid overcooking or overthawing. They should never cover more than 30% of the food, should be flat and unwrinkled and kept clear of oven walls to avoid arcing which could damage the oven. If necessary, secure the pieces of foil to the food with wooden toothpicks. Commercially frozen convenience foods in *shallow* foil containers may be defrosted and reheated by microwave. Remove any foil covers and replace with microwave-safe plastic wrap. Loosen plastic-coated paper board lids to allow steam to escape.

TO CLEAN THE MICROWAVE OVEN

If food is covered, either lightly with paper towels or closely with plastic wrap or a lid, the oven should stay reasonably clean. However, should some spattering of food or a spill-over occur, wipe out with a damp cloth. If the food spots are stubborn, allow a cup of water to boil in the oven for 2–3 minutes to create some steam to help loosen the food and then wipe again with a warm damp cloth.

If these efforts are unsuccessful, try either a creamy liquid cleaner applied to a damp cloth or a metal cleaner recommended for use on stainless steel, used as directed on the container.

If a fishy odour remains after cooking seafood, add two or three slices of lemon or a few drops of vanilla essence to a small bowl of water and boil for several minutes.

CONVERTING YOUR FAVOURITE RECIPES

Many favourite recipes can be converted for the microwave oven, but it is not recommended that you try these conversions until you become familiar with microwave cooking in general. Once you become reasonably comfortable with the general principles, find a microwave recipe that bears some resemblance to one of your own favourites and take it from there.

SAVOURY DISHES

When converting savoury dishes you'll need to reduce some flavourings and seasonings. Herbs and spices are stronger in microwave cookery so use a lighter hand when adding these.

Because many microwave cooking procedures take half and in some instances even a third the cooking time of a conventional oven, there will frequently be less evaporation, so as a general rule when converting recipes with a reasonable amount of liquid among the ingredients, use one-third less liquid when cooking by microwave.

Ensure that meat pieces in casserole-type recipes are covered by liquid to prevent the meat drying out. If necessary, place a sheet of baking paper over the surface and immerse any exposed meat in the liquid. Cut meat and vegetables into fairly small, uniform pieces for quicker and more even cooking.

When adding seafood to other ingredients, do so at the last possible moment so that the flesh, which cooks very quickly by microwave, does not overcook and toughen.

For best results with roasts you will certainly need a browning dish — see recipe for Stuffed Loin of Lamb (page 133) for correct use.

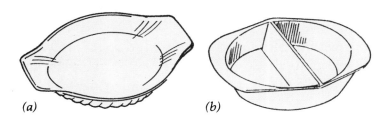

(a)   (b)

(a) Vegetable dish. Suitable for cooking and serving au gratin vegetables.
(b) Divided vegetable dish.

VEGETABLES

When preparing vegetable dishes, take into account the speed of microwave cooking and don't cook the vegetables too far ahead of the time you wish to serve them. In fact, if the vegetables have been prepared in advance and are in their container ready for the oven, it may not be necessary for you to begin to cook them until a few minutes before serving the meal. This timing may not work out perfectly for the first two or three trial runs, but in no time it will become a matter of routine.

BAKING

Where baking is concerned a few basic rules will soon give you a clear understanding of the best types of mixture for good results with cakes and biscuits. See the introduction to the Scones, Cakes, Biscuits and Sweets chapter.

DESSERTS

Baked desserts, particularly with a cake-like base, are best cooked in a ring pan. This applies also to those that are self-saucing and those that have a base of fruit set in a pattern and are turned out to serve.

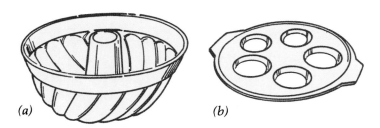

(a)   (b)

(a) Fluted microwave-safe glass ring dish. Used for cakes and desserts.
(b) Plastic patty pan. For muffins and cupcakes.

RECIPES NOT SUITABLE FOR MICROWAVING

Never attempt to deep-fry in the microwave oven. Oils reach dangerously high temperatures in the microwave oven and, in any case, the whole principle of deep-frying could not be carried out in an enclosed oven.

Pies and other pastry items rely for their success on crisp textures and well-browned surfaces. The microwave oven will not produce satisfactory results for these items. Crisp, crusted Yorkshire pudding and soufflés, along with pizzas, are also unsuccessful. Pizza bases of a sort may be cooked, but they will not produce a truly crisp crust.

STANDING TIME

The action of microwaves on food causes cooking to continue after food is taken from the oven. It is wise to remove many foods from the oven before they appear fully cooked and then allow them to stand. Cooking will continue during this time.

This may seem rather complicated but you will soon become an expert at knowing the exact time to stop cooking. For example, baked custards should be removed from the oven before they seem fully set.

Jacket potatoes should not have a 'sagged' look after cooking — in fact they should feel quite firm. If the potato 'gives' when pressed lightly, it is almost certain you have overcooked it. Test instead with a fine metal cake tester. If it will pass through the potato with barely any resistance, wrap the potato in foil and let it stand for up to 5 minutes, when it should be perfectly cooked. If not, remove the foil and give it another half minute in the oven.

You will soon learn that cooking, particularly in foods that have a skin, such as potatoes, will continue for some time after the power has been turned off. So don't be tempted to give that extra minute for good measure!

Many foods need standing time after microwave cooking — the larger the food mass, the longer the suggested standing time. (See Food Defrosting Guide for extra periods of standing time recommended for some foods, page 235.)

STEP-BY-STEP MENU PLANNING

You need a different approach to meal planning when you begin to use a microwave oven so that everything comes together at the right time with the minimum of fuss. These tips will help you achieve just that. Once you have cooked and perfected a few simple dishes in the microwave oven you'll want to combine various dishes to make a complete meal. The aim is to use your oven as much as you can.

The problem is that the speed of the microwave often confuses the cook used to timing things conventionally. As well, you must include standing time to complete cooking.

The idea is to cook in steps.

Most of the time you once spent preparing and cooking is now spent planning. Dishes you once cooked last may now be done well ahead and reheated at the last minute. You can cook vegetables, for example, while the meat is completing cooking (standing time) outside the oven. As you become more confident, planning becomes second nature.

These six simple steps will show you how:
1. Allow plenty of time to plan your first few meals so you won't feel rushed. Try to have one of the courses cold — either the entrée or dessert — so you can prepare in advance. Many soups, like vichyssoise, carrot and tomato are equally delicious hot or cold. Heating up only takes minutes, in any case.
2. Preparation — peeling, cutting and placing of vegetables in cooking containers, partial cooking of some meats — can be done several hours ahead and left, covered, in the refrigerator. Casseroles, once cooked, don't dry out when they are reheated gently in the oven. You can heat them while you

are eating the preceding course of the meal.
3. As a main course, joints of meat that require standing time offer the beginner the most flexibility. They can stand and continue to cook, under foil, outside the oven while vegetables are cooking inside the oven. Some vegetables, like jacket potatoes and sweet corn, when wrapped in foil retain their heat for 15 minutes.
4. Soups and gravies can be cooked well in advance. Put them in a serving dish and gently reheat as required.
5. Place bread rolls in a cotton or linen-lined straw basket and warm through at the last moment. (A straw basket is quite safe to use here as it will only be in the oven for a few seconds.) Over-warming causes rolls to dry out and become unpalatable.
6. Always try to cook food in the dish you plan to serve it in. This helps retain heat during standing time and it can be popped back in the oven for a quick, last-minute warming before serving.

KEEP IN MIND THE FOLLOWING:
Some foods should be cooked only once. Vegetables are best cooked just before serving, especially cabbage, Brussels sprouts and broccoli which become soggy if reheated.

Seafood, egg and cheese dishes cook very quickly and should be done at the last minute to prevent toughening.

Egg and cheese dishes can sometimes separate on reheating.

Fish dishes, especially without a covering sauce, dry out and overcook easily on reheating. Fish doesn't reheat well, so it is always best cooked at the last minute.

Dishes that benefit from using the conventional oven and the microwave in conjunction with each other include roast or baked dinners. Only small quantities of roast potatoes and roast pumpkin can be cooked successfully by microwave — and do not attempt to cook Yorkshire pudding in the microwave oven. Therefore it makes sense to use the conventional oven for roasting the meat and other suitable dishes such as Yorkshire pudding, leaving the microwave free to cook additional accompanying vegetables or the dessert.

Rice and pasta dishes, too, cook well in the microwave, but take the same length of time as they would if cooked conventionally. It makes sense then to cook the pasta or rice on top of the stove and prepare the sauce in the microwave. You'll still be saving a lot of time.

Appetisers, Snacks and Soups

SIMPLE SNACKS

Snack foods for family eating are more quickly available with a microwave oven. Using a base of toast, large cracker biscuits, pita bread or toasted muffins, any number of tasty snacks can be had in the space of a couple of minutes. Try a thin spread of commercial pasta sauce or a slice of tomato topped with a little chopped onion or spring onion and grated cheese on any of these bases and heat in the microwave oven for a minute, or until the cheese begins to melt. If you prefer the base to remain crisp, take a bowl of a similar mixture of ingredients, adding a dash of Tabasco or other favourite seasoning, heat by microwave and let everyone spoon on his or her own topping.

APPETISERS

One of the problems of planning the type and quantity of appetisers, particularly when catering for a crowd, is the uncertainty of just how many will be required. The microwave oven, in conjunction with the freezer, can be a great asset on these occasions. Choose at least some appetisers that freeze well, such as mini meatballs and the sauce that is to accompany them, mini pizzas and savoury tartlets. Because you can rely on the microwave to heat them quickly, there will be no need to have them all available at the same time. In this way there will be no wastage, and treats available for a future occasion.

Seafood appetisers are the least durable of the finger foods served to guests, so it's wise to pass these around first. On the other hand, when seafood is served as a first course at a sit-down occasion, the problem of leftovers doesn't arise. It's not a bad idea, however, to have an alternative first course waiting in the wings — it's surprising how many people are allergic to certain seafoods and you can feel confident that you have something else to take its place and a microwave oven to get it to the table in near record time.

SOUP

Many soups can be frozen successfully. Freeze leftovers in small freezer bags or in servings for two or four, according to your lifestyle. Remember when cooking soup, to use a large cooking container, preferably one that is deep with straight sides. Stir well and often, to ensure that ingredients cook evenly and the soup won't boil over. If converting your own recipes for microwave, remember very little evaporation takes place so cut down on any liquid used by one-third. Shorten cooking time by always adding hot or boiling stock and never season with salt until cooking is complete. When adding herbs remember that these flavours are a little more concentrated when used in microwave recipes.

● *Previous pages, clockwise from top:* Chestnut Charlotte Russe (page 187); Chicken and Asparagus Mornay (page 89); Kipper Pâté (page 27) with Melba Toast (page 27)

● Cheese Fondue

Cheese Fondue

A fondue is a great way to integrate a group of guests who don't know each other. Tradition has it that those who lose their bread piece in the fondue have to pay a forfeit — invent forfeits in advance to suit the company!
The fondue mixture thickens slightly on standing. Care should be taken not to overcook the cheese as it will become stringy.

4 cups (500 g/1 lb) grated Swiss cheese
5 tspns cornflour
1 garlic clove, crushed
freshly ground black pepper
1 tspn ground nutmeg
pinch paprika
1½ cups (375 ml/12 fl oz) dry white wine
French bread for dipping

SERVES 4–6

*I*n a large mixing bowl, combine cheese, cornflour, garlic, pepper, nutmeg and paprika.

Pour the wine into a large 2–3 l (2–3 qt) microwave-safe dish or casserole and heat on HIGH (100%) for 3 minutes, until it begins to steam. Stirring continuously, gradually add half the cheese mixture. Cook, uncovered, on MEDIUM (50%) for 3 minutes. Stir in remaining cheese mixture and continue cooking on MEDIUM for 5–6 minutes, until all cheese is melted and mixture is thick. Stir well.

Pour into a suitable dish or fondue dish and serve with chunks of bread for dipping.

Chicken and Camembert Mousse

A delicious mousse to serve at a summer buffet, or as a luncheon dish with a mixed green salad.

1 cup (125 g/4 oz) Camembert cheese
½ cup (125 ml/4 fl oz) mayonnaise
1 cup (155 ml/5 fl oz) natural yoghurt
¼ cup chopped fresh chives
1 tspn Dijon mustard
1 tspn mixed herbs
2 cups (250 g/8 oz) cooked chicken breast, minced
3 tspns gelatine
⅓ cup (90 ml/3 fl oz) chicken stock

SERVES 12

*C*ombine all ingredients except chicken, gelatine and stock in a food processor; or chop the cheese finely, then beat with the mayonnaise, yoghurt, herbs and mustard until smooth. Mix the gelatine and stock together in a small microwave-safe bowl. Heat on HIGH (100%) for 1 minute to warm stock, then stir well until gelatine is dissolved. Stir into cheese mixture, then gently fold in chicken.

Pour mixture into a wetted 500 ml (16 fl oz) shaped mould. Chill overnight to allow flavours to develop.

Potted Cheese Pâté

A hearty pâté, ideal to serve before a light meal or on crusty bread with soup.

2 cups (250 g/8 oz) grated strongly flavoured Cheddar cheese
3 tbspns strong beer
⅓ cup (90 g/3 oz) butter
pinch mixed dried herbs
caraway seeds
white pepper
4 bay leaves

SERVES 4

*M*elt the cheese, beer, 2 tbspns (45 g/1½ oz) of the butter and seasonings very gently together in a 1 l (1 qt) microwave-safe dish on MEDIUM (50%) for 5–6 minutes, stirring well every minute until melted and thoroughly combined. Remove from oven and beat well until very smooth.

Spoon into individual serving dishes. Allow to set in the refrigerator. Place a bay leaf on top of each dish. Melt remaining butter in a small microwave-safe bowl on HIGH (100%) for 1 minute. Use to seal the cheese.

Chill well before serving. Serve with crackers or hot toast. (See photo page 29.)

Kipper Pâté

3 kipper fillets, skinned and boned
½ cup (125 ml/4 fl oz) thickened cream
black pepper to taste
1 tbspn lemon juice
fresh parsley
twists of lemon

SERVES 4

*P*lace the fish fillets, cream, pepper and lemon juice into a 1 l (1 qt) microwave-safe dish. Cook on MEDIUM (50%) for 10–15 minutes, mashing and mixing several times to blend the cream with the fish. Place in single dish or in four individual dishes. Chill until required. Serve garnished with parsley sprigs and lemon twists and accompanied by Melba Toast. (See photo pages 24–25.)

Melba Toast

This is the ideal partner for your favourite pâté.

½ large, thin-sliced wholemeal loaf of bread

SERVES 4

*R*emove crusts from bread. Cut into triangles and place bread around the outer edge of the turntable of oven or a flat microwave-safe plate. Cook on HIGH (100%) for 2–3 minutes until bread has dried out and is crisp. Repeat process until all bread is used up. Store in an airtight container.

Avocado Seafood

The delicate flavour of avocados is very easily spoilt by overheating. Ensure that the filling rather than the avocados is heated just prior to serving.

100 g (3½ oz) Tasmanian scallops, trimmed, beards removed and well washed
155 g (5 oz) shelled prawns, deveined and well washed
½ cup (125 ml/4 fl oz) water
½ cup (125 ml/4 fl oz) dry white wine
1 tbspn (20 g/¾ oz) butter
4 spring onions, chopped
90 g (3 oz) button mushrooms, wiped and sliced
2 tbspns flour

1 cup (250 ml/8 fl oz) milk
black pepper to taste
few drops chilli sauce (if desired, to taste)
2 large ripe avocados
chopped parsley for garnish

SERVES 4

*P*lace the scallops, prawns, water and wine into a 1 l (1 qt) microwave-safe dish. Cover with a well-fitting lid or plastic wrap and cook on HIGH (100%) for 3 minutes. Remove seafood from the dish and continue heating the cooking liquid for 5 minutes, until the liquid boils and reduces by at least half. Set liquid aside.

Melt the butter in dish on HIGH for 1 minute. Add the spring onions, re-cover dish and cook on HIGH for 2 minutes. Stir in the mushrooms and continue cooking on HIGH for 1–2 minutes until mushrooms are tender. Remove dish from oven. Stir in the flour, milk, reserved cooking liquid and pepper. Heat on HIGH for 4–5 minutes, stirring every 1 minute until liquid boils and thickens. Stir in seafood. Adjust seasonings to taste, adding a little chilli sauce if desired.

Cut avocados in half, remove stones and place each half in a microwave-safe dish. Divide seafood sauce between the avocados and place in stone cavities. Set on outer edge of turntable. Heat on HIGH for 5 minutes until heated through. Sprinkle with chopped parsley. Serve hot.

Stuffed Mushrooms

*The lemon rind and juice give these mushrooms a real zing.
Great at a barbecue or served as a first course at a dinner
party.*

8 medium-sized mushrooms, wiped clean
1 tbspn (20 g/¾ oz) butter or margarine
1 rasher bacon, rind removed and chopped
¾ cup (45 g/1½ oz) fresh breadcrumbs
2 tspns chopped fresh parsley
1 hardboiled egg, finely chopped
grated rind of ½ lemon
1 tspn lemon juice
freshly ground pepper
½ cup (60 g/2 oz) finely grated Cheddar cheese

SERVES 4

Remove stalks from mushrooms and chop stalks
finely. Combine butter or margarine, mushroom
stalks and bacon in a 1 l (1 qt) casserole and cook,
covered, on HIGH (100%) for 1–1½ minutes. Add
breadcrumbs, parsley, chopped egg, lemon rind
and juice. Season with pepper.

Place mushroom caps on a flat, round plate.
Divide mixture evenly between the mushrooms,
piling the mixture in a peak. Top with grated
cheese and cook on MEDIUM HIGH (70%) for 3–5
minutes. Serve hot.

Artichokes with Lemons

4 large artichokes
3 tbspns olive oil
1 tspn fennel
juice and finely grated rind of 1 large lemon
1 garlic clove, crushed
freshly ground black pepper to taste
lemon wedges for garnish

SERVES 4

Rinse artichokes in cold water and cut off stems
close to base. Remove any loose or discoloured
leaves at the base. Cut off about 2 cm (¾ in) from
the top of each artichoke and trim the outside
leaves.

Wrap each artichoke in plastic wrap and place
in oven on the outer edge of the turntable. Cook
on HIGH (100%) for 16–20 minutes, or until tender
and leaves pull away easily. Split each artichoke in
half lengthways and place in a large, shallow serving dish.

Combine the olive oil, fennel, lemon juice and

rind, garlic and black pepper in a jar. Seal with a
well-fitting lid and shake well until all ingredients
are well blended. Pour sauce over artichokes.

Serve warm or cold, garnished with lemon
wedges.

Coquille St Jacques

1 tbspn (20 g/¾ oz) butter
1 onion, finely chopped
500 g (1 lb) scallops, washed
90 g (3 oz) mushrooms, wiped and sliced
2 tbspns plain flour
black pepper to taste
¼ cup (60 ml/2 fl oz) cream
¼ cup (60 ml/2 fl oz) white wine
1 cup (125 g/4 oz) dry breadcrumbs
2 tbspns (45 g/1½ oz) extra butter
⅓ cup (45 g/1½ oz) grated Swiss cheese
fresh parsley, chopped

SERVES 4–6

Place butter and onion in a large 2–3 l (2–3 qt)
microwave-safe dish or casserole. Cover with a
well-fitting lid or plastic wrap. Cook on HIGH
(100%) for 2 minutes, until onion is tender. Add
scallops and mushrooms, re-cover dish and continue cooking on MEDIUM (50%) for 2 minutes.

Stir in flour, pepper, cream and wine. Continue
cooking, covered, on MEDIUM for 4–6 minutes, stirring well after 3–4 minutes, until sauce just boils
and thickens slightly. Adjust seasoning to taste if
necessary.

Divide mixture between 4–6 scallop shells or
ramekin dishes.

Place breadcrumbs and extra butter in a small
microwave-safe bowl. Cook, uncovered, on HIGH
for 1 minute. Stir well and continue cooking for
1 minute.

Top scallop mixture with breadcrumbs, cheese
and a little chopped parsley.

Place dishes around the outer edge of the turntable and cook on HIGH for 1–2 minutes, until cheese
begins to melt. Serve immediately.

● Artichokes with Lemons; Potted Cheese Pâté (page 26)

Escargots with Garlic Butter

An ideal starter for your gourmet friends. Snails should be available from gourmet grocery stores and specialist supermarkets.

⅓ cup (90 g/3 oz) butter
2 spring onions, finely chopped
1 tspn finely chopped fresh parsley
1 garlic clove, crushed
24 snail shells
24 snails, canned

SERVES 4

Cream the butter, spring onions, parsley and garlic together in a small mixing bowl.

Place ¼ tspn of the herbed butter into each snail shell. Top with one well-drained snail, then fill each shell to the brim with herbed butter.

Place filled snail shells on escargot or other small plates (6 to a plate). Place two plates on the turntable of oven. Cook on MEDIUM (50%) for 2–3 minutes, until butter is melted and snails are heated through. Place foil over the cooked snails and cook the remaining 2 plates of snails in the same way.

Serve hot with crusty bread.

● Escargots with Garlic Butter

Seafood Ramekins

Place the seafood in ramekins in the refrigerator well in advance, along with the combined sauce ingredients ready for a quick turn in the microwave.

16 green prawns, shelled and deveined
24 scallops, cleaned
1½ tbspns water per ramekin
200 g (6½ oz) tub soft cream cheese
½ tspn prepared mild French mustard
juice of 1 lemon
¼ cup finely chopped spring onion
1 tbspn brandy (optional)
freshly ground black pepper to taste
½ cup (60 g/2 oz) grated Cheddar cheese
lemon twists
fennel or dill sprigs

SERVES 4

Place 4 prawns, 6 scallops and water in each of 4 ramekins; cover dishes loosely with plastic wrap and cook each dish in microwave on MEDIUM HIGH (70%) for 1½–2 minutes. Drain off all water.

In a large microwave-safe dish, combine cream cheese, mustard, lemon juice, spring onion, brandy, pepper and cheese. Cover loosely with plastic wrap and cook on MEDIUM HIGH for 2–3 minutes. Stir until cheese is melted and sauce is well combined. Pour a quarter of the sauce over seafood in each ramekin. Bake each dish on MEDIUM HIGH for 2–3 minutes. Garnish with a lemon twist and a sprig of fennel or dill. Serve with steamed rice.

Oysters Kilpatrick

Take great care not to overcook the oysters. They have been known to explode in the microwave, so pierce each one with a cocktail stick before cooking and cover with a sheet of absorbent kitchen paper to catch any spatters.

24 oysters in shells, opened
juice of 1 lemon
2 tspns Worcestershire sauce
black pepper to taste
4 rashers bacon

SERVES 4

Cook bacon on HIGH (100%) until almost crisp, then chop. Set 12 of the oysters around the edge of a large microwave-safe plate. Sprinkle each with lemon juice, Worcestershire sauce and pepper.

Sprinkle a little of the bacon over each oyster. Cook on HIGH (100%) for 2–3 minutes, until oysters are hot. Repeat process with remaining oysters. Serve immediately with bread and butter.

Cheesy Toast Fingers

1 slice hot buttered toast
1 tbspn commercial tomato-based pasta sauce
1 tbspn grated tasty cheese, or — for the very young — shredded processed cheese

SERVES 1

Spread the toast with the pasta sauce and sprinkle with cheese. Place on a paper towel on a plate and heat on HIGH (100%) for 1 minute or until cheese melts to your liking.

VARIATIONS Add some chopped spring onions or chives before the cheese; cook a chopped bacon rasher between 2 sheets of paper towel for 1 or more minutes (depending on how crisp you like it) and sprinkle over before the cheese; try chopped olives or anchovies for more mature tastes.

Grapefruit Appetiser

1 grapefruit
2–4 tspns brown sugar, or to taste
pinch ground cinnamon (optional)
1 tbspn dry sherry

SERVES 1 or 2

Halve grapefruit and cut segments away from skin with a curved grapefruit knife. Cut between segments from centre, remove central core and lift segments a little. Sprinkle each half with brown sugar, a little cinnamon and the dry sherry. Cook each half, on a small serving plate, on HIGH (100%) for 1–2 minutes, depending on size.

Boiled Eggs

There are several reasons why boiled eggs need special care when cooked by microwave. If cooked in the microwave oven by the method one would normally use — in water on top of the stove — there's a very real danger that the egg will explode. To avoid this happening the egg is wrapped completely in aluminium foil, with hot water added to the container. The heat of the water is transferred through the foil to the egg itself. You will soon acquire the art of moulding the foil to completely cover the egg with not even a little of the shell showing. (The foil acts as a *de*flector of microwaves while it *re*flects the heat of the water through to the egg.)

After wrapping the egg, place in a 2 cup (500 ml/16 fl oz) jug or small basin, add approximately 1 cup (250 ml/8 fl oz) of hot water and cook on HIGH (100%) for 4–5 minutes for softboiled or 5–6 minutes for hardboiled.

The second reason that special care needs to be taken when boiling eggs — or for that matter cooking eggs by any method by microwave — is that it takes only seconds in some instances to overdo the cooking, resulting in remarkably tough eggs.

The following chart will help you to get the right results if you're cooking more than one egg at a time.

2 foil-wrapped eggs — 5–7 minutes for soft-boiled
2 foil-wrapped eggs — 5–8 minutes for hard-boiled
3 foil-wrapped eggs — 8–10 minutes for soft-boiled
3 foil-wrapped eggs — 10–12 minutes for hard-boiled

● Garlic Bread

the oven turntable. Heat on HIGH (100%) for 30 seconds until warm. Serve dusted with icing sugar.
Health Food Spread centres with cream cheese, fill with grated carrot, sultanas and roughly chopped mixed nuts. Place croissants on a piece of absorbent kitchen paper on the oven turntable. Heat on HIGH (100%) for 30 seconds until warm.

Garlic Bread

1 small crusty French stick
¼ cup (60 g/2 oz) butter
2 cloves garlic, crushed
1 tbspn chopped fresh parsley

SERVES 4

Cut the loaf into 1 cm (⅓ in) slices, not quite cutting all the way through, so that bread still remains in one piece.

Soften the butter on HIGH (100%) for 15 seconds, then blend in garlic and parsley.

Spread a little flavoured butter onto each slice of bread. Wrap whole loaf in kitchen paper and heat through on HIGH for 1 minute. Serve warm.
VARIATION In place of garlic add ½ tspn dried mixed herbs and 2 tspns snipped fresh chives.

Croissants

Cut croissants almost in half and fill with one of the following suggestions.

Cheese and Ham Fill croissants with slices of ham and thinly-sliced Cheddar cheese. Place a piece of absorbent kitchen paper on the oven turntable. Place croissants on paper. Heat on HIGH (100%) for 30–40 seconds, until cheese melts. Serve immediately. Two croissants will take approximately 45–50 seconds for cheese to melt and to warm croissants through.
Seafood Spread centres with a little mayonnaise, fill with tomato and cucumber slices and freshly cooked and shelled prawns, tuna or crab meat. Place croissants on a piece of absorbent kitchen paper on the oven turntable. Heat on HIGH (100%) for 20–30 seconds until warm.
Franzipan Fill centres with thin slices of almond marzipan and some fresh or canned apricot halves. Place croissants on a piece of absorbent kitchen paper on the oven turntable. Heat on HIGH (100%) for 30 seconds until warm. Serve dusted with icing sugar.
Chocolate and Banana Spread centres with grated chocolate or chocolate spread, top with ½ mashed banana and some chopped walnuts. Place croissants on a piece of absorbent kitchen paper on

Pizzas

1 packet (6) Lebanese bread
500 g (1 lb) jar tomato-based pasta sauce
200 g (6½ oz) tomato paste sachet
2 cups (250 g/8 oz) grated tasty cheese
1 large onion, thinly sliced or chopped
1 each red and green capsicum, seeded and sliced
125 g (4 oz) mushrooms, sliced
250 g (8 oz) cabanossi, sliced
olives (optional)
125 g (4 oz) bacon rashers, rind removed and chopped
anchovy fillets (optional)
2 cups (250 g/8 oz) shredded mozzarella cheese

SERVES 6

Place a round of bread on each plate. For each round take 2 tbspns pasta sauce mixed with 2 tspns tomato paste and spread over bread. Top with grated cheese and a selection of the other topping ingredients, finishing with mozzarella cheese. Cook each pizza on HIGH (100%) for 3 minutes or until cheese melts. For a browned topping, use a conventional griller.

Tacos

500 g (1 lb) topside minced steak
1 medium onion, chopped finely
1 tbspn oil
1 packet taco seasoning mix
½ cup (125 ml/4 fl oz) water
1 packet taco shells (about 12)
shredded lettuce
onion rings or chopped spring onions
grated cheese

SERVES 6

In a medium-sized microwave-safe dish, combine minced steak, onion and oil. Break up mince with a fork. Cook on HIGH (100%) for 5–6 minutes, stirring with a fork several times. Add taco mix and stir well, then add water and stir to combine. Microwave on HIGH for 7–8 minutes or until meat is cooked, stirring regularly.

To serve, place taco shells, 6 at a time, upright in a fairly narrow, rectangular dish and place a heaped spoonful of mixture in each shell. Heat on HIGH for 1–2 minutes. Top each shell with a little shredded lettuce, onion and grated cheese. Repeat with remaining 6 shells.

Meatballs with Thai Dipping Sauce

500 g (1 lb) beef or pork and veal mince
1 onion, finely chopped
1 egg, beaten
¾ cup (45 g/1½ oz) fresh breadcrumbs
1 small clove garlic, finely chopped
¼ tspn nutmeg
1 tbspn finely chopped coriander or parsley
salt and pepper to taste

SAUCE

1 tbspn sweet chilli sauce
1 small clove garlic, crushed
2 tbspns fish sauce
1 tbspn lime juice
2 tbspns water
2 tbspns finely crushed peanuts

SERVES 4

To make meatballs, combine all ingredients and form into small balls about 2–2.5 cm (¾–1 in) in diameter. Arrange around the outer edge of a large microwave-safe platter and cook on MEDIUM HIGH (70%) for 12–16 minutes or until cooked, rearranging halfway through cooking time. Cover with aluminium foil while preparing sauce.

Combine all sauce ingredients except peanuts and cook on MEDIUM (50%) for 2 minutes. Add peanuts and cook on MEDIUM for a further minute. Use sauce as a dip for the meatballs.

Slimmers' Flan

BASE

1¼ cups (155 g/5 oz) plain flour, sifted
3 tbspns (60 g/2 oz) butter or margarine
½ cup (30 g/1 oz) processed bran cereal such as Kellogg's All-Bran
1 tbspn grated Parmesan cheese
¼ cup (60 ml/2 fl oz) cold water

FILLING

1 tbspn (20 g/¾ oz) butter
6 spring onions, finely chopped
1 stick celery, sliced
½ green capsicum, seeded and sliced
½ cup seeded, chopped cucumber
250 g (8 oz) tub ricotta cheese
2 eggs, lightly beaten
½ cup (125 ml/4 fl oz) skim milk
200 g (6½ oz) cooked prawns, peeled and roughly chopped
black pepper to taste

SERVES 4–6

Sift the flour into a large mixing bowl. Rub in the butter or margarine until the mixture resembles fine breadcrumbs. Stir in the bran cereal and Parmesan cheese. Gradually add the cold water, 1 tbspn at a time, until mixture can be formed into a stiff dough. Knead dough into a smooth ball.

Roll dough out very thinly on a lightly floured surface and use to line the base and sides of a 20–23 cm (8–9 in) microwave-safe flan dish. Allow pastry to rest in refrigerator for 30 minutes.

Prick base of pastry with a fork. Line base with a piece of absorbent kitchen paper. Bake on an elevated cooking rack or upturned saucer on HIGH

Reheat filled pastries very carefully. Because sugar and fat attract microwaves, the filling may become very hot while the surface temperature of the pastry remains cool. Pastries should be allowed to stand after reheating to equalise the internal and external temperatures. Eating them straight from the microwave may result in burnt mouths.

(100%) for 1½–2 minutes, until pastry looks opaque. Remove paper from base and allow to stand while filling is prepared.

Place butter, spring onions, celery, capsicum and cucumber into a 1 l (1 qt) microwave-safe dish. Cover with a well-fitting lid or plastic wrap. Cook on HIGH for 3–4 minutes, stirring well after 2 minutes, until soft. Remove from oven and stir in remaining ingredients. Pour filling into prepared flan case. Bake on MEDIUM (50%) for 15–20 minutes until filling is set. Serve hot or cold.

Mushroom Quiche

BASE

¾ cup (90 g/3 oz) plain flour
¼ cup (30 g/1 oz) plain wholemeal flour
⅓ cup (90 g/3 oz) butter or hard margarine, cut into pieces
¼ cup (60 ml/2 fl oz) cold buttermilk

FILLING

1 tbspn (20 g/¾ oz) butter
1 onion, chopped
125 g (4 oz) mushrooms, chopped
½ tspn chopped fresh basil or dill
pepper to taste
1 cup (125 g/4 oz) grated Swiss cheese
3 eggs
1 cup (250 ml/8 fl oz) hot milk
2 tbspns plain flour
1 tspn prepared horseradish
¼ tspn dry mustard
paprika
few mushroom slices for garnish
fresh herbs for garnish

SERVES 4–6

Mix flours for base together in a large bowl. Rub in the butter or margarine until mixture resembles fine breadcrumbs. Add enough buttermilk so that mixture holds together in a firm ball. Chill for 1 hour. Roll pastry out thinly on a lightly floured surface and use to line a 23 cm (9 in) pie or quiche plate. Prick bottom and sides of pastry all over with a fork. Cook on MEDIUM HIGH (70%) for 6–8 minutes, until pastry appears dry and opaque.

Place remaining butter for filling together with onion, mushrooms, basil or dill and pepper in a large bowl, cover and cook on HIGH (100%) for 1–2 minutes, until tender.

Cover pastry with cheese, then with mushroom mixture. Beat eggs, milk, flour, horseradish and mustard together in a large bowl. Pour over mushrooms and finish with a sprinkling of paprika.

Place quiche on a microwave baking sheet and cook on MEDIUM (50%) for 10–15 minutes until set. Centre will look slightly soft. Allow to stand for 5 minutes before serving, garnished with mushroom slices and fresh herbs.

Oyster Soup

This is an ideal starter when you are entertaining and have little time.

1 tbspn (20 g/¾ oz) butter
2 tbspns plain flour
2 cups (500 ml/16 fl oz) chicken stock
1 cup (250 ml/8 fl oz) fish stock or water
½ cup (125 ml/4 fl oz) cream
24 bottled oysters, well drained
white pepper
snipped chives to garnish

SERVES 4

*P*lace the butter and flour in a 2 l (2 qt) microwave-safe dish or casserole. Heat on HIGH (100%) for 1 minute, stirring after 30 seconds. Add chicken and fish stock or water, and stir well. Cook on HIGH for 5–6 minutes, stirring every minute until liquid boils and thickens.

Stir in cream, oysters and seasoning to taste. Cook on MEDIUM (50%) for 1–2 minutes, until heated through.

Spoon into serving dishes and serve garnished with chives.

Prawn Bisque

1 tbspn (20 g/¾ oz) butter
315 g (10 oz) shelled green prawns, deveined (weight after shelling)
1 small onion, finely chopped
1 small carrot, grated or finely chopped
1 stick celery, chopped
1 tbspn tomato purée
½ cup (90 g/3 oz) long-grain rice
1 bouquet garni
¼ cup (60 ml/2 fl oz) white wine
2 tbspns brandy
4 cups (1 l/1 qt) fish stock
black pepper to taste
2 tbspns cream

SERVES 4–6

● Oyster Soup

*M*elt the butter in a 3 l (3 qt) microwave-safe dish or casserole, on HIGH (100%) for 45 seconds. Add the prawns and toss well to coat in the butter. Cook for 1 minute. Stir in the onion, carrot and celery. Cover dish with a well-fitting lid or plastic wrap and cook on HIGH for 2–3 minutes.

Stir in the tomato purée, rice, bouquet garni, white wine, brandy and half the stock. Re-cover dish and cook for 10–12 minutes, until rice is tender.

Remove 4 of the prawns. Purée the remainder of the soup in a liquidiser or food processor. Return to the casserole. Dilute to required consistency with remaining stock. Adjust seasonings to taste.

Reheat on HIGH for 2–3 minutes. Stir in the cream. Pour into individual serving bowls and serve each bowl garnished with a prawn and croûtons if desired.

Mediterranean Seafood Soup

2 tspns butter
1 large onion, sliced
3 leeks, thoroughly washed and thinly sliced
2 carrots, peeled and thinly sliced
1 stick celery, washed and thinly sliced
1 green capsicum, seeded and thinly sliced
1 l (1 qt) water, fish stock or diluted chicken stock,
boiling
1 bay leaf
1 tspn dried thyme
4 sprigs fresh parsley washed
pinch powdered saffron
2 cloves garlic, crushed
6 fish steaks (gemfish or kingfish), uncooked
100 g (3½ oz) shelled green prawns, washed
6 fresh oysters, shelled (or fresh bottled)
black pepper to taste

SERVES 4–6

*P*lace butter in a 2.5–3 l (2½–3 qt) casserole. Melt in the microwave on HIGH (100%) for 45 seconds. Add the onion, leeks, carrots, celery and capsicum. Stir and toss well to coat vegetables with butter. Cover dish and cook on HIGH for 5 minutes; stir vegetables and add boiling water, fish or chicken stock, together with bay leaf, thyme, parsley, saffron and crushed garlic. Cover dish and cook on HIGH for 5 minutes. (Water or stock must be boiling when added to vegetables to quickly bring out flavours that would otherwise take a while to extract.) Give vegetables a thorough stir, then gently add fish steaks. Replace lid and cook, covered, on HIGH for 5 minutes. Stir in the green prawns and oysters. Cook on HIGH for 1 minute. Adjust seasonings to taste, adding salt if desired.

Serve immediately as a meal in itself, with lots of crusty bread.

Split Pea and Bacon Soup

1½ cups (315 g/10 oz) split green peas
2.25 l (2¼ qt) water
2 medium-sized bacon rashers
1 large onion, chopped
1 large carrot, chopped
1 stick celery, chopped
1 medium potato, chopped
½ tspn dried thyme
2 bacon stock cubes
½ tspn pepper
1 bay leaf

250 g (8 oz) bacon bones
salt, if required
cooked bacon rasher for garnish

SERVES 6–8

*P*ut peas in a 4 l (4 qt) microwave-safe casserole with 4 cups (1 1/1 qt) of water. Cook on HIGH (100%) for 10 minutes, stirring after 5 minutes. Cover and put aside. Chop bacon and cook 1 minute on HIGH in a smaller casserole. Add chopped vegetables and cook, covered, for 5 minutes on HIGH. Crumble stock cubes into the large casserole containing the peas and add remaining water, the cooked vegetables and bacon. Add remaining ingredients and cook on HIGH for 25 minutes, stirring twice.

Remove bones and return any meat to the soup. Blend soup, if desired, after removing bay leaf. Serve garnished with cooked bacon rasher.

Curried Pumpkin Soup

1 kg (2 lb) pumpkin, peeled and cut into 2.5 cm (1 in)
dice
2 cups (500 ml/16 fl oz) water
1 chicken stock cube, or 1 heaped tspn stock powder
1 clove garlic, crushed
1 tspn curry powder (or to taste)
black pepper to taste
⅔ cup (185 ml/6 fl oz) thickened cream
croûtons (see recipe on page 41)
ground nutmeg
sprig of tarragon for garnish

SERVES 4

*P*lace the diced pumpkin in a 2–3 l (2–3 qt) microwave-safe dish or casserole with water, stock cube, garlic and curry powder. Cover with a well-fitting lid or plastic wrap and cook on HIGH (100%) for 12–14 minutes, until pumpkin is broken down. Stir well after 6 minutes.

Allow to cool for 2–3 minutes, then purée pumpkin and liquid in a blender or food processor until smooth. Pour soup back into casserole, then stir in seasoning to taste and cream. Cook uncovered on HIGH for 4–5 minutes, until heated through.

Serve with croutons, sprinkle with nutmeg and garnish with sprig of tarragon.

● *Clockwise from top:* Curried Pumpkin Soup; Split Pea and Bacon Soup; Minestrone (page 40)

Hearty Tomato and Zucchini Soup

This chunky fresh soup is a meal in itself. It can also be puréed to make a smooth soup.

750 g (1½ lb) tomatoes, blanched, peeled and chopped
4 medium zucchini, finely sliced
4 cups (1 l/1 qt) chicken stock, boiling
1 tbspn plain flour
black pepper to taste
2 tbspns (45 g/1½ oz) butter
1 tspn ground nutmeg
1 tbspn chopped fresh parsley
1 tbspn chopped fresh dill
½ cup (125 ml/4 fl oz) sour cream

SERVES 6

Place tomatoes, zucchini and half of the boiling chicken stock into a 3 l (3 qt) microwave-safe dish or casserole. Cook on HIGH (100%) for 10 minutes, stirring occasionally until the soup comes to the boil. Continue cooking on MEDIUM (50%) for 10 minutes, until vegetables cook and soften.

Meanwhile combine flour, black pepper and butter in a small bowl. Cook on HIGH (100%) for 1 minute, stirring after 30 seconds. Stir in nutmeg, parsley and dill. Pour a little of the soup into the bowl, stir to combine and return to casserole with remaining chicken stock. Cook on HIGH for 3–4 minutes until soup returns to the boil and thickens slightly.

Serve hot with fresh crusty bread and garnished with sour cream.

Beef and Vegetable Soup

A hearty family soup for chilly evenings.

500 g (1 lb) minced steak
1 large onion, chopped
8 cups (2 1/2 qt) beef stock
1 cup (155 g/5 oz) macaroni
1 large potato, chopped
1 large carrot, chopped
2 sticks celery, chopped
1 tbspn chopped parsley
1 cup shredded cabbage
4 large cooking tomatoes, skinned and chopped
½ teaspoon dried oregano or marjoram
salt and pepper to taste
½ cup (75 g/2½ oz) frozen peas (optional)

SERVES 8–10

Place minced steak in a 4 l (4 qt) microwave-safe casserole. Break up meat with a fork and add onion. Cover and cook on MEDIUM HIGH (70%) for 6 minutes. Stir to break up meat and cook a further 6 minutes on MEDIUM HIGH. Add remaining ingredients, except peas, and cook a further 25–30 minutes on MEDIUM HIGH. (Add peas 10 minutes before end of cooking time.) Allow soup to stand, covered, for 15 minutes. Skim off any fat before serving.

Beetroot and Orange Soup

Though usually served chilled, this soup may be served hot if preferred.

500 g (1 lb) fresh beetroot, peeled and cut into 2 cm (¾ in) dice
finely grated rind and juice of 1 orange
2 cups (500 ml/16 fl oz) hot chicken stock (or use stock cubes and water)
1 cup (250 ml/8 fl oz) tomato juice
black pepper to taste

GARNISH

⅓ cup (90 ml/3 fl oz) sour cream
snipped chives

SERVES 4

Place beetroot into a 2–3 l (2–3 qt) microwave-safe dish or casserole. Cover with a well-fitting lid or plastic wrap and cook on HIGH (100%) for 6–8 minutes until tender. Allow to cool for 5 minutes while remaining ingredients are prepared.

Place beetroot plus any cooking liquid into a blender or liquidiser and blend until smooth.

Transfer beetroot purée back into casserole dish, with orange rind and juice, stock, tomato juice and pepper. Stir well. Heat through on HIGH for 5 minutes, stirring occasionally, until liquid boils. Reduce power and continue cooking on MEDIUM (50%) for 5 minutes, stirring occasionally until soup is thick and well combined. Remove from oven. Leave to cool, then chill.

Serve well chilled, garnished with sour cream and snipped chives.

Stock for soups can be quickly made by cooking meat or chicken scraps and bones with seasonings and water. For each 2 cups (500 ml/16 fl oz) of liquid allow 5 minutes on HIGH (100%), then 10 minutes on MEDIUM (50%). Allow to stand for 10 minutes and strain.

Gingered Carrot Soup

600 g (1¼ lb) carrots, peeled and cut into 1 cm (½ in) lengths
2 cups (500 ml/16 fl oz) hot chicken stock
finely grated rind and juice of 2 oranges
1 cup (250 ml/8 fl oz) water
1 tspn ground ginger
½ tspn ground mace
⅔ cup (185 ml/6 fl oz) cream
black pepper to taste

SERVES 4–5

Place the carrots in a 2–3 l (2–3 qt) microwave-safe dish or casserole. Cover with a well-fitting lid or plastic wrap and cook on HIGH (100%) for 5–6 minutes, until soft. Stir in the chicken stock, orange rind and juice, water and spices. Continue heating on HIGH for 6–8 minutes until the liquid boils, stirring occasionally during cooking.

Leave to cool for 5 minutes, then transfer soup in batches to a blender or liquidiser. Blend until smooth.

Stir in half the cream. Adjust seasonings to taste, then place in refrigerator.

Serve well chilled, garnished with a little of the reserved cream.

Mushroom Soup

Though delicious, mushroom soup could not be described as colourful. Garnishing it with a lemon slice and chopped chives adds interest.

2 tbspns (45 g/1½ oz) butter or margarine
½ cup finely chopped spring onions
2 cups (185 g/6 oz) mushrooms, finely chopped
1½ cups (375 ml/12 fl oz) chicken stock
1½ cups (375 ml/12 fl oz) milk
1 tbspn plain flour
⅓ cup (90 ml/3 fl oz) cream
1 egg yolk
chopped chives
lemon slices (optional)

SERVES 4–6

Place butter or margarine, onions and mushrooms in a deep 3 l (3 qt) microwave-safe casserole dish. Cover and cook on HIGH (100%) for 3 minutes. Stir in chicken stock and milk. Cook on HIGH for 3 minutes or until bubbly around edge. Blend flour with a little water until smooth. Stir into the soup. Cook on HIGH for 2 minutes. In a bowl, whisk cream and egg yolk together. Stir in a little of the hot soup. Mix cream mixture into soup. Cook on HIGH for 3 minutes or until bubbly around edge. Stir before serving. Garnish with chives and a slice of lemon, if desired.

Spicy Indian Cauliflower Soup

2 cups (125 g/4 oz) small cauliflower florets
½ medium red capsicum
2 tbspns (45 g/1½ oz) ghee or butter
1 large onion, finely chopped
2 tspns turmeric
¼–½ tspn chilli powder (or to taste)
2 cups (500 ml/16 fl oz) hot strong chicken stock (or use stock cubes and water)
2 tbspns besan (chickpea flour)
1 cup (250 ml/8 fl oz) milk
1 cup (185 g/6 oz) natural yoghurt
1 tspn garam masala
salt to taste
2 tbspns chopped fresh coriander or parsley

SERVES 6

Make a small cut in the base of the cauliflower floret stems; seed capsicum and cut into thin strips. In a casserole, heat ghee or butter on HIGH (100%)

for 1 minute or until melted. Add capsicum, cauliflower and onion and cook, covered, on HIGH for 5 minutes, stirring after 3 minutes. Add turmeric, chilli powder and chicken stock, stir well and cook, covered, on HIGH for 8 minutes, stirring several times. Meanwhile, blend besan with a little of the milk to make a paste, gradually add remaining milk and stir into soup. Cover and heat on HIGH until just boiling. Stir in yoghurt and seasonings well, then reheat on HIGH until almost boiling.

Just before serving, stir through chopped coriander or parsley.

French Onion Soup

2 tbspns (45 g/1½ oz) butter or margarine
2 large onions, sliced
1 tbspn plain flour
3 cups (750 ml/24 fl oz) beef stock (or use stock cubes and water)
¼ cup (60 ml/2 fl oz) white wine
1 bay leaf
freshly ground black pepper to taste
60 g (2 oz) Gruyère or Cheddar cheese, grated
4 thick slices French bread

SERVES 4

Melt butter in a 2 l (2 qt) microwave-safe casserole on HIGH (100%) for 1 minute, stir in onions and cook, covered, for 5 minutes. Add flour and stir well. Cook, covered, on HIGH for 1 minute. Gradually stir in stock, wine, bay leaf and black pepper. Cook on HIGH for 10 minutes. Add salt if desired.

Meanwhile, sprinkle grated cheese on the slices of bread. Place under a hot grill until cheese bubbles and melts. Pour soup into soup bowls and top each bowl with a slice of bread and melted cheese. Serve immediately.

Minestrone

2 tbspns olive oil
1 large onion, finely chopped
2 cloves garlic, crushed
2 medium potatoes, peeled and cut into 2 cm (¾ in) dice
2 medium carrots, peeled and cut into 1 cm (½ in) lengths
2 sticks celery, sliced
2 cups shredded cabbage
3 tomatoes, peeled and chopped
4 cups (1 l/1 qt) hot chicken stock

1 bouquet garni
315 g (10 oz) can 4 bean mix, washed and well drained
1 cup (155 g/5 oz) small macaroni
90 g (3 oz) ham off the bone, diced
½ tspn paprika
black pepper to taste
1 medium-sized zucchini, diced
½ cup (60 g/2 oz) grated Parmesan cheese
sprigs of thyme for garnish

SERVES 4-6

*P*our the oil into a 3–4 l (3–4 qt) microwave-safe dish or casserole. Heat on HIGH (100%) for 1–2 minutes, until hot. Quickly add the onion and garlic. Cook, covered with a well-fitting lid or plastic wrap, on HIGH for 2 minutes. Stir in the potatoes, carrots and celery. Re-cover dish and cook on HIGH for 5 minutes. Stir in the cabbage and tomatoes, then stir in the chicken stock, bouquet garni, drained beans, macaroni, ham, paprika and seasoning. Re-cover and cook on HIGH for 20 minutes, stirring after 5, 10 and 15 minutes, until vegetables are cooked through and macaroni is tender. Stir well.

Remove bouquet garni and stir in zucchini. Cook on HIGH for 5 minutes.

Serve hot, sprinkled with Parmesan cheese and garnished with sprigs of thyme.(See photo page 37.)

Thick Lentil Soup

For a fresh, unusual flavour substitute a sprig of mint for the allspice in this soup. Remove before serving. Or, for a Middle Eastern flavour, add 1 tspn ground cumin. For an even more substantial meal, stir through some cooked small pasta (heat on HIGH [100%] for a few minutes before serving).

1 cup (185 g/6 oz) brown lentils, well washed
1 tbspn (20 g/¾ oz) butter
1 large onion, finely chopped
1 clove garlic, crushed
1 large carrot, thinly sliced
4 cups (1 l/1 qt) water, boiling
1 tbspn chicken stock powder
black pepper to taste
pinch allspice
1 tbspn chopped fresh parsley

SERVES 4

*S*oak the lentils in water while remaining ingredients are being prepared.

Melt the butter in a 3 l (3 qt) microwave-safe dish or casserole on HIGH (100%) for 1 minute. Stir in the onion, garlic and carrot. Cover dish with a well-fitting lid or plastic wrap and cook on HIGH for 2 minutes. Stir in the drained lentils. Re-cover dish and cook on HIGH for 2 minutes. Stir in boiling water, stock powder, seasoning, allspice (or alternative) and parsley. Cook uncovered on MEDIUM (50%) for 15–20 minutes, until lentils are soft.

If desired, purée the soup, return to cooking container and adjust seasonings to taste.

Croûtons

Croûtons are a welcome accompaniment to soup — and that pleasant crunchiness is so easy to achieve in the microwave. Use wholemeal or multigrain bread, as white bread will not give as appetising a result.

2 tbspns (45 g/1½ oz) butter or margarine
3 thick slices wholemeal bread, cubed

SERVES 4

*M*elt the butter in a shallow, microwave-safe dish on HIGH (100%) for 2 minutes. Stir in the diced bread. Cook on HIGH for 4–5 minutes, turning and tossing the bread occasionally during cooking, until crisp.

Pasta and Rice

There is no great time saving in cooking pasta and rice in the microwave. However, there is the convenience of being able to cook and serve in the same dish, if desired.

PASTA

Like rice, pasta will cook well in the microwave oven. However, there is no time saving and because of the amount of water required for cooking pasta it is only possible to cook 250 g (8 oz) at a time. If serving pasta, it is usually a better proposition to cook the accompanying sauce by microwave while the pasta cooks on the stove-top.

To cook pasta you must use a large casserole — at least 3 l (3 qt) capacity. For 250 g (8 oz) of pasta add 6 cups (1.5 l/1½ qt) boiling water, salt to taste and 1 tablespoon oil. Bring back to boil on HIGH (100%), stirring several times to separate pasta, and cook, uncovered, on HIGH for approximately 8–10 minutes. Drain and return to cooking container or a heated serving dish, add a little oil and stir lightly if not serving immediately.

If using *fresh pasta* cook for only 4–6 minutes.

It is not possible to give accurate times for cooking pasta. Different brands of the same pasta have varying cooking times. One must test after the minimum suggested time and continue cooking if necessary.

Cooked pasta that has been frozen and defrosted does not have the same quality as freshly cooked pasta. If you need to freeze a quantity of pasta, package as for rice, extracting as much air as possible.

RICE

When cooking rice by microwave, use the absorption method for best results. Timings given are approximate, since opinions differ as to how soft the cooked grain should be. If you like the grains to be quite separate and find this is not the case with microwaved rice, all you need to do is to hold the colander of cooked rice under the hot tap for a few seconds and then drain well.

An alternative is to add a teaspoon of butter when cooking the rice — this helps to some extent to keep the grains separate. Of course if the rice is to be used in a recipe for which separated grains are not demanded, such as rice pudding or creamy rice, neither of these options is necessary.

If you prefer rice with a softer than average grain, add a little more water than suggested in the following cooking table and cook until the rice is to your taste. For a firmer grain, use a little less water. The ideal quantity of rice to cook by microwave is 1 cup. Use a container with a capacity of at least 2 l (2 qt).

Rice may be frozen and if it is carefully defrosted it loses little of its original cooked quality. When freezing, do not place it in a container too large for the quantity of rice. If this happens, the rice tends to dehydrate and develops a rather unpleasant texture.

The best method of freezing is to pack the rice in freezer bags in the quantities you plan to use it at a later stage. Extract as much air as possible, preferably using the small vacuum pumps available in most kitchenware departments, or extract the air by pressing down on the rice (without depressing it too much), twisting the bag closed and securing with a metal tie.

DEFROSTING RICE

To defrost, remove the metal tie but leave the bag closed, simply tucking under the end and placing on a plate. Heat on DEFROST (30%) until rice is thawed and hot, moving the rice several times by pushing the bag gently with a wooden spoon to assist even heating, without uncovering the rice. The trapped steam does a dual job of hastening the thawing and keeping the rice moist.

If you are cooking and freezing rice in advance for a dinner party, undercook slightly and when thawing, sprinkle the rice with a little water and cover very closely while it defrosts.

RICE COOKING GUIDE				
VARIETY	**QUANTITY**	**HOT WATER**	**COOKING TIME ON HIGH (100%)**	**STANDING TIME COVERED**
Calrose (short grain)	1 cup (185 g/6 oz)	2 cups (500 ml/16 fl oz)	10–12 mins, uncovered	5 mins
Long grain	1 cup (200 g/6½ oz)	2 cups (500 ml/16 fl oz)	10–12 mins, uncovered	5 mins
Brown	1 cup (220 g/7 oz)	3 cups (750 ml/24 fl oz)	30 minutes, covered, with steam vent, stirring twice	10 mins
Quick brown	1 cup (200 g/6½ oz)	2⅓ cups (600 ml/19 fl oz) boiling water	15–18 mins, covered, with steam vent, stirring twice	10 mins

Spaghetti Bolognese

This perennial favourite is a good main course for a budget menu. Make the sauce the night before — it saves time and tastes better.

250 g (8 oz) spaghetti
4 rashers bacon, finely chopped
1 onion, chopped
2 cloves garlic, crushed
345 g (11 oz) minced beef
1 medium-sized carrot, grated
410 g (13 oz) can tomatoes
2 tspns each fresh chopped marjoram and oregano, or 1 tspn mixed dried herbs
2 tbspns tomato paste
1 tbspn Worcestershire sauce
1 tbspn chopped fresh parsley
black pepper to taste
90 g (3 oz) mushrooms, chopped
grated Parmesan cheese

SERVES 4

Cook spaghetti on stove-top until tender.

Place bacon, onion and garlic in a 2–3 l (2–3 qt) microwave-safe casserole, cover and cook for 3 minutes on HIGH (100%) until onion is soft. Stir in minced beef, mashing with a fork to separate. Re-cover and cook for 5 minutes, until meat loses its pink colour. Drain off any excess fat and add remaining ingredients, except mushrooms and cheese, stirring well to combine. Cover dish and cook on MEDIUM HIGH (70%) for 15 minutes, stirring after 5 and 10 minutes. Stir in mushrooms. Cook on HIGH for 3 minutes.

Serve hot pasta topped with sauce and sprinkled with grated Parmesan cheese.

Spaghetti with Tuna Sauce

250 g (8 oz) spaghetti
¼ cup (30 g/1 oz) plain flour
1 cup (125 g/4 oz) grated Cheddar cheese
1 small onion, grated or finely chopped
1 clove garlic, crushed
1½ cups (375 ml/12 fl oz) dry white wine or mixture of white wine and stock
425 g (13½ oz) can tuna, drained and roughly flaked
½ tspn curry powder
6 green stuffed olives, roughly chopped

SERVES 4

Cook pasta on stove-top until tender.

Combine the flour and cheese in a 1–2 l (1–2 qt) microwave-safe dish or jug. Stir the onion and garlic into the wine or wine and stock mixture, and then stir this into the cheese mixture. Heat on MEDIUM (50%) for 3 minutes, stir well, then continue cooking on MEDIUM for 5–6 minutes. Stir occasionally, until all the cheese has melted and the mixture is thick. Beat well until mixture is smooth. Stir in the tuna, curry powder and olives. Heat through on MEDIUM for 3–4 minutes.

Serve hot with spaghetti.

Spaghetti Siciliana

A spaghetti main course with a decidedly Mediterranean character. Have on hand a bottle of Italian red wine and some crusty bread to mop up any excess sauce.

250 g (8 oz) spaghetti
4 tomatoes, peeled and chopped
1 red and 1 green capsicum, seeded and chopped
6 spring onions, finely chopped

¼ cup (45 g/1½ oz) black olives, seeded and chopped
2 tbspns green olives, chopped
45 g (1½ oz) can anchovy fillets, chopped
freshly ground black pepper to taste
juice of ½ lemon
2 tbspns olive oil
fresh parsley, chopped
grated Parmesan cheese

SERVES 4

Cook spaghetti on stove-top until tender.

Meanwhile, mix tomatoes, capsicums, spring onions, olives, anchovy fillets, seasoning and lemon juice together in a 2–3 l (2–3 qt) microwave-safe dish. Cover and cook on HIGH (100%) for 5 minutes, until mixture bubbles, stirring well after about 2–3 minutes to redistribute ingredients.

Drain spaghetti and stir in olive oil. Add spaghetti to tomato mixture in dish. Re-cover dish and heat through on HIGH for 3–4 minutes.

Just before serving garnish with chopped parsley and grated Parmesan cheese. (See photo page 49.)

Tortellini with Cream Sauce

250 g (8 oz) tortellini
1 tbspn (20 g/¾ oz) butter
4 rashers bacon, chopped
1 green capsicum, seeded and sliced
155 g (5 oz) mushrooms, wiped and sliced
1 tbspn plain flour
2 tspns dry mustard
freshly ground black pepper to taste
1 cup (250 ml/8 fl oz) milk
½ cup (125 ml/4 fl oz) cream
½ cup (60 g/2 oz) grated Cheddar or Parmesan cheese

SERVES 4

Cook tortellini on stove-top until tender.

Meanwhile, melt butter in a shallow 1 l (1 qt) microwave-safe dish on HIGH (100%) for 1 minute. Add bacon and capsicum and cook, uncovered, on HIGH for 2 minutes, until capsicum softens. Stir in mushrooms, flour, mustard and seasoning. Cook on HIGH for 1 minute, stirring once. Gently stir in milk. Cook on HIGH for 3–4 minutes, until sauce boils and thickens, stirring well after 2 minutes. Stir in cream and continue cooking for 1 minute.

Drain tortellini and place on a warmed serving plate. Pour sauce over pasta. Sprinkle with grated cheese. Cheese may be browned quickly under a hot grill before serving if a crisp top is preferred.

Tagliatelle with Ham and Ricotta Sauce

Tomato tagliatelle makes an interesting change, but plain or spinach pasta can of course be substituted.

375 g (12 oz) pack tomato tagliatelle
2 tbspns (45 g/1½ oz) butter (melted) or cooking oil
⅔ cup (155 g/5 oz) ricotta cheese
220 g (7 oz) ham, diced
6 spring onions, finely chopped
¼ tspn cayenne pepper
freshly ground black pepper to taste
220 g (7 oz) mushrooms, wiped and sliced
¾ cup (90 g/3 oz) grated Parmesan cheese
¼ cup (60 ml/2 fl oz) cream
fresh parsley for garnish

SERVES 4–5

Cook tagliatelle on stove-top until tender.

While pasta is cooking, add melted butter or cooking oil to a 1–2 l (1–2 qt) microwave-safe dish or casserole and cook on HIGH (100%) for 2 minutes, until bubbling. Stir in ricotta cheese, diced ham, spring onions, peppers, mushrooms and Parmesan cheese, mix well and cook on MEDIUM (50%) for 3–4 minutes.

Fold the mushroom and ham mixture through the hot pasta, together with the cream. Serve hot, garnished with parsley sprigs. (See photo page 49.)

Spinach Tagliatelle with Smoked Salmon and Broccoli

Smoked salmon and broccoli florets add colour to this delicious pasta sauce.

250 g (8 oz) spinach tagliatelle
2 cups (125 g/4 oz) sliced broccoli florets
1 tbspn (20 g/¾ oz) butter
1 tbspn plain flour
½ cup (125 ml/4 fl oz) milk
½ cup (125 ml/4 fl oz) cream
125 g (4 oz) smoked salmon, cut into thin strips
garlic to taste
salt and pepper to taste

SERVES 4 as a light entrée

Cook pasta on stove-top until tender.

Cook broccoli for 1½–2 minutes or until just tender. (See Vegetable Cooking Guide, page 144.) Keep covered while making sauce.

Melt butter in a medium-sized bowl on HIGH (100%) for 30 seconds. Stir in flour and cook for 1 minute, stirring after 30 seconds. Add milk, garlic, seasoning and cream and stir briskly with a wire whisk. Continue to cook on HIGH for 2 minutes, stirring regularly, until thickened. Add smoked salmon, broccoli and seasonings and reheat on HIGH for about 30 seconds.

Serve over cooked tagliatelle.

> To peel tomatoes easily, lightly slash or prick the skin, place on a microwave-safe plate and heat on HIGH (100%) for 10–40 seconds per tomato, depending on its ripeness, size and firmness. Remove the skin with a small knife.

Tomato and Fennel Fettucine

Try a mixture of plain and spinach pasta for a different look in this all-vegetable pasta sauce.

250 g (8 oz) each plain and spinach-flavoured fettucine
1 medium onion, finely chopped
1 fennel bulb, sliced thinly
1 clove garlic, crushed
½ cup (125 ml/4 fl oz) water
1 tbspn (20 g/¾ oz) butter or margarine
500 g (1 lb) tomatoes, peeled and chopped
¼ cup thinly sliced red capsicum
2 tbspns tomato paste

¼ cup (60 ml/2 fl oz) white wine or water
1 tspn dried basil
salt, pepper and sugar to taste

SERVES 4–6

Cook pasta on stove-top until tender.

Place onion, fennel, garlic, water, and butter or margarine in a microwave-safe casserole and cook, covered, on HIGH (100%) for 5 minutes.

Add remaining ingredients, excluding the pasta and cook, covered, for a further 10 minutes on HIGH, stirring once during cooking.

Place plain and spinach fettucine decoratively on a serving plate and spoon over the tomato sauce. Serve with crusty bread. (See photo page 155.)

Fettucine with Pesto Sauce

Just for a change this recipe cooks the pasta in the microwave while preparing the sauce conventionally.

250 g (8 oz) fettucine
1 tbspn pinenuts, chopped
½ cup finely chopped and crushed fresh basil
⅓ cup chopped fresh parsley
2 cloves garlic, crushed
½ cup (60 g/2 oz) grated Parmesan cheese
1 cup (250 ml/8 fl oz) olive oil

SERVES 4

Place 8 cups (2 1/2 qt) of boiling water into a 3–4 l (3–4 qt) microwave-safe casserole. Add fettucine and stir well to distribute. Cook, uncovered, on HIGH (100%) until pasta is tender. (Fresh fettucine will take approximately 3–4 minutes, dried will take approximately 6–8 minutes to cook.) Allow to stand for 3–4 minutes before draining.

Meanwhile, mix together remaining ingredients except oil in a bowl. Gradually add oil, a little at a time, stirring and mixing constantly.

Drain pasta and stir pesto sauce through. Serve immediately.

QUICK TIP USING THE FOOD PROCESSOR Chop pinenuts in processor, using metal blade; add basil, parsley and crushed garlic, while machine is running. Process until herbs are finely chopped, if necessary scraping down sides of bowl after 1 minute; add cheese. While still processing, combine oil by pouring in a constant stream through top opening. Process for 1 second. Stir sauce through pasta.

● *From top: Fettucine with Pesto Sauce; Spaghetti Siciliana (page 46); Tagliatelle with Ham and Ricotta Sauce (page 47)*

Ditalini with Tomato and Bacon Sauce

250 g (8 oz) ditalini (short pasta tubes)
4 bacon rashers
1 kg (2 lb) ripe tomatoes, peeled and seeded, or 2 cups (500 ml/16 fl oz) canned tomatoes with juice
1 clove garlic, crushed
1 medium onion, finely chopped
2 tbspns olive oil
1 tbspn chopped fresh oregano, or ½ tspn dried oregano
½ green capsicum, seeded and cut into thin strips
2 tspns sugar
½ cup (90 g/3 oz) sliced black olives
freshly ground black pepper to taste
salt, if required

SERVES 4

Cook ditalini in boiling water on stove-top until tender.

Remove rind from bacon and snip the fat to prevent bacon from curling during cooking. Place on a microwave-safe plate between 4 sheets of absorbent kitchen paper. Cook on HIGH (100%) for 2½–3 minutes (or a little longer if you want the bacon crisp) and allow to stand for about 1 minute. Cut the bacon rashers into small pieces with kitchen scissors.

Combine all ingredients, except pasta and salt, in a 2–3 l (2–3 qt) microwave-safe casserole and cook, uncovered, on HIGH for about 15 minutes or until sauce is of desired thickness. Check seasoning before adding salt.

Serve with the cooked pasta and a green salad.

Penne with Fiery Tomato Sauce

410 g (13 oz) penne
1 tbspn olive oil
2 cloves garlic, crushed
sliced fresh chilli pepper, or chilli powder, to taste
½ cup (125 ml/4 fl oz) tomato purée
black pepper to taste
fresh basil, chopped

SERVES 4

Cook penne on stove-top until tender.

Meanwhile, heat oil in a 1–2 l (1–2 qt) microwave-safe casserole on HIGH (100%) for 2 minutes, until hot. Add garlic and chilli pepper. Cook, covered, on HIGH for 1 minute to release flavours, stir in tomato purée and continue cooking on HIGH for 2 minutes until sauce bubbles.

Drain pasta, stir in sauce, add seasoning to taste and serve sprinkled generously with basil.

Ravioli with Tomato and Garlic Sauce

250 g (8 oz) fresh ravioli
2 tbspns olive oil
2 cloves garlic, crushed
410 g (13 oz) can tomatoes, sieved
½ tspn ground allspice
black pepper to taste

SERVES 4

Cook ravioli on stove-top until tender.

Meanwhile, heat oil in a 2 l (2 qt) microwave-safe casserole on HIGH (100%) for 2 minutes. Quickly add garlic and stir well to release flavours, then stir in remaining ingredients. Cook, uncovered, on HIGH for 6–8 minutes until sauce bubbles. Stir well after 3–4 minutes. Adjust seasonings to taste and add salt if desired.

Drain ravioli and gently stir into tomato sauce. Cover dish and warm on MEDIUM HIGH (70%) until heated through. Serve with fresh crusty bread.

Pasta Carbonara

250 g (8 oz) pasta shells
½ cup (125 ml/4 fl oz) cream
3 eggs
¼ cup (30 g/1 oz) grated Parmesan cheese
2 tbspns tomato sauce
2 tbspns white wine
1 tbspn (20 g/¾ oz) butter or margarine
2 cloves garlic, crushed
1 tspn dried oregano

6 spring onions, roughly chopped
8 slices ham, cut into thin strips
2 tomatoes, peeled and chopped
fresh parsley for garnish

SERVES 4

*B*oil the pasta shells on stove-top until tender.

Meanwhile, prepare remaining ingredients.

Lightly beat the cream, eggs, cheese, tomato sauce and wine together in a medium-sized jug, then set aside.

Melt the butter or margarine in a 3 l (3 qt) microwave-safe dish or casserole on HIGH (100%) for 1 minute, until hot. Stir in garlic, oregano and spring onions. Cover dish with a well-fitting lid or plastic wrap and continue cooking on HIGH for 2 minutes. Stir in the ham and tomatoes. Re-cover dish and continue heating on MEDIUM HIGH (70%) for 4–5 minutes, until heated through, stirring occasionally.

Drain pasta shells and stir into the ham mixture together with the cream and eggs mixture. Continue cooking on MEDIUM (50%) for 4–6 minutes, stirring every 2 minutes until the sauce begins to thicken.

Serve hot, garnished with chopped parsley.

Pasta Marinara

Marinara mix should be available from most fish shops.

250 g (8 oz) trivelle (pasta spirals)
2 tbspns (45 g/1½ oz) butter
1 clove garlic, crushed
2 tomatoes, peeled and chopped
1 tbspn tomato paste
¼ cup (60 ml/2 fl oz) white wine
1 tspn chopped fresh basil
black pepper to taste
1 tbspn chopped fresh parsley
750 g (1½ lb) marinara mix, thoroughly washed

SERVES 4

Cook pasta on stove-top until tender.

Place butter and garlic in a 1–2 l (1–2 qt) microwave-safe dish or casserole. Cook on HIGH (100%) for 1 minute, stir in tomatoes, tomato paste, white wine, basil, black pepper and chopped parsley. Cook on HIGH for 5 minutes, stirring well after 2 minutes. Purée the tomato mixture in a blender or food processor. Return to cooking container and stir in seafood. Heat on MEDIUM (50%) for about 5–7 minutes. Serve hot on a bed of pasta.

Cannelloni

16 cannelloni tubes

FILLING

1 tbspn olive oil
1 large onion, finely chopped
1 clove garlic, crushed
410 g (13 oz) minced beef
½ tspn dried oregano
½ tspn chopped fresh basil
2 tspns tomato paste
90 g (3 oz) mushrooms, chopped
1 egg, lightly beaten
black pepper to taste

SAUCE

1 tbspn olive oil
1 clove garlic, crushed
2 tbspns chopped fresh parsley
410 g (13 oz) can tomatoes, sieved
2 tbspns tomato paste
½ cup (125 ml/4 fl oz) dry white wine or chicken stock
90 g (3 oz) button mushrooms, sliced
black pepper to taste
¼ cup (30 g/1 oz) grated Parmesan cheese

SERVES 4

Cook cannelloni on stove-top until tender.

To prepare filling: Heat oil in a 2 l (2 qt) microwave-safe casserole on HIGH (100%) for 2 minutes until hot. Stir in onion and garlic. Cook, uncovered, on HIGH for 1 minute to soften. Add minced beef, oregano, basil and tomato paste and stir well to combine. Cover dish and cook on HIGH for 6–8 minutes, until meat loses its pink colour. Stir in mushrooms, egg and seasoning. Cook on HIGH for a further 1 minute. Set aside while making sauce.

To prepare sauce: Heat oil in a shallow microwave-safe dish on HIGH for 2 minutes until hot. Quickly stir in garlic and parsley to release flavours, stir in sieved tomatoes, tomato paste, and wine or chicken stock. Cook on HIGH for 3–4 minutes until sauce bubbles; stir well after 2 minutes. Stir in mushrooms.

> **If cooked pasta has to stand for a time before being served add 1 tablespoon of oil after draining it, stir and cover. This will prevent the pasta from sticking together.**

Add seasoning to taste as required.

To assemble: Drain pasta and spoon meat mixture into tubes. Place a plastic oven roasting bag on a shallow baking dish and place filled tubes in one layer in bag. Hold the bag open and pour tomato sauce over cannelloni. Tie bag with an elastic band or piece of string. Cook on HIGH for 10–12 minutes, until heated through.

Carefully transfer cannelloni and sauce to a warmed serving dish. Sprinkle with grated Parmesan cheese just before serving.

Creamy Pork Lasagne

1 tbspn (20 g/¾ oz) butter or margarine
1 onion, chopped
2 cups (250 g/8 oz) cooked, chopped pork
2 tbspns plain flour
¾ cup (185 ml/6 fl oz) hot chicken stock
½ tspn nutmeg
freshly ground black pepper to taste
90 g (3 oz) mushrooms, wiped and sliced
½ bunch spinach leaves, well washed and finely shredded
2 tbspns cream
6 sheets of instant lasagne
470 g (15 oz) can condensed cream of chicken soup
1½ cups (185 g/6 oz) grated Cheddar cheese

SERVES 4–6

Melt the butter or margarine in a 3 l (3 qt) microwave-safe dish or casserole on HIGH (100%) for 1 minute. Stir in the onion, cover dish with a well-fitting lid or plastic wrap and cook on HIGH for 2 minutes. Add the pork, flour, stock, nutmeg and seasoning. Stir well, then continue cooking on HIGH for 3–4 minutes, stirring well after 2 minutes, until the sauce boils and thickens. Stir in the mushrooms, spinach and cream. Re-cover dish and continue cooking on HIGH for 3–4 minutes.

Cover the base of a greased large, shallow microwave-safe baking dish with a layer of the pork mixture. Top with a layer of lasagne, then ⅓ of the can of soup, then ⅓ of the cheese. Continue layering meat mixture, lasagne, soup and cheese until all ingredients are used up, finishing with a layer of cheese.

Cook on MEDIUM (50%) for 20–25 minutes, until all the ingredients are heated through, the pasta is cooked and the cheese has melted on the top.

If desired, brown the top quickly under a hot grill before serving. Serve hot.

Pastitso

If you are looking for a pasta meal for a large family, then this recipe could be just the one for you. Reminiscent of lasagne, it has a meat and cream sauce.

500 g (1 lb) elbow macaroni
2 tspns oil
3 eggs, lightly beaten
1 cup (125 g/4 oz) grated tasty cheese

MEAT SAUCE

1 tbspn (20 g/¾ oz) butter
2 large onions, finely chopped
500 g (1 lb) topside minced beef or lamb
250 g (8 oz) tomato paste
60 g (2 oz) salami, finely chopped
½ cup (125 ml/4 fl oz) water or dry white wine
½ tspn sugar
salt and freshly ground black pepper to taste

CREAM SAUCE

¼ cup (60 g/2 oz) butter
¼ cup (30 g/1 oz) plain flour
2 cups (500 ml/16 fl oz) milk
2 eggs, lightly beaten
1 cup (125 g/4 oz) grated tasty cheese
pinch of nutmeg
salt and freshly ground black pepper to taste

TOPPING

1 tbspn grated Parmesan cheese
½ cup (60 g/2 oz) grated tasty cheese
freshly ground black pepper to taste

SERVES 6–8

*P*lace macaroni in a large microwave-safe dish, pour over 2.5 l (2½ qt) of boiling water and add oil. Cook, covered, on HIGH (100%) for approximately 12 minutes. Rinse well with hot water, drain and fold through lightly beaten eggs, tasty cheese and salt if desired. Cover and let stand while cooking meat sauce and cream sauce.

To prepare meat sauce: Melt butter in a shallow 2 l (2 qt) microwave-safe dish on HIGH for 1 minute, add chopped onions and cook, uncovered, on HIGH for 2 minutes. Add mince and mix well. Cook on HIGH for about 5 minutes or until meat changes colour. Stir to break up any meat lumps. Add remaining ingredients, then cook on MEDIUM HIGH (70%) for a further 8 minutes or until cooked. Cover and let stand.

To prepare cream sauce: Melt butter in a deep 1 l (1 qt) microwave-safe container, add flour and mix to a smooth paste. Gradually add milk, mixing well, until smooth. Cook on HIGH until sauce thickens, for approximately 6 minutes, stirring after 2–3 minutes. Add beaten eggs and mix well. Fold in cheese, nutmeg and seasonings.

Using a 3 l (3 qt) oval, microwave-safe casserole dish, spread half of the prepared macaroni evenly over the base. Pour the meat sauce over the macaroni, covering it well. Cover with remaining macaroni, levelling the surface. Pour cream sauce over macaroni to cover the surface evenly.

Top with tasty and Parmesan cheeses. Sprinkle with freshly ground black pepper. Cook on MEDIUM HIGH for 15–20 minutes. If desired, brown in a conventional oven for approximately 20 minutes.

● Macaroni Casserole

Macaroni Casserole

For a quickly prepared pasta meal this simple combination of mushrooms, ham and tomatoes is ideal. Add a salad for summer meals, or a side-serving of garlic bread for chilly days.

250 g (8 oz) macaroni
¼ cup (60 g/2 oz) butter
1 onion, thinly sliced
1 clove garlic, crushed
90 g (3 oz) mushrooms, sliced
3 tomatoes, skinned and chopped
¼ cup tomato paste
250 g (8 oz) ham, finely chopped
⅓ cup (90 ml/3 fl oz) dry white wine
black pepper to taste
fresh parsley, chopped
Parmesan cheese, grated

SERVES 4

Cook macaroni in boiling water on stove-top until tender.

Meanwhile, melt butter in a 2–2.5 l (2–2½ qt) casserole on HIGH (100%) for 1 minute. Stir in onion and garlic. Cook, covered, on HIGH for 2 minutes. Stir in remaining ingredients, except parsley and Parmesan cheese. Cook on HIGH for 4–5 minutes.

Drain macaroni, then stir into casserole mixture. Re-cover dish and heat on MEDIUM HIGH for 3–4 minutes.

Sprinkle with Parmesan cheese and parsley and serve with fresh crusty bread.

Macaroni Cheese

250 g (8 oz) macaroni
1 tspn oil
SAUCE
¼ cup (60 g/2 oz) butter or margarine
⅓ cup (45 g/1½ oz) plain flour
2½ cups (625 ml/20 fl oz) milk
½ tspn prepared English mustard
salt and freshly ground black pepper to taste
1½ cups (185 g/6 oz) grated tasty Cheddar cheese
paprika (optional)

SERVES 3–4

Cook macaroni, uncovered, on HIGH (100%) in a 1.5 l (1½ qt) microwave-safe container with boiling water and the oil for 6 minutes or until tender. Drain, return to container, cover and set aside.

To prepare sauce: Place butter in a 1 l (1 qt) microwave-safe bowl and heat, uncovered, on HIGH for 1 minute or until melted. Stir in flour until well blended and cook for 1 minute on HIGH, stirring once. Stir in milk, mustard and seasoning until well blended and cook, uncovered, on HIGH for 5–6 minutes, or until thickened, stirring every minute. Stir in 1 cup of cheese and heat on HIGH for 30 seconds.

Combine sauce with macaroni in a serving dish and sprinkle over the remaining ½ cup of cheese. Cook, uncovered, on HIGH for 2–3 minutes. Sprinkle with a little paprika. If preferred, omit paprika and brown lightly under a heated grill.

Golden Coconut Rice

If you don't know how to make coconut milk (and it isn't the liquid inside the coconut!), buy a can of coconut cream and dilute it by half with water.

2½ cups (625 ml/20 fl oz) coconut milk
½ cup (125 ml/4 fl oz) chicken stock
1 tspn turmeric
1 bay leaf (or 1 daun salam)
1½ cups (250 g/8 oz) Basmati long-grain rice
½ cup (90 g/3 oz) sultanas
½ cup (60 g/2 oz) slivered almonds, toasted
GARNISH
red and green fresh chillis
SERVES 8

Mix coconut milk, stock, turmeric and bay leaf together in a 3 l (3 qt) microwave-safe dish or casserole. Heat on HIGH (100%) for 6–8 minutes, until liquid begins to boil. Stir in the drained rice, sul-

tanas and almonds. Cook, uncovered, on HIGH for 12–14 minutes, stirring occasionally, until rice is tender and has absorbed all the liquid.

While rice is cooking, make chilli flowers by cutting the chillis approximately 2 cm (¾ in) from stem end. Using a sharp knife, shred the flesh downwards without cutting into stem. Place in a bowl of iced water so that the 'petals' curl.

When rice is cooked, cover and allow to stand for 5 minutes. Serve hot, garnished with chilli flowers. (See photo pages 91 and 162.)

Pilau Rice

1 tbspn (20 g/¾ oz) butter
1 onion, chopped
2 cups (315 g/10 oz) long-grain rice

freshly ground black pepper to taste
4 cups (1 l/1 qt) boiling chicken stock (or use stock cubes and water)
⅓ cup (45 g/1½ oz) cashew nuts
⅓ cup (60 g/2 oz) sultanas

SERVES 4–6

Melt butter in a 3 l (3 qt) casserole on HIGH (100%) for 30 seconds. Add onion, cover dish and cook on HIGH for 2 minutes until soft. Stir in rice and seasoning and cook, covered, on HIGH for 1 minute. Stir in boiling stock and cook, uncovered, for 12–14 minutes until tender. Continue cooking 1 minute at a time if not cooked to desired taste. Remove from oven and let stand, covered, for 5 minutes. Pour off excess liquid (if any). Stir through cashew nuts and sultanas.

Serve hot with poultry, fish or curries.

Smoked Ham Risotto

2 cups (500 ml/16 fl oz) chicken stock
1 cup (155 g/5 oz) long-grain rice
2 tbspns (40 g/1½ oz) butter
2 large onions, finely chopped
2 red capsicums, seeded and chopped
500 g (16 oz) mushrooms, wiped and sliced
155 g (5 oz) smoked ham, roughly chopped
4 tbspns chopped blanched almonds
4 tbspns chopped fresh parsley
black pepper to taste

SERVES 4

Pour chicken stock into a 3 l (3 qt) microwave-safe casserole or dish. Cook on HIGH (100%) for 3 minutes, until liquid boils.

Stir in the rice, cover dish and cook on HIGH for 10 minutes. Remove dish from oven and allow to stand, covered, while other ingredients are cooked.

Mix together butter, onion and capsicum in a small microwave-safe bowl. Cover and cook on HIGH for 4 minutes, stirring after 2 minutes.

Add onion and capsicum to rice, together with mushrooms, ham, almonds, parsley and pepper. Cook, uncovered, on HIGH for 2–3 minutes, stirring occasionally.

Nasi Goreng

This is a classic Indonesian dish with well-flavoured rice combined with meat, poultry or seafood.

¼ cup (60 ml/2 fl oz) cooking oil
1 large onion, chopped
2 cloves garlic, crushed
1 tspn finely chopped fresh chilli pepper
½ tspn shrimp paste
6 cups cooked rice (approx. 2 cups/410 g/13 oz raw)
1 tbspn soy sauce
1 tbspn tamarind sauce
1 tbspn curry sauce
1 cup (125 g/4 oz) cooked and chopped beef, pork, chicken or seafood (or use a combination)
¼ cup (45 g/1½ oz) raw peanuts
2 eggs

SERVES 4

Place the oil, onion, garlic, chilli and shrimp paste in a 2–3 l (2–3 qt) microwave-safe dish. Cover with a well-fitting lid or plastic wrap. Cook on HIGH (100%) for 3 minutes, stirring well after 2 minutes, until onion is soft.

● Smoked Ham Risotto

Stir in the rice and cook, uncovered, for 3 minutes. Stir in remaining ingredients, except the eggs. Cook for 5 minutes, stirring occasionally until all ingredients are heated through and well combined.

Cover and set aside for 2–3 minutes. Place eggs into a small microwave-safe bowl. Beat until frothy. Cook on HIGH for 30 seconds. Stir well and continue cooking on HIGH for 45 seconds. When egg is set, roughly chop and stir into rice.

Serve immediately.

Tuna Slice

3 cups cooked long-grain rice (approx. 1 cup/155 g/ 5 oz raw)
2 eggs, beaten separately
1 small onion, chopped
¼ cup (60 g/2 oz) butter, melted
470 g (15 oz) tuna, drained and flaked
2 tbspns plain flour
1½ cups (375 ml/12 fl oz) milk
1 tspn dry mustard
1 tspn paprika
black pepper to taste
½ cup (60 g/2 oz) grated Cheddar cheese
¼ cup chopped fresh parsley
2 tspns lemon juice
GARNISH
1 tomato, sliced
sprigs of watercress

SERVES 4–6

Combine the cooked rice, 1 of the beaten eggs, onion and 1 tbspn of the melted butter in a medium-sized mixing bowl. Press well onto the base and sides of a well-greased 22 × 14 cm (9 × 5 in) microwave-safe loaf pan. Press the tuna well onto rice base.

Place remaining melted butter, flour, milk, mustard and paprika into a 1–2 l (1–2 qt) microwave-safe dish or jug. Heat on HIGH (100%) for 3–4 minutes, stirring every minute until sauce boils and thickens. Add seasoning, then stir in remaining egg, cheese, parsley and lemon juice. Stir until well combined.

Pour sauce into tuna-lined dish. Cook on HIGH for 3 minutes, then reduce power and cook on MEDIUM (50%) for 10 minutes, until top is set. Cover dish loosely with foil and allow to stand for 5 minutes before turning out onto a serving plate.

Serve hot or well chilled, garnished with tomato slices and sprigs of watercress.

Paella

Rice features in the classic dishes of several countries of the world. In Spain paella is traditional.

90 g (3 oz) green prawns, shelled and deveined
90 g (3 oz) mussels, shelled
90 g (3 oz) white fish fillets, roughly chopped
1 tbspn (20 g/ ¾ oz) butter
2 tbspns olive oil
1 onion, chopped
410 g (13 oz) chicken, cut into pieces
1 tomato, skinned and chopped
1 green capsicum, seeded and sliced
1 clove garlic, crushed
pinch paprika
1 tspn powdered saffron, or to taste
1½ cups (250 g/8 oz) long-grain rice
2 cups (500 ml/16 fl oz) water, boiling
1 cup (155 g/5 oz) frozen peas
90 g (3 oz) calamari, cut into rings
3-4 cooked spicy sausages

SERVES 4-6

*P*lace the prawns, mussels and fish fillets into a shallow microwave-safe dish. Dot with the butter. Cover with a well-fitting lid or plastic wrap and cook on HIGH (100%) for 3-4 minutes, until fish is tender. Set aside.

Heat the oil and onion together in a 3 l (3 qt) microwave-safe dish or casserole, covered, on HIGH for 2 minutes, until onion is tender. Add chicken and continue cooking on HIGH for 3 minutes. Stir in tomato, capsicum, garlic and paprika. Cook, covered, on HIGH for 5 minutes. Add saffron, rice, boiling water, peas and calamari. Stir well and cook, uncovered, on MEDIUM (50%) for 15-20 minutes, until water is absorbed and rice is cooked.

Carefully stir in cooked seafood and cooked sausages. Heat through on MEDIUM for 2-3 minutes before serving.

Beef and Rice Hotpot

250 g (8 oz) minced steak
¼ tspn mixed dried herbs, or 1 tbspn chopped fresh herbs
½ small onion, chopped
½ cup (90 g/3 oz) raw rice
1 beef stock cube
410 g (13 oz) can tomatoes, undrained
75 g (2½ oz) mushrooms, sliced
1 cup (125 g/4 oz) grated cheese
2 tbspns chopped fresh parsley

¾ cup sliced French beans
¾ cup small cauliflower florets
2 tspns butter
squeeze of lemon juice

SERVES 2

*C*ook mince in a 1 l (1 qt) microwave-safe casserole for about 5 minutes on HIGH (100%) or until no longer pink, stirring with a fork several times to break up meat. Add herbs, onion, rice, stock cube, tomatoes and mushrooms. Cover and cook on HIGH for 20 minutes, stirring every 5 minutes. (Add a little more stock if the mixture shows signs of drying out.) Stand, covered, while preparing and cooking vegetables.

Place beans and cauliflower in a small container, just large enough to hold them, cover tightly with plastic wrap and cook on HIGH for 2-3 minutes; keep container covered. Combine cheese with chopped parsley and sprinkle over the hotpot. Cook on HIGH for about 1½ minutes or until cheese melts, or brown under a heated griller. Uncover vegetables, add butter and lemon juice and toss.

Serve vegetables with hotpot.

Rice and Vegetable Loaf

2 sticks celery, chopped
½ red or green capsicum, seeded and chopped
1 carrot, grated
3-4 large mushrooms, wiped and chopped
1 onion, chopped
¼ tspn dried oregano or mixed dried herbs
1 cup (125 g/4 oz) grated Cheddar cheese
1 clove garlic, crushed (optional)
3 cups cooked and rinsed brown rice (approx. 1 cup/ 155 g/5 oz raw)
½ cup (90 g/3 oz) peanuts, chopped
2 eggs, beaten
2 tspns Worcestershire sauce, or to taste

GARNISH
½ cup (60 g/2 oz) grated Cheddar cheese

SERVES 4

*M*ix all loaf ingredients thoroughly and place in a microwave-safe loaf or ring pan. Cook on HIGH (100%) for 5 minutes, reduce power to MEDIUM (50%) and cook for 10-12 minutes, until almost firm to touch. Allow to stand for 5 minutes, until firm. Turn out of mould onto serving plate.

Serve hot or cold, garnished with extra grated cheese, as an accompaniment to cold meat or pâté.

● Seafood Risotto

Seafood Risotto

2 tbspns cooking oil
1 onion, sliced
1 red and 1 green capsicum, seeded and thinly sliced
1 cup (155 g/5 oz) long-grain rice, rinsed
2 large tomatoes, peeled and roughly chopped
2 cups (500 ml/16 fl oz) hot fish or chicken stock
250 g (8 oz) marinara mix, fresh or canned
90 g (3 oz) mushrooms, wiped and sliced

GARNISH

freshly grated Parmesan cheese
chopped fresh parsley

SERVES 4 as a lunch or supper dish

*P*lace the oil, onion and capsicums into a 3 l (3 qt) microwave-safe dish or casserole. Cover with a well-fitting lid or plastic wrap and cook on HIGH (100%) for 2 minutes. Stir in the rice and cook, covered, on HIGH for a further 2 minutes. Stir in the tomatoes and stock. Re-cover dish and continue cooking on HIGH for 10–12 minutes until all the stock is absorbed and rice is tender. Stir well with a fork to separate rice grains. Stir in the marinara mix and mushrooms, then continue cooking on MEDIUM (50%) for 3–4 minutes until heated through.

Serve garnished with a sprinkle of Parmesan cheese and chopped parsley.

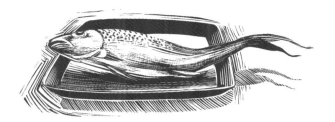

Fish and Seafood

PRECISION COOKING FOR BEST RESULTS

If there is one vital point to keep in mind when cooking seafood, it is that it should *never* be even *slightly* overcooked, because of its delicate flesh. This applies equally to conventional *and* microwave cooking, but because of the speed of microwave cooking it is even more important to bear this in mind when cooking by microwave.

To ensure the best possible results, always cover fish, especially fillets, to lessen moisture loss. Unvented microwave-safe plastic wrap is an ideal covering, particularly for fillets, if no moisture such as lemon juice or melted butter is added. Check fish a little before the recommended cooking time and remove from the oven when the flesh will *barely* flake when tested with a fork. Since fish continues to cook briefly after microwaving, if it is allowed to continue cooking until the flesh will flake readily, it will very likely be overcooked when served.

FISH FILLETS

A fish fillet cooked absolutely alone on a plate greased with a little melted butter, will bring out the true but delicate flavour of fish as nothing else can. Add a light squeeze of lemon or lime juice and a brief grinding of pepper and if you're a true fish fan you'll agree that this simple preparation is hard to beat. If preferred, brush the fish fillets with a little melted butter before cooking.

AVOID UNEVEN COOKING

If fish fillets have a thin, tapering end, place the fillets in the cooking dish so that the thin ends are tucked under themselves or sections of other fillets to avoid overcooking. Otherwise, shield the thin sections with small strips of aluminium foil, ensuring that the foil does not come in contact with the metal walls of the oven. When cooking fillets of

uneven size, it may be necessary to rearrange the fish at least once during cooking or to remove a smaller fillet as it is cooked.

CONVERTING YOUR OWN RECIPES

When converting a recipe from conventional to microwave cooking, where fish is one of a number of ingredients remember that because of the speed with which it cooks, fish should be added towards the end of the cooking time, or, if preferred, cook the fish separately then add it to the other ingredients or sauce and reheat briefly just before serving.

WHOLE FISH

When buying a whole fish remember to check that it will fit in your oven. Of course the head could be removed if necessary. The tail of a whole fish and the flesh close to the head will probably need to be shielded with strips of foil for part of the cooking time to prevent them overcooking. To ensure that the fish will not split as the skin shrinks during cooking, cut several slits with a sharp knife through the skin just into the flesh. Brush with combined melted butter and lemon juice and cover lightly with baking paper. Juices from the fish after cooking may be used as the basis of a sauce.

STUFFED WHOLE FISH

When cooking a fish with stuffing, it is wise to partly cook the stuffing before placing it in the fish cavity. For example, cook chopped onion in a little butter until softened, add crumbs, toss and cook in the butter and onion mixture until lightly coloured, add remaining ingredients and pack lightly into the fish cavity. If too tightly packed, the stuffing may swell during cooking and cause the fish to split. Remove or pierce fish eyes before cooking to prevent a build-up of steam.

SHELLFISH

Shellfish must be cooked with great care to avoid toughening the delicate flesh. Microwaves pass

● *Clockwise from top:* Moules Marinière (page 66); Tasmanian Salmon with Mousseline Sauce (page 78); Burmese Seafood Curry (page 81)

through the shells to cook the flesh, so there is no need for shelling before cooking. Thin sections must be shielded with foil to avoid overcooking. When preparing crayfish and crabs for cooking, tie legs close to the body. Shellfish is cooked when the shells change colour and the flesh is almost opaque.

OPENING SHELLFISH

To open oysters and mussels, cook a few at a time on HIGH (100%), removing each as its shell opens. The last or unopened shells should be prised open and checked for freshness. Take particular care with oysters and mussels — even brief overcooking will toughen and spoil the flesh.

TO DEFROST FISH

Remove fish from its freezer wrapping, place on a rack in a casserole to raise it above any collecting juices. For best results only partially defrost fish in the microwave oven. Let stand at room temperature to thaw completely. Leave covered and refrigerate immediately thawing is completed. Over-defrosting by microwave can start the cooking process in the thinner sections of the fish. Pat the fish dry with paper towels before cooking. If you like you can reserve any thawed juices and use them in sauces. (See also Food Defrosting Guide on page 235.)

REHEATING COOKED FISH

Cover the fish loosely and reheat at MEDIUM-MEDIUM HIGH (50–70%) power for the shortest possible time, as the delicate texture of fish can be quickly destroyed. For fish served with sauce, reheat each separately where possible and combine before serving.

TYPE OF SEAFOOD	QUANTITY	PREPARATION	POWER LEVEL	COOKING TIME IN MINUTES	STANDING TIME IN MINUTES
Fish Fillets	500 g/1 lb	Place in greased dish, dot with butter and cover loosely.	70%	5–6	2–3
Steaks or cutlets	500 g/1 lb	Place in greased dish, brush with melted butter and cover closely.	70%	6–8	3–4
Whole fish small	250 g/8 oz to 500 g/1 lb	Slash skin in thick section, brush with melted butter and cover loosely.	70%	3–5	2–3
large	750 g/1 ¾ lb to 1 kg/2 lb	Slash skin in thick section, brush with melted butter and cover loosely.	70%	10–12	3–4
Prawns, shelled	500 g/1 lb	Devein and drizzle melted butter or lemon juice over, cover loosely.	70%	5–6	2–3
unshelled	1 kg/2 lb	Drizzle lemon juice over and cover loosely.	70%	8–10	3–4
Lobster/crayfish, whole	750 g/1 ½ lb to 1 kg/2 lb	Tie legs securely and protect legs with aluminium foil. Cover loosely.	100% then 70%	5 10–12	5–6
Scallops, shelled	500 g/1 lb	Place in shallow dish, add ½ cup water or stock and cover closely.	70%	5–7	1–2
Mussels in shell	250 g/8 oz	Scrub shells and remove beards. Remove as shells open.	100%	2–3	
Oysters	250 g/8 oz	Scrub shells, remove as shells open.	100%	2–3	
Crabs, small (2)	1 kg/2 lb	Tie legs securely and protect legs with aluminium foil.	100% then 70%	5 5–6	4–5
Squid rings/calamari	500 g/1 lb	Clean and trim; place in greased dish with a little water and cover loosely.	70%	5–6	2–3

Pineapple Honey Prawns

2 tbspns (45 g/1½ oz) butter
500 g (1 lb) green prawns, shelled and deveined
1 tspn finely chopped fresh root ginger
1 clove garlic, crushed
4 spring onions, cut into 2 cm (¾ in) lengths
1 red capsicum, seeded and cut into thin strips
*440 g (14 oz) can pineapple pieces, juice reserved and
blended with 2 tspns cornflour or arrowroot*
2 tspns soy sauce
1 tbspn sherry (optional)
2 tspns chicken stock powder
1 tbspn honey

SERVES 2–3

*P*lace butter into a 1–2 l (1–2 qt) microwave-safe dish or casserole. Heat on HIGH (100%) for 1 minute, until bubbling and hot. Add prawns and quickly toss to coat in melted butter. Cook on HIGH for 2 minutes, remove from dish, set aside and cover with foil to keep warm.

Add ginger, garlic, spring onions and capsicum to dish, cover and cook on HIGH for 1 minute. Stir in pineapple pieces and cook for 2 minutes. Stir in remaining ingredients and cook on HIGH for 3–4 minutes until sauce boils and thickens. Return

● Pineapple Honey Prawns

prawns to dish and stir well to coat with sauce and spices. Heat through on HIGH for 2 minutes. Stir well. Serve hot on a bed of plain boiled rice.

Garlic Prawns

2 tbspns (40 g/1½ oz) butter
2 tbspns chopped fresh parsley, or 1 tspn dried parsley
2 tbspns lemon juice
2 cloves garlic, crushed
*500 g (1 lb) shelled, cleaned raw king prawns (approx.
750 g/1½ lb prawns in shell)*

SERVES 4

*P*lace butter in a large, shallow casserole. Melt in the microwave on HIGH (100%) for 30–40 seconds, then stir in parsley, lemon juice and garlic. Gently add prawns and toss to coat with butter. Cover dish and cook on HIGH for 3½–5 minutes, until prawns are pink, opaque, and cooked through when tested with a sharp knife. Check after minimum cooking time as they toughen if overcooked.

Serve as a starter with fresh, buttered brown bread or crusty French loaf slices.

Prawn Kebabs

*1 kg (2 lb) fresh, cooked king prawns, shelled and
deveined (approx. 750 g/1½ lb shelled)*
⅓ cup (90 ml/3 fl oz) Chinese oyster sauce
⅓ cup (90 ml/3 fl oz) soy sauce
⅓ cup (90 ml/3 fl oz) vegetable oil
few drops of chilli or Tabasco sauce
*1 red and 1 green capsicum, seeded and cut into 2 cm
(¾ in) squares*
500 g (1 lb) whole button mushrooms, wiped
lemon slices

SERVES 4

Combine oyster sauce, soy sauce, vegetable oil,
and chilli or Tabasco sauce in a medium-sized
bowl. Add the prawns, stir well, cover and marinate overnight in the refrigerator.

Thread prawns, capsicum and mushrooms onto
wooden cocktail sticks; arrange on a roasting rack
set in a shallow microwave-safe dish.

Cook on HIGH (100%) for 2–3 minutes, turning
once during cooking.

Serve garnished with lemon slices.

Moules Marinière

*Keep in mind the speed of microwave cooking when dealing
with seafood. Mussels will toughen if overcooked, so remove
each one as it opens.*

2 kg (4 lb) mussels
1 tbspn (20 g/¾ oz) butter
4 spring onions, finely chopped
1 clove garlic, crushed
1¼ cups (310 ml/10 fl oz) dry white wine
2 tbspns finely chopped fresh parsley
2 fresh thyme sprigs, or a pinch of dried thyme
1 bay leaf
freshly ground black pepper to taste
*extra chopped fresh parsley and crusty French bread for
serving*

SERVES 4

Wash mussels under cold, running water. Remove
all traces of mud, seaweed and barnacles with a
brush or knife. Remove beards. If mussels have

● Perch Fillets with Saffron Rice

cracked or broken shells, discard them. If any are slightly open, tap sharply and if they do not close, discard. Place butter in a 2–3 l (2–3 qt) microwave-safe casserole dish. Melt in the microwave on HIGH (100%) for 45 seconds. Stir in spring onions and garlic, and cook on HIGH for 1 minute. Stir in wine, parsley, thyme, bay leaf and pepper. Cook on HIGH for 2 minutes. Stir well. Add mussels, tightly cover dish and cook on HIGH for 2 minutes, giving dish a good stir or shake after 30 seconds to redistribute mussels and cooking juices.

The shells will open as the mussels cook. If necessary, lift cooked mussels out of dish and continue cooking remainder for a further 30 seconds–1 minute on HIGH. Never overcook mussels as they will become dry and tough. Place all mussels in a large serving dish, cover with plastic wrap and allow to stand for 2–3 minutes.

Put casserole dish and cooking liquid back into microwave and cook on HIGH for 2–3 minutes until liquid comes back to the boil. Boil for 2 minutes. Taste, and adjust seasonings if necessary. Pour liquid over mussels.

Serve garnished with chopped parsley and fresh crusty bread. (See photo page 62.)

Scallops in Wine

750 g (1½ lb) scallops, washed
155 g (5 oz) mushrooms, wiped and sliced
¼ cup chopped fresh parsley
1 tbspn white wine
1 tbspn lemon juice
black pepper, to taste
¼ cup (30 g/1 oz) dry breadcrumbs
2 tbspns (45 g/1½ oz) butter

SERVES 4–6

Divide scallops between 4 or 6 large scallop shells or microwave-safe ramekin dishes. Top each with the mushrooms and parsley. Sprinkle each dish with wine, lemon juice and pepper to taste.

Place dishes around the outer edge of turntable and cook on HIGH (100%) for 5 minutes. Stir scallops gently, rearrange dishes and continue cooking, uncovered, on HIGH for 3–4 minutes until scallops are tender. Set aside.

Combine breadcrumbs and butter in a small microwave-safe bowl. Cook on HIGH for 1½ minutes until butter is melted. Stir well and spoon a little of this breadcrumb topping over each scallop dish. Serve hot.

Perch Fillets with Saffron Rice

2 cups (375 g/12 oz) Calrose rice
3 cups (750 ml/24 fl oz) chicken stock
pinch saffron, or ½ tspn turmeric

SAUCE

1 tbspn cooking oil
½ small green and ½ small red capsicum, seeded and thinly sliced
1 carrot, peeled and cut into julienne strips
4 spring onions, peeled and thinly sliced
1 cup pineapple pieces, drained
½ cup (90 g/3 oz) sultanas
1 tspn finely diced fresh root ginger
⅓ cup (90 ml/3 fl oz) malt vinegar
1 tbspn soy sauce
¾ cup (185 ml/6 fl oz) chicken or fish stock (or use stock cubes and water)
1 tbspn cornflour (blended with a little of the stock)

FISH

4 fillets perch or other white fish
lemon pepper to taste
1 tspn butter

SERVES 4

Cook the rice in chicken stock with saffron or turmeric on stove-top for 15 minutes, stirring occasionally until tender and all liquid is absorbed.

Meanwhile prepare sauce and fish in microwave.

To prepare sauce: Heat the oil in a 2–3 l (2–3 qt) microwave-safe casserole or dish on HIGH (100%) for 1 minute, until hot. Add capsicum, carrot and spring onions, cover with a well-fitting lid or plastic wrap. Cook on HIGH for 2 minutes. Stir in pineapple, sultanas, ginger, vinegar, soy sauce, stock and cornflour. Cook on HIGH for 3–4 minutes until sauce boils and thickens, stirring well after 2 minutes. Cover and set aside while fish is being cooked.

To prepare fish: Place fish fillets in the base of a shallow microwave-safe dish, sprinkle with lemon pepper and top each with a little of the butter. Cover with plastic wrap. Cook on HIGH for 4 minutes until tender (fish should barely flake when tested with a fork.) Allow to stand for 2 minutes.

Return sauce to oven, heat on MEDIUM HIGH (70%) for 1 minute. Stir rice with a fork to fluff it up. Pile rice onto serving platter, place cooked fish on rice and top with sauce.

Spiced Perch

finely grated rind and juice of 1 orange
½ cup (125 ml/4 fl oz) wine
1 tbspn finely chopped fresh ginger
1 tspn green peppercorns
500 g (1 lb) perch fillets
fresh chives, chopped

SERVES 4

Combine orange rind and juice, wine, ginger and peppercorns in a large, shallow microwave-safe dish. Cook on HIGH (100%) for 3 minutes. Stir once during cooking.

Place fish in poaching liquid. Cover dish with a well-fitting lid or plastic wrap and cook on HIGH for 3–4 minutes until fish is tender and barely flakes when tested with a fork. Stand, covered, for 2 minutes.

Remove fish from liquid and serve garnished with chives and with a little of the poaching liquid poured over.

Tuna Terrine

LAYER ONE

440 g (14 oz) can tuna, drained (reserve liquid)
1–2 tbspns chopped fresh dill, or 1–2 tspns dried dill
freshly ground black pepper to taste
220 g (7 oz) can reduced cream (use half the can)
3 tspns gelatine

LAYER TWO

500 g (1 lb) fish fillets, e.g. John Dory, flake, trout
1 tbspn lemon juice
remaining half can of reduced cream

● Tuna Terrine

freshly ground black pepper to taste
¼ cup (60 ml/2 fl oz) mayonnaise
¼ cup (60 ml/2 fl oz) water
extra 3 tspns gelatine

SERVES 6 as an entrée or luncheon dish, or 15–20 as a snack

To make first layer, place tuna, dill, pepper and reduced cream into food processor or blender. Blend until smooth. Place ¼ cup (60 ml/2 fl oz) reserved tuna liquid in a medium-sized microwave-safe bowl. Sprinkle gelatine over. Heat on HIGH (100%) for 1 minute to soften. Whisk well to dissolve gelatine completely. Blend into tuna mixture in processor or blender.

Line a 5 cup loaf tin, 20 × 10 × 6 cm (8 × 4 × 3 in), with plastic wrap. Pour in tuna mixture and smooth top, using a small knife or spatula. Refrigerate while preparing second layer.

To make second layer, place fish fillets in a large, flat microwave-safe dish with thin ends towards centre. Add 1 tbspn water and cover. Cook on MEDIUM HIGH (70%) for 5 minutes. Allow to cool slightly.

Remove flesh from fish, discarding any bones and skin. Place in a food processor or blender with lemon juice, cream, black pepper and mayonnaise. Blend until smooth.

Place ¼ cup water in a medium-sized microwave-safe bowl. Sprinkle over extra gelatine. Heat on HIGH for 1 minute to soften. Whisk well to dissolve gelatine completely. Blend into fish mixture.

Pour fish mixture into loaf tin over tuna mixture. Cover and chill until very firm, preferably overnight. Turn out onto a platter and serve with crackers or crusty bread. Alternatively, slice and serve with salad and a dressing of your choice.

Tunabalaya

¼ cup (60 g/2 oz) butter
1 onion, thinly sliced
1 clove garlic, crushed
1 red or green capsicum, finely sliced
440 g (14 oz) can tuna, drained and flaked (reserve liquid)
440 ml (14 fl oz) can tomato juice
½ cup (125 ml/4 fl oz) dry white wine or chicken stock
½ tspn dried thyme
½ tspn dried basil
1 cup (155 g/5 oz) long-grain rice, washed
lemon wedges

SERVES 4–6

Heat butter, onion, garlic and capsicum together in a 1–2 l (1–2 qt) microwave-safe dish on HIGH (100%) for 2–3 minutes. Add reserved liquid from tuna, tomato juice, wine or stock, and seasonings. Stir well and heat on HIGH for 3–4 minutes, until liquid begins to boil. Stir in rice. Cover with a well-fitting lid or plastic wrap and cook on HIGH for a further 10–12 minutes.

Remove dish from the oven and stir through tuna. Re-cover dish and let stand for 10 minutes.

Serve with lemon wedges and a tossed salad.

Seafood Mousse with Avocado Sauce

4 spring onions, finely chopped
1 tbspn (20 g/ ¾ oz) butter
4 eggs
1½ cups (375 ml/12 fl oz) milk
½ cup (125 ml/4 fl oz) cream
220 g (7 oz) can prawns, tuna, salmon or crab meat, drained
dash of Tabasco sauce
freshly ground black pepper to taste

AVOCADO SAUCE

1 ripe avocado, peeled
black pepper to taste
dash of Tabasco sauce
approx. ½ cup (125 ml/4 fl oz) cream

SERVES 4–6

Place spring onions and butter in a 1 l (1 qt) microwave-safe bowl or jug. Cook on HIGH (100%) for 1 minute. Add the eggs, milk, cream, seafood, Tabasco, and black pepper. Beat until well combined.

Divide mixture between 4 well-greased teacups or 6 microwave-safe ramekin dishes. Place around edge of turntable in oven. Cook on MEDIUM (50%) for 8–10 minutes, until just set. Allow to stand, covered with foil, for 2–3 minutes.

While mousses are standing, prepare sauce. Place avocado flesh in a small microwave-safe mixing bowl and mash until smooth. Add seasonings and enough of the cream to make a soft pouring consistency. Heat on DEFROST (30%) for 2 minutes.

Turn out mousses onto serving plates. Serve garnished with avocado sauce.

Potato-topped Fish Casserole

2 large potatoes, peeled and chopped into 2 cm (¾ in)
pieces
2 tbspns (45 g/1½ oz) butter
2 rashers bacon, chopped
½ cup (60 g/2 oz) grated Cheddar cheese
1 onion, thinly sliced
1 stick celery, chopped
600 g (1¼ lb) trevally or ling fish fillets, skinned and
cut into large pieces
90 g (3 oz) button mushrooms, wiped and sliced
4 tomatoes, quartered
1 tbspn Worcestershire sauce
black pepper to taste

SERVES 4

Place potatoes in a microwave-safe bowl. Cover with a well-fitting lid or plastic wrap and cook on HIGH (100%) for 6 minutes, until tender. Mash with half the butter.

Place bacon between 2 sheets of absorbent kitchen paper. Cook on HIGH for 2 minutes. Stir bacon and cheese into mashed potato. Set aside.

Heat the remaining butter in a 2 l (2 qt) microwave-safe dish or casserole. Cook on HIGH for 1 minute. Add onion and celery. Cover dish with a well-fitting lid and cook on HIGH for 2 minutes, then stir in fish, mushrooms, tomatoes, Worcestershire sauce and pepper. Re-cover dish and cook on MEDIUM HIGH (70%) for 3 minutes, stirring once during cooking.

Top fish with mashed potatoes. Cook, uncovered, on MEDIUM HIGH for 10 minutes, or until fish barely flakes when tested with a fork.

Spinach and Smoked Salmon Roulade

This is a light-textured, colourful dish requiring some care in its handling to ensure a neat roll. Treat it like a Swiss-roll and you will have no trouble.

⅓ cup (90 ml/3 fl oz) thick sour cream
60 g (2 oz) smoked salmon, roughly chopped
1 tbspn chopped fresh dill, or 1 tspn dried dill
220 g (7 oz) washed and trimmed spinach
1 tspn butter
freshly ground black pepper to taste
pinch nutmeg
2 eggs, separated

SERVES 2–3

> **Strong or stale food odours can be removed from the microwave by heating a cup of water containing 4 or 5 slices of lemon (or 2 tablespoons of vinegar) on HIGH (100%) for 6–8 minutes, then wiping out the interior of the oven with a clean, dry cloth. Leave the door open for at least 5 minutes.**

Make a baking tray for the roulade by turning up and folding the four sides of a piece of baking paper, holding corners firm with a piece of adhesive tape, so that finished size of rectangle is approximately 23 × 18 cm (9 × 7 in). Place tray on a microwave-safe plate and make sure it can turn freely on the microwave turntable. Brush carefully with oil.

Mix together sour cream, smoked salmon and dill. Chill until required.

Place the well-washed spinach in a small microwave-safe container, with only the water that remains on the leaves. Cover tightly with a well-fitting lid or plastic wrap. Cook on HIGH (100%) for 4 minutes. Give dish a good shake. Let stand for 1 minute, then squeeze spinach and drain off any excess liquid. (It is important to remove all moisture from the spinach at this stage, in order to get a light result.) Chop spinach finely. Place in a medium-sized bowl and stir in butter, seasonings and egg yolks.

Whisk the egg whites until stiff, but still glossy and not quite dry. Gently fold into spinach mixture. Carefully spoon spinach mixture into prepared baking tray. Cook on HIGH for 3 minutes, until top is just set and centre is still a little sticky to touch. Sides should be just spongy. Leave to stand for 1 minute.

Turn out the roulade onto a piece of baking or greaseproof paper. (Work quickly at this stage so that roulade is rolled while it is still warm, to prevent it from cracking.) Spread the salmon filling onto the roulade and roll up, like a Swiss roll, using the paper as a lift and guide. Wet the baking paper and wrap around roulade. Secure well, then allow roulade to cool and set.

Serve warm (heat on MEDIUM HIGH [70%] for 2 minutes) or chilled, sliced and garnished with sprigs of fresh dill. (See photo pages 104–105.)

Ling Fillets with Apples and Pinenuts

This unusual combination is delicious. If ling fillets are unavailable, use any sweet-fleshed fish.

4 ling fillets
1 tbspn lemon juice
freshly ground black pepper to taste
2 tbspns pinenuts, toasted
2 tspns butter
2 tspns brown sugar
2 tbspns finely chopped spring onions
2 small or 1 large apple, peeled, cored and thinly sliced
2 tbspns cream
1 tbspn snipped fresh dill, or 1 tspn dried dill

SERVES 4

Wipe fish fillets and pat dry with absorbent kitchen paper. Place fish in a large, shallow microwave-safe casserole. Sprinkle with lemon juice and pepper. Cover dish with plastic wrap or a well-fitting lid. Cook on MEDIUM (50%) for 6–8 minutes, or until fish barely flakes when tested with a fork. Sprinkle with toasted pinenuts.

Place butter, sugar and spring onions in a small microwave-safe dish or casserole and cook on HIGH (100%) for 2 minutes. Add apple slices, cover loosely with plastic wrap and cook on HIGH for 2 minutes. Gently pour in cream and stir well, being careful not to break up apples. Serve apple mixture next to fish sprinkled with dill.

Lemon Whiting

1 tbspn (20 g/ ¾ oz) butter
½ cup (30 g/1 oz) soft breadcrumbs
1 tbspn finely chopped fresh parsley
finely grated rind and juice 1 lemon
¼ tspn ground nutmeg
¼ tspn black pepper
1 egg, lightly beaten
2 medium-sized whiting, gutted, scaled and thoroughly washed
lemon and cucumber slices

SERVES 2

Melt butter in a microwave-safe bowl in the microwave on HIGH (100%) for 30 seconds. Stir in the next 6 ingredients.

Pack the stuffing into the cavities of the prepared whiting. If necessary, secure edges together with wooden cocktail sticks.

Wrap stuffed whiting in plastic wrap and cook on HIGH for approximately 4 minutes, turning fish over after 2 minutes. The fish should barely flake when tested with a fork. Allow to stand for 2–3 minutes before unwrapping.

Garnish with lemon and cucumber slices.

● Lemon Whiting

Spicy Fish

Choose a fairly firm-fleshed fish such as gemfish or ling. For best results the fish should be of even thickness.

2 large onions, finely chopped
3 cloves garlic, crushed
1 tspn chilli powder
1 tbspn chopped fresh basil
1 tbspn finely chopped fresh root ginger
½ tspn dried shrimp paste
1 small piece tamarind, or 1 tspn tamarind paste
1 cup (250 ml/8 fl oz) thick coconut milk
4 fillets of white fish, skinned, boned and each cut into 4 equal pieces
lemon or lime wedges

SERVES 8

Combine all ingredients, except fish and lemon or lime wedges, in a large bowl, or process together in a food processor. Pour over fish and stir well, so that all pieces of fish are well coated with marinade. Cover and leave to marinate in the refrigerator for at least 30 minutes or overnight.

Transfer fish and marinade to a shallow microwave-safe dish. Cook on HIGH (100%) for 4–5 minutes, turning fish over after 2 minutes. Check that fish is cooked after minimum cooking time. (It should barely flake when tested with a fork.)

Serve fish in hot marinade, garnished with lemon or lime wedges.

Dijon Trout

This dish is suitable for oven bag cooking. The delicate flesh of trout will be protected by this moist cooking style.

5 tbspns (100 g/3½ oz) butter, softened
2 tbspns Dijon mustard
black pepper to taste
4 medium-sized trout
juice of 1 lemon
2 tbspns finely chopped fresh dill, or 1 tspn dried dill

SERVES 4

Blend 2 tbspns (45 g/1½ oz) of the butter with the mustard and black pepper. Lightly spread mixture over the fish. Place a plastic oven bag into a shallow microwave-safe dish and gently insert the fish into the bag. Close bag tightly with the strip of plastic provided with the bag, a piece of string or elastic band. Cook on HIGH (100%) for 6 minutes, until fish barely flakes when tested with a fork.

While fish is cooking, blend remaining butter with lemon juice and dill. Form into pats and chill in freezer. Serve cooked fish with dill butter.

● Dijon Trout

Ricotta-stuffed Trout

Take care not to overcook these beautifully textured fish. Serve with hot parsley rice and microwaved snow peas.

2 rashers bacon, chopped
1 tbspn chopped fresh chives
⅓ cup (90 g/3 oz) ricotta cheese
1 tbspn sour cream
black pepper to taste
2 whole trout, boned, with head removed and tail trimmed

SERVES 2

Place bacon between 2 sheets of absorbent kitchen paper. Cook on HIGH (100%) for 1 minute. Combine bacon with chives, cheese, sour cream and pepper. Spoon the filling into the boned cavity of the prepared fish.

Place fish in a shallow microwave-safe dish. Shield tail with a piece of foil. Cover dish with a well-fitting lid or plastic wrap. Cook on MEDIUM HIGH (70%) for 5–6 minutes, until flesh barely flakes when tested with a fork. Remove foil after 2–3 minutes.

● Whole Snapper in Capsicum and Black Bean Sauce

Whole Snapper in Capsicum and Black Bean Sauce

1 large snapper, scaled, gutted, head removed and
thoroughly washed
finely grated rind and juice of 2 large lemons
2 tbspns black beans in soy sauce, mashed lightly
1 tbspn soy sauce
1 slice fresh ginger, finely diced or minced
2 tbspns red and 2 tbspns green capsicum, seeded and
roughly chopped
1 small onion, quartered

SERVES 4

Place fish in a large, shallow microwave-safe casserole; pour lemon juice over fish. Cover tail with a small piece of foil to prevent overcooking. Cover dish and cook in microwave on HIGH (100%) for 6 minutes. Turn fish over halfway through cooking time and remove foil. Fish should barely flake when tested with a fork. Cover the dish and stand while sauce is prepared.

Mix black beans, soy sauce, ginger, capsicum and onion together in a small microwave-safe dish. Cover and cook on HIGH for 3 minutes, stirring or giving the dish a good shake halfway through cooking time to redistribute ingredients.

Transfer fish to a serving plate and serve immediately topped with sauce.

Fish Turbans

Ensure that you buy even, thin fish fillets for these turbans.
It will make filling and rolling the fish much easier.

8 white fish fillets (about 750 g/1½ lb)
1 tspn dried thyme
1 tbspn chopped fresh parsley
1 tbspn lemon juice
black pepper to taste
90 g (3 oz) smoked salmon, thinly sliced
½ cup (125 ml/4 fl oz) white wine
8 capers
8 sprigs fresh parsley

SERVES 4 as a main course
or 6 as an entrée

Lay fish fillets out flat. Combine thyme, parsley, lemon juice and pepper. Spread herb mixture over each fish fillet.

Trim salmon into pieces similar in width to the fish fillets and lay each piece flat over a fillet. Roll each fish fillet and secure with wooden cocktail stick. Place fish rolls in a large, shallow, microwave-safe casserole dish. Pour wine over the fish and cook, covered, on MEDIUM HIGH (70%) for 6–8 minutes. Remove fish turbans to a warm serving plate and garnish with capers and parsley.

Serve with wedges of lemon accompanied by steamed carrots and zucchini, if desired.

Tropical Coconut Redfish

When cooking coated fish in the microwave, it is important
to press crumb mixture firmly onto the fish. Always chill the
coated fish while browning dish is being heated.

2 large, very ripe bananas
2 tbspns lemon juice
sprinkle of lemon pepper
1 cup (125 g/4 oz) dry breadcrumbs
½ cup (60 g/2 oz) ground almonds
½ cup (45 g/1½ oz) desiccated coconut
500 g (1 lb) redfish fillets, skinned
2 tbspns seasoned plain flour
2 tbspns cooking oil

SERVES 4

Mash bananas with lemon juice and lemon pepper. Combine breadcrumbs with almonds and coconut for coating. Coat redfish fillets with flour and dip into banana mixture, then coat with breadcrumb mixture, pressing crumbs on firmly. Shake lightly to remove excess coating. Chill while heating browning dish.

Heat a browning dish on HIGH (100%) for 7 minutes until hot. Add oil and heat for 1 minute. Place fish in hot dish. Cook on HIGH for 2 minutes. Turn fish over and cook on HIGH for 1 minute. Drain on absorbent kitchen paper.

Serve immediately.

NOTE Should the fillets not fit into your dish in one batch, discard the used cooking oil and wipe out the dish. Reheat dish on HIGH for 4 minutes, add 2 tbspns of cooking oil, heat on HIGH for 1 minute, add remaining fish and cook as above.

Redfish with Spinach Stuffing

¼ cup cooked and chopped spinach
½ cup (125 g/4 oz) ricotta cheese
2 tbspns grated Parmesan cheese
1 small onion, chopped
1 egg, lightly beaten

1 tbspn chopped fresh dill
1 tbspn chopped fresh parsley
pepper to taste
8 redfish or butterfish fillets, skinned and boned
½ cup (30 g/1 oz) processed bran cereal
2 tbspns vegetable oil

SERVES 4

Mix together spinach, ricotta and Parmesan cheese, onion, egg, herbs and seasoning. Preheat a browning dish on HIGH (100%) for 6 minutes, until hot. Meanwhile, spread a little of the stuffing mixture over each fish fillet and sprinkle with bran cereal. Roll up the fillets and secure with small wooden cocktail sticks. Add the oil to the browning dish and continue heating on HIGH for 1 minute. Quickly add the stuffed fish fillets and cook on HIGH for 2 minutes. Turn fillets over and cook on HIGH for a further 2–3 minutes, until fish is tender.

Serve hot with cooked fresh vegetables.

● Fish Turbans

Fish Capricorn

750 g (1½ lb) white fish, cut into 2.5 cm (1 in) pieces
440 g (14 oz) can pineapple pieces, drained and
½ cup (125 ml/4 fl oz) juice reserved
2 tbspns cornflour
125 g (4 oz) mushrooms, wiped and chopped
2.5 cm (1 in) piece fresh ginger, thinly sliced
2 tbspns soy sauce
½ green capsicum, chopped

SERVES 4 as a main course
or **6** as an entrée

Place fish into a shallow, microwave-safe casserole. Cover and cook on MEDIUM HIGH (70%) for 4–6 minutes. Stand, covered, while making the sauce.

In a bowl combine the pineapple pieces, reserved juice blended with the cornflour, mushrooms, ginger and soy sauce. Cook on HIGH (100%) for 4–6 minutes, stirring halfway through and at the end of cooking, until thickened.

Drain the reserved fish and add to the pineapple sauce with the capsicum. Cook on HIGH a further 2 minutes.

Serve immediately.

Fish in Orange Sauce with Fettucine

250 g (8 oz) fettucine, spinach or plain
2 tomatoes, chopped
2–3 sticks celery, sliced
155 g (5 oz) mushrooms, wiped and sliced
220 g (7 oz) can sweet corn, drained
1–2 tbspns no-oil dressing
4 white fish fillets
sprinkle of lemon pepper
1 tspn butter
finely grated rind and juice of 1 large orange
1 tspn chopped capers
⅓ cup (90 ml/3 fl oz) cream
1 egg yolk
1 orange, sliced, for garnish

SERVES 4

Cook the fettucine on stove-top until tender.

To prepare salad: Chop tomatoes, celery and mushrooms together. Stir in sweet corn. Pour on a little salad dressing. Place in serving dish and set aside.

Place the fish fillets in a large, shallow microwave-safe dish. Sprinkle with lemon pepper and dot each with a little of the butter. Cover with a well-fitting lid or plastic wrap. Cook on HIGH (100%) for 2 minutes, turn fish over, re-cover and continue cooking on HIGH for 2–3 minutes. Fish is cooked when it barely flakes when tested with a fork.

Remove fish from dish, cover and keep warm on serving plate. Add orange rind and juice and capers to dish. Heat on HIGH for 1 minute, until orange juice and fish juices come to the boil. Add the cream and egg yolk. Stir carefully but thoroughly until egg yolk is well combined. Heat on DEFROST (30%) for 2–3 minutes, stirring after every minute, until sauce thickens.

Drain fettucine and place on a large serving plate. Serve fish on pasta, with a little of the sauce poured over and the remainder in a sauce boat. Serve salad separately.

Crab-stuffed Fish

1½ tbspns (30 g/1 oz) soft margarine
⅓ cup (20 g/¾ oz) soft breadcrumbs
pinch paprika
freshly ground black pepper to taste
125 g (4 oz) can crabmeat, drained
¼ cup chopped fresh parsley
4 spring onions, finely chopped
1 large egg white
1 tspn lemon juice
4 white fish fillets (approx. 125 g/4 oz each)

SERVES 4

Place margarine in a small microwave-safe bowl. Melt on HIGH (100%) for 30 seconds. Stir in 1½ tbspns of the breadcrumbs, the paprika and pepper to taste. Set aside.

Mix together the remaining breadcrumbs, the crabmeat, parsley, spring onions, egg white and lemon juice in a small bowl.

Spoon ¼ of the crab filling onto the centre of each fillet. Loosely roll up each piece of fish, enclosing stuffing in centre. Secure with wooden cocktail sticks and place in a shallow microwave-safe dish. Spoon reserved crumb mixture evenly over the top of each fish roll. Cover dish with a well-fitting lid or plastic wrap and cook on HIGH (100%) for 5 minutes, or until fish is barely tender and filling is hot. Stand, covered, for about 2 minutes.

Remove cocktail sticks before serving.

Kingfish with Herb and Lemon Butter

2 tbspns (45 g/1½ oz) butter
2 tbspns lemon juice
4 kingfish cutlets
2 tbspns finely chopped fresh mixed herbs
black pepper to taste

SERVES 4

*P*lace butter and lemon juice into a large shallow microwave-safe dish. Cook on HIGH (100%) for 2 minutes. Add kingfish to dish. Cover dish with a well-fitting lid or plastic wrap and cook on MEDIUM HIGH (70%) for 7–8 minutes, turning fish once during cooking.

Place fish on a warmed serving dish. Stir fresh herbs and pepper into the hot butter and juices. Spoon a little juice over each cutlet before serving.

Fish Cutlets with Pesto

2 cloves garlic, crushed
1 tbspn pinenuts
¼ cup chopped fresh basil, or 1 tbspn dried basil
¾ cup (90 g/3 oz) grated Parmesan cheese
2 tbspns olive oil
4 fish cutlets, e.g. snapper, kingfish or jewfish (approx. 1 kg/2 lb)
1 small onion, chopped
2 tspns olive oil
2 tomatoes, peeled and finely chopped
4 anchovy fillets, drained and chopped
freshly ground pepper to taste

SERVES 4

*T*o make the pesto, pound the garlic and pinenuts in a mortar and pestle or use a food processor. Add basil and continue pounding or processing. Add Parmesan. Slowly add the oil, until the sauce has the consistency of thick cream.

●
To warm hand towels for dinner guests, oriental style, soak 4–6 small towels in scented water. Squeeze them well and roll each separately before covering them with plastic wrap. Heat on HIGH (100%) for about 2 minutes.
●

Place the fish cutlets in a shallow, microwave-safe casserole and cook, covered, on MEDIUM HIGH (70%) for 8–10 minutes, turning halfway through cooking, until fish barely flakes when tested with a fork. Allow to stand, covered, while completing the sauce.

Place the onion and 2 tspns of oil in a bowl and cook on HIGH (100%) for 2 minutes. Add the tomatoes, anchovies and pepper to taste. Cook on HIGH a further 3–4 minutes or until tomatoes are tender. Stir the pesto into the tomato sauce and heat on HIGH a further 1 minute or until hot.

Pour sauce over the fish cutlets. Garnish with sliced lemon and sprigs of fresh parsley if desired.

Tasmanian Salmon with Mousseline Sauce

Unfortunately the wonderful Tasmanian salmon isn't available fresh all year round so it's good to know that ocean trout is considered by some to be its equal.

2 cutlets Tasmanian Atlantic salmon or ocean trout (total weight 315–345 g/10–11 oz)
2 tbspns (45 g/1½ oz) butter, melted
MOUSSELINE SAUCE
2 tbspns (45 g/1½ oz) butter
2 egg yolks, beaten
1 tbspn lemon juice
½ cup (125 ml/4 fl oz) cream
salt and pepper to taste

SERVES 2

*H*eat browning dish on HIGH (100%) for 6 minutes. Brush cutlets on both sides with melted butter. Press down in browning dish, reduce power to MEDIUM HIGH (70%) and cook for 3–4 minutes, or until fish barely flakes. Do not cook on both sides. Remove to heated serving dish and cover with aluminium foil while making sauce.

To prepare sauce: Heat butter in a small bowl on MEDIUM HIGH for 1 minute. Add beaten egg yolks, lemon juice and half the cream; season to taste. Cook on MEDIUM (50%) for 1 minute, stirring four or five times. Remove from oven and beat briskly with a small wire whisk until thick and fluffy. Whip remaining cream until thick, fold quickly into sauce and heat about 30 seconds, stirring once. Pour over cutlets and reheat on MEDIUM for 20–25 seconds. (See photo page 62.)

● *From top:* Lemon Mustard Jewfish (page 80); Kingfish with Herb and Lemon Butter

Lemon Mustard Jewfish

1 tbspn (20 g/¾ oz) butter
1 small onion, finely chopped
½ cup (60 g/2 oz) dry breadcrumbs
2 tspns mustard seeds
1 tspn Dijon mustard
finely grated rind and juice of 1 lemon
black pepper to taste
2 large or 4 small jewfish cutlets
lemon slices to garnish

SERVES 4

Melt the butter in a small microwave-safe dish on HIGH (100%) for 45 seconds; stir in the onion. Cook on HIGH for 2 minutes. Stir in the breadcrumbs, mustard seeds, Dijon mustard, lemon rind and juice, and pepper to taste.

Place fish in a shallow microwave-safe dish. Top with the lemon and mustard mixture. Cover dish with a well-fitting lid or plastic wrap and cook on HIGH for 6–7 minutes until fish is tender.

Garnish with lemon slices. (See photo page 79.)

Fish Curry

Frozen fish can be used in this curry just as easily as fresh and can be cooked in the portions taken from the pack. Just adjust cooking times accordingly. The curry is also superb when prepared with prawns or squid.

2 onions, finely chopped
1½ tbspns (30 g/1 oz) butter or margarine
garlic to taste
curry powder to taste
¾ tspn ground coriander
¾ tspn ground cumin
¾ tspn ground ginger
paprika to taste
salt to taste
440 g (14 oz) can tomatoes
750 g (1½ lb) fish fillets, skinned and boned

SERVES 2–3

Place the onions, butter or margarine, garlic and curry powder in a microwave-safe bowl. Cook on HIGH (100%) for 1½ minutes. Stir in the remaining spices and seasonings, add the tomatoes and cook on DEFROST (30%) for 6 minutes.

Cut fish into strips and stir into the sauce. Cover and cook on MEDIUM HIGH (70%) for 5 minutes or until just cooked.

Serve with saffron or turmeric rice garnished with lemon.

Creamy Oyster Casserole

¼ cup (60 g/2 oz) butter or margarine
½ cup (60 g/2 oz) dry breadcrumbs
pinch paprika
1 stick celery, finely chopped
24 fresh oysters, washed and opened, or 24 bottled oysters
1 cup (250 ml/8 fl oz) chicken soup
2 tbspns cream
1 tbspn chopped fresh parsley
black pepper to taste

SERVES 4

Place 2 tbspns (45 g/1½ oz) of the butter or margarine into a small microwave-safe dish and heat on HIGH (100%) for 30 seconds until just melted. Stir in the breadcrumbs and paprika. Set aside.

Place celery and remaining butter into a larger microwave-safe bowl. Cover with a well-fitting lid or plastic wrap and cook on HIGH for 1–1½ minutes, until celery is softened.

Stir in the well-drained oysters, re-cover dish and continue cooking on MEDIUM (50%) for 3–4 minutes, until the edges of the oysters just begin to curl and they are heated through.

Stir in the soup, cream, parsley and pepper to taste. Continue cooking on MEDIUM for 5–6 minutes, stirring occasionally until the liquid starts to bubble.

Sprinkle top of dish with reserved buttered breadcrumbs, then cook on MEDIUM HIGH (70%) for 2 minutes, until top is crisp. Serve hot or cold.

Burmese Seafood Curry

The prawns used in this recipe are already cooked. Take care to barely heat them through to avoid overcooking.

2 large onions
3 cloves garlic
5 cm (2 in) piece green ginger
⅓ cup (90 ml/3 fl oz) oil
2 tspns turmeric
2 cm (¾ in) piece prawn paste (blachan), chopped fine
1 green capsicum, seeded and cut in thin strips
¼ tspn chilli powder (optional)
4 large tomatoes, chopped
1 cup (250 ml/8 fl oz) chicken stock
1 kg (2 lb) cooked prawns, shelled and deveined but with tails intact
chopped fresh coriander or parsley

SERVES 4

*F*inely mince or chop the onions, garlic and ginger. Heat oil in a large, microwave-safe casserole on HIGH (100%) for 2 minutes. Add onions, garlic and ginger and cook on HIGH for 5 minutes, stirring several times. Add turmeric, prawn paste, capsicum, chilli powder, tomatoes and chicken stock. Cook, uncovered, on HIGH for 20 minutes.

Add prawns and heat on HIGH for 2–3 minutes, or until prawns are just heated through — don't overcook the prawns or they'll become tough. Stir through coriander or parsley and serve. (See photo page 62.)

Poultry and Game

Whether roasting poultry or cooking poultry pieces as part of a favourite recipe, the microwave oven will do the job splendidly. As with large meat cuts, a whole bird will brown slightly when cooked by microwave but there are several ways of enhancing the colour if the bird is to be served without a covering sauce.

BROWNING POULTRY

Special microwave browning agents are available for use in browning poultry, some commercial and some of your own making. Check out any marinade mixtures you might use for barbecuing — these would probably do a very satisfactory job on a whole chicken or chicken pieces. Glazes based on soy sauce and honey mixtures go well with chicken. If you're really pressed for time, a little melted butter and paprika can give a bird a pleasant, light golden glow. If the family enjoys roasted or pan-fried poultry, consider acquiring a browning dish or grill for a close-to authentic baked appearance and flavour.

GETTING THE BASICS RIGHT

While poultry pieces may be cooked very successfully on 100% power, whole birds should be cooked on MEDIUM HIGH (70%) for best results.

As many people purchase frozen poultry it is important to emphasise the need for thorough defrosting — whole birds, particularly, and also poultry pieces.

● *Previous pages, clockwise from top:* Glazed Christmas Ham (page 131); Christmas Pudding (page 176) with Brandy Sauce (page 221); Christmas Cake (page 205); Kumara with Sherried Orange Sauce (page 160); Cranberry Sauce (page 220); Piquant Beans (page 146); Roast Turkey (page 98); Onions in Cheese Sauce (page 155); Pavlova (page 189)

When thawing poultry, ensure that the bird defrosts evenly, even if it means slowing down the process of defrosting with an extra resting period or two to allow even thawing throughout the bird. Rinse, particularly the cavity, with hot or even boiling water after thawing to ensure the job has been done thoroughly.

If the bird is to be stuffed, remember to take the weight of the stuffing into account when working out the required cooking time. Stuffings may be partly cooked first, and remember that there may be some expansion of the ingredients during cooking, so stuff loosely rather than tightly packed.

Truss the bird neatly so that wings and legs are tied close to the body. Cover wing and leg ends as well as the breast with strips of foil to prevent overcooking and leave in place for about half the cooking time. Keep the foil in place with wooden cocktail sticks and ensure that it will at no time come into contact with the walls of the oven.

To cook, use either a browning dish (following the manufacturer's instructions) or place the bird on a roasting rack in a casserole, to ensure that the bird will not be sitting in the juices that gather during cooking. (To avoid having the bird cooking in too moist an atmosphere, use a bulb baster to siphon off the juices from the bottom of the dish several times. These can be reserved and used later, after skimming off excess fat, to prepare gravy or sauce.)

FOLLOW A SET ROUTINE

A few simple rules will ensure that poultry stays moist and tender. Always begin cooking with the bird breast down and turn it over for the last half of the cooking time. A single turn is sufficient for a chicken but it is preferable to turn a duck twice and a turkey three or four times — both sides, breast down then breast up.

For enhanced flavour and colour, baste the bird during cooking, either with a commercial preparation or your own mixture.

SELF-BASTING TURKEYS AND CHICKENS

During cooking, the skin of these birds must be pierced to release the fat placed under the skin to encourage browning and help keep the flesh moist. Pierce the skin each time the bird is turned.

WHEN IS THE BIRD COOKED?

It is important that poultry be thoroughly cooked. When the cooking time is almost completed, take the bird from the oven and check. When the juices begin to run clear and leg joints move easily in their sockets, cover the bird with a 'tent' of foil and stand for 10–12 minutes. Before carving, check again that juices run clear. If there is a delay of any more than a few minutes before carving, cover closely with foil to keep warm. Refrigerate any leftovers promptly.

OVEN-BAG COOKERY

This is a very satisfactory method for cooking either whole birds or portions, particularly the large or less tender. Add a little liquid and seasonings during cooking. If you wish you may marinate the bird in the oven bag prior to cooking. Follow the manufacturer's directions for use of the bag but we suggest that you reduce the amount of flour used in the bag to 2 to 3 teaspoons.

PAN-FRYING

Poultry pieces cook well when pan-fried in a browning dish or grill. Brown lightly when the dish has been heated and complete cooking at MEDIUM-MEDIUM HIGH) (50–70%) power.

BOILING-FOWLS

If cooking a boiling-fowl, choose the conventional method of gentle simmering on the stove-top for best results.

TO DEFROST POULTRY

Remove from wrapping, place the bird, breast down, on a rack in a suitable dish. If defrosting pieces, place on a rack with thicker pieces towards the outside. Cover loosely with kitchen paper towel. Defrost according to directions in your oven manual. (See also Food Defrosting Guide, page 235.)

POULTRY COOKING GUIDE					
POULTRY	**1ST SETTING**	**COOKING TIME**	**2ND SETTING**	**COOKING TIME**	**STANDING TIME**
Chicken					
Whole	100%	3–4 mins	70%	10–12 mins per 500 g (1 lb)	10–12 mins
Pieces	100%	3–4 mins	100%	6–8 mins per 500 g (1 lb)	10–12 mins
Fillets			70%	7–9 mins per 500 g (1 lb)	6–8 mins
Duck					
Whole	100%	4–5 mins	50%	8–10 mins per 500 g (1 lb)	10–15 mins
Pieces	100%	4–5 mins	100%	6–8 mins per 500 g (1 lb)	10–15 mins
Turkey					
Whole (up to 4 kg/8 lb)	100%	10–12 mins	50%	10–12 mins per 500 g (1 lb)	15–20 mins
Breasts	100%	4–5 mins	50%	10–12 mins per 500 g (1 lb)	15–20 mins
Drumsticks	100%	4–5 mins	50%	14–16 mins per 500 g (1 lb)	15–20 mins
Game birds					
Duck, pheasant, quail			50%	6–8 mins per 500 g (1 lb)	8–10 mins

After one-third of defrosting time, turn the bird and inspect for warm spots; protect these with foil strips. Rearrange pieces if required. Proceed with defrosting.

Do not try to hurry defrosting, particularly with large birds. It is better to let the bird stand for 5 to 10 minutes during defrosting to allow the heat to equalise rather than risk partly cooking some sections while others remain frozen.

TO REHEAT COOKED POULTRY

Take care not to dry out poultry when reheating. Cover with a little gravy or sauce if available, otherwise cover with a light mist of water and use unvented plastic wrap over the plate or dish. For sliced poultry heat on MEDIUM HIGH (70%) and on MEDIUM (50%) for larger pieces, turning them for even heating.

PROTECT THE OVEN DURING BAKING

To protect the oven from spattering, cover poultry with baking paper after leaving the bird uncovered for a period to encourage browning. If you're not happy with a roast unless it's well browned and crisp, you could of course give it a quick burst (after cooking is complete by microwave) under a heated grill or in the oven of your conventional range.

Roast Chicken Dinner

1 × size 15 (1.5 kg/3 lb) chicken, washed and wiped dry
2 tbspns (45 g/1½ oz) butter, melted
500 g (1 lb) broccoli, washed and cut into small florets
4–6 medium-sized potatoes, peeled and quartered
345 g (11 oz) can asparagus spears
2 tspns cornflour or gravy powder

SERVES 4

Brush chicken all over with melted butter. Place breast side down on a microwave roasting rack or upturned saucer, set in a microwave-safe dish. Cook in microwave on HIGH (100%) for 8 minutes. Turn bird over and cover wing tips and ends of legs with foil to prevent further cooking and drying out. Continue cooking on HIGH for 4 minutes. Baste chicken with juices. Cook for a further 5–8 minutes on HIGH, until juices run clear in thigh when pierced with a sharp knife. Remove chicken from dish, cover with foil and allow to stand for 15 minutes.

Set juices aside, allow fat to rise to surface and skim off.

To cook vegetables: Place broccoli at one end of a large, shallow, microwave-safe dish. Place potatoes at other end. Cover dish tightly with plastic wrap. Cook on HIGH for 8 minutes. Turn potatoes over in dish, putting cooked ones towards centre of dish. Carefully place asparagus in centre of dish. Re-cover with plastic wrap. Cook for 3 minutes on HIGH. Remove dish from the oven. Allow to stand for 5 minutes. If desired, sauté potatoes in a frying pan on stove-top.

Mix juices and ¼ cup (60 ml/2 fl oz) boiling water with cornflour or gravy powder blended with a little cold water. Microwave on HIGH for 3–5 minutes, stirring after every minute, until gravy boils and thickens. If necessary strain into a gravy boat.

Place chicken on a serving platter, accompanied by potatoes, broccoli and asparagus.

Honey-baked Chicken

1 × size 15 (1.5 kg/3 lb) chicken
2 sprigs parsley
1 sprig thyme
2 sprigs celery tops
1 bay leaf
⅓ cup (125 g/4 oz) honey
1 tbspn (20 g/¾ oz) butter
1 tbspn lemon juice
salt and freshly ground pepper to taste

SERVES 4–5

Rinse chicken inside and out with hot water and dry thoroughly, particularly inside, with absorbent kitchen paper towels. Tie herbs together and place in chicken cavity. Draw neck skin over back of chicken and secure with wooden cocktail sticks. Tuck wings behind chicken and tie legs. Place chicken on roasting rack in a shallow microwave-safe casserole.

Combine honey, butter and lemon juice in a small dish and heat on HIGH (100%) for 2 minutes or until blended, stirring after 1 minute. Brush glaze over chicken and turn, breast down, on roasting rack. Cover thin ends of drumsticks and wings with small strips of aluminium foil. Cook on HIGH 4 minutes, reduce to MEDIUM HIGH (70%) and cook a further 15–18 minutes. Remove foil strips, turn chicken breast side up and brush with honey glaze. Cook on MEDIUM HIGH a further 15–18 minutes or until cooked, brushing with glaze several times. Remove to heated serving dish, brush once more with glaze, cover with a 'tent' of foil and let stand 10–12 minutes before serving.

● Chicken Marengo

Chicken Marengo

4 chicken maryland joints, cut into drumsticks and thigh joints
1 tbspn seasoned, plain flour*
1 tbspn (20 g/¾ oz) butter
1 large tomato, chopped
½ cup (125 ml/4 fl oz) dry white wine
1 tbspn tomato paste
1 tspn chicken stock powder
1 clove garlic, crushed
155 g (5 oz) button mushrooms, wiped and sliced
chopped fresh parsley

SERVES 4

Coat chicken in flour.

Melt butter in a suitable frying pan on top of stove. Add chicken pieces and fry quickly for 2 minutes until brown. Turn pieces over and brown other sides for 2 minutes. Transfer to a 1.5–2 l (1½–2 qt) microwave-safe dish; add tomato.

Mix wine, tomato paste, stock powder, garlic and ¼ cup water together. Pour over chicken. Cover with a well-fitting lid or plastic wrap. Cook on HIGH (100%) for 5 minutes, stirring well after 3 minutes to redistribute ingredients. Test to see if chicken is cooked. Meat juices should run clear when pierced with a sharp knife.

Stir in mushrooms and chopped parsley, re-cover and cook for a further 2 minutes.

*NOTE A microwave seasoning mix for chicken is good for coating or adding to flour, as it colours as well as lightly flavours the meat.

Chicken and Asparagus Mornay

4 large chicken pieces or breasts, skinned, boned and washed
sprinkle of lemon pepper or microwave browner
1 tbspn (20 g/¾ oz) butter or cooking oil
1½ tbspns plain flour
1 tspn prepared mustard
1 cup (250 ml/8 fl oz) condensed chicken soup
¾ cup (185 ml/6 fl oz) milk
1 tbspn mayonnaise
2 tbspns chopped fresh parsley
black pepper to taste
425 g (13½ oz) can asparagus spears, drained
2 cups (315 g/10 oz) long-grain rice
¼ cup chopped fresh parsley
2 × 25 g pkts cheese corn chips, crushed

SERVES 4

Cut the chicken pieces in half and place in a large, shallow microwave-safe dish. Sprinkle with lemon pepper or microwave browner and cover with a well-fitting lid or plastic wrap. Cook on HIGH (100%) for 4 minutes, turning meat over after 2 minutes. Leave to stand while sauce is being made.

Melt the butter (or pour cooking oil) in a 1–2 l (1–2 qt) microwave-safe dish or jug on HIGH for 45 seconds. Stir in the flour and mustard and cook on HIGH for 30 seconds, stirring once. Add juice from the chicken and stir well until sauce is thick but smooth. Cook on HIGH for 1 minute. Stir in the soup, milk, mayonnaise, parsley and seasoning to taste.

Place asparagus in dish with chicken. Pour sauce over chicken.

Prepared dish can be covered and left in the refrigerator at this stage, ready to cook later.

To cook, place the rice in a saucepan of boiling water on top of stove. Cook for 10–15 minutes, until tender. Drain and stir in parsley.

Sprinkle crushed corn chips on top of the sauce and chicken. Cook on HIGH for 2 minutes, reduce power and continue cooking on MEDIUM (50%) for 8–10 minutes, until heated through.

Serve hot on a bed of hot parsley rice. (See photo pages 24–25.)

NOTE To serve six people use six chicken pieces and increase sauce by using 1½ cups (375 ml/ 12 fl oz) of condensed chicken soup. Cook chicken for 4–6 minutes then cook completed dish on HIGH for 4 minutes; complete cooking time as in the above method.

Chicken Paprika

1 tbspn (20 g/¾ oz) butter
1 tbspn oil
1 large onion, chopped
1 clove garlic, crushed
2 tspns paprika (or more according to taste)
1 cup (250 ml/8 fl oz) strong chicken stock, hot
2 kg (4 lb) chicken pieces, skinned
1 tspn plain flour
½ cup (125 ml/4 fl oz) sour cream

SERVES 4–6

Add butter and oil to a medium-sized microwave-safe casserole. Stir in onion, garlic and paprika and cook on HIGH (100%) until onion is transparent and begins to colour slightly. Add stock and stir. Add chicken and cook on HIGH for 6–8 minutes, rearranging chicken after 4 minutes. Reduce to MEDIUM HIGH (70%) and cook for 10 minutes or until chicken is cooked, rearranging chicken pieces after 5 minutes.

Stir flour into sour cream and add to dish gradually, stirring in well. Reheat on MEDIUM HIGH only until at serving temperature.

Serve with boiled noodles or rice. Accompany with a salad or a green vegetable.

● Chicken Satay

Valencia Chicken

Citrus fruits bring out the flavour of chicken and this recipe is no exception. Valencia Chicken is a Spanish dish which is adapted here for the microwave.

2 tbspns plain flour
½ tspn paprika
4 large chicken joints, skinned
½ cup (125 ml/4 fl oz) orange juice
1 tbspn Worcestershire sauce
½ cup (125 ml/4 fl oz) dry white wine or chicken stock
¼ tspn celery salt
155 g (5 oz) mushrooms, wiped and trimmed
¼ cup (45 g/1½ oz) black olives, seeded and halved
fried orange wedges for garnish

SERVES 4

Combine flour and paprika, use to coat the chicken. Place in a 2–3 l (2–3 qt) microwave-safe casserole.

Mix orange juice, Worcestershire sauce, wine or stock and seasoning with any remaining seasoned flour. Pour liquid over chicken. Cover dish and cook on HIGH (100%) for 5 minutes, stir chicken and sauce well. Re-cover dish and continue cooking on MEDIUM (50%) for 25 minutes, until chicken is tender.

Stir in mushrooms and black olives. Re-cover and cook on MEDIUM for 3–4 minutes until mushrooms are heated through.

Serve hot with noodles or preferred pasta, garnished with orange wedges.

Chicken Satay

600 g (1¼ lb) chicken fillets, cut into 2.5 cm (1 in) chunks
bamboo skewers
1 tbspn cooking oil
MARINADE
1 tspn caraway seeds
1 tspn ground coriander
1 clove garlic, crushed
1 tbspn brown sugar
1 tbspn soy sauce
1 tbspn lemon juice
SATAY SAUCE
3 red chillies, seeded and finely chopped (or to taste)
2 cloves garlic, crushed
1 tspn fresh ginger, grated
¼ cup (60 g/2 oz) peanut butter
1 cup (250 ml/8 fl oz) water
¼ cup (45 g/1½ oz) sultanas
¼ cup (30 g/1 oz) raisins
½ cup (125 ml/4 fl oz) vinegar
½ cup (125 g/4 oz) sugar
½ cup (90 g/3 oz) peanuts
1 tbspn fruit chutney

SERVES 4

Combine all marinade ingredients in a large mixing bowl. Add chicken and cover bowl with plastic wrap. Leave for at least 1 hour in the refrigerator.

Mix all the sauce ingredients together in a 1–2 l (1–2 qt) microwave-safe jug and cook on HIGH (100%) for 10–12 minutes, stirring halfway through cooking time. Push mixture through a fine sieve, or purée sauce in a food processor or liquidiser. Set aside.

Preheat a browning dish on HIGH for 7 minutes until hot. Meanwhile thread chicken cubes onto skewers. Quickly add the oil to hot browning dish and swirl to coat, add chicken pieces. Cook on HIGH for 2 minutes, turning chicken over and continue cooking on HIGH for a further 3 minutes. You may have to do this in a few batches.

Serve chicken hot with satay sauce. (To reheat sauce, cook on HIGH for 1–2 minutes. Stir well before serving.)

NOTE This recipe serves four but for two people, use two chicken breasts, boned and skinned. Halve remaining ingredients and cook as above.

● *From top:* Valencia Chicken; Roast Duckling with Cherry Sauce (Page 100)

Chicken and Spinach Stir-fry

3 tspns soy sauce
1 tbspn cold water
2 tspns cornflour
2 tspns dry sherry
½ tspn honey
¼ tspn ground ginger
pinch ground nutmeg
315 g (10 oz) chicken breast fillets, cut into 5 cm (2 in) strips
2 tspns soft margarine
1 stick celery, thinly sliced
3 cups torn spinach leaves, well washed and drained
1 cup cooked long-grain rice, hot (approx. ⅓ cup/60 g/ 2 oz) raw

SERVES 2

*F*or the marinade, combine soy sauce, water, corn-flour, sherry, honey, ginger and nutmeg in a large mixing bowl. Add chicken and cover with plastic wrap. Set aside for 30 minutes, or overnight in the refrigerator.

Preheat a microwave-safe browning dish on HIGH (100%) for 6–7 minutes, quickly add the margarine and swirl to coat the dish. Add the chicken and marinade. Stir well and cook on HIGH for 2 minutes. Stir in celery and cover dish. Continue cooking on HIGH for 2 minutes. Stir in spinach. Re-cover dish and cook for 2–4 minutes, stirring once during cooking, until vegetables are tender to taste.

Serve each portion of chicken over half a cup hot cooked rice.

NOTE This recipe serves two, but for four people, double recipe. Cook chicken on HIGH in preheated microwave-safe browning dish for 5 minutes. Cook completed dish for 6–8 minutes.

Coq au Vin

2 rashers bacon, diced
1 large onion, finely chopped
4 large chicken joints, skinned and cut into 8 equal pieces
1 tbspn seasoned flour
2 tbspns brandy
1 cup (250 ml/8 fl oz) red wine
½ cup (125 ml/4 fl oz) chicken stock
1 tbspn tomato paste
1 clove garlic, crushed
1 bouquet garni
155 g (5 oz) mushrooms, wiped and sliced

SERVES 4

*P*lace the bacon in a 3 l (3 qt) microwave-safe dish or casserole. Cover with a well-fitting lid or plastic wrap and cook on HIGH (100%) for 1 minute. Add the onion and stir well. Re-cover dish and cook for 2 minutes.

Toss chicken in the seasoned flour and add to the bacon and onion in dish. Cook on HIGH for 5 minutes. Stir well, then stir in remaining ingredients except mushrooms. Re-cover dish and cook on MEDIUM (50%) for 20 minutes until chicken is tender and juice is thick. Remove bouquet garni and stir in mushrooms. Cook, uncovered, for a further 5 minutes. Serve with new potatoes or rice.

Chicken Livers with Wine and Herbs

1 onion, chopped
1 tbspn (20 g/¾ oz) butter
750 g (1½ lb) chicken livers, washed and halved
¾ cup (185 ml/6 fl oz) red wine
¼ cup (30 g/1 oz) plain flour
2 tbspns chopped fresh parsley
2 tbspns tomato sauce
1 tspn dried oregano
pinch dry mustard

SERVES 4–6

*P*lace onion and butter in a 1–2 l (1–2 qt) microwave-safe dish or casserole. Cover with a well-fitting lid or plastic wrap and cook on HIGH (100%) for 2 minutes until onion is tender. Stir in remaining ingredients. Re-cover dish and cook on MEDIUM (50%) for 20–25 minutes, stirring every 5 minutes until liver is tender and flavours have been absorbed.

Serve hot with jacket potatoes and green beans.

● Chicken Curry on Golden Coconut Rice (page 54)

Chicken Curry

This mild curry recipe originates from northern India. Coconut milk may be substituted for the yoghurt and more garam masala may be added if desired.

1 tspn turmeric
2 tspns garam masala
1 tspn chilli powder
1 kg (2 lb) chicken pieces: drumsticks, thighs, and/or wings, washed and dried with absorbent kitchen paper
2 tbspns (45 g/1½ oz) ghee or butter
1 large onion, sliced
1 tbspn fresh ginger, finely diced
2 cloves garlic, crushed
½ tspn freshly ground black pepper
1 tspn ground cinnamon
1 tspn ground cardamom
200 ml (6½ fl oz) carton natural yoghurt
fresh coriander leaves for garnish

SERVES 8

Mix turmeric, garam masala and chilli powder, rub into chicken pieces. Heat ghee or butter with onion, ginger and garlic in a 3 l (3 qt) microwave-safe dish or casserole, covered with a well-fitting lid or plastic wrap, on HIGH (100%) for 2 minutes. Stir in black pepper, cinnamon and cardamom. Keep uncovered and cook on HIGH for a further 1 minute. Stir in yoghurt, then stir in chicken pieces. Re-cover dish and cook on MEDIUM (50%) for 30 minutes, stirring well after 10 and 20 minutes, until chicken is tender.

Serve with Golden Coconut Rice (see page 54) and garnish with coriander leaves.

Chicken Oregano with Green Beans and Tagliatelle

1 tbspn (20 g/¾ oz) butter
1 large onion, sliced
1 kg (2 lb) chicken pieces
1 tbspn seasoned, plain flour
440 g (14 oz) can tomatoes
½ cup (125 ml/4 fl oz) chicken stock
2 tspns dried oregano
1 tbspn tomato paste
black pepper to taste
1 green capsicum, seeded and thinly sliced
250 g (8 oz) tagliatelle
500 g (1 lb) green beans, topped and tailed

SERVES 4

Melt the butter in a 3 l (3 qt) microwave-safe dish or casserole on HIGH (100%) for 1 minute. Add the onion and cook on HIGH for 2 minutes.

Toss the chicken in the flour and add to the onions, quickly tossing to coat in butter. Cover dish with a well-fitting lid or plastic wrap and cook on HIGH for 5 minutes. Stir in tomatoes, stock, oregano, tomato paste, seasoning and capsicum. Cook on HIGH for 5 minutes, then re-cover dish and cook on MEDIUM (50%) for 12–15 minutes, until chicken is tender and flavours have been absorbed. Adjust seasoning to taste. Let stand, covered.

Meanwhile, cook pasta in a saucepan of boiling water on stove-top for 10–12 minutes, until tender.

Wash and prepare green beans. Place in a shallow microwave-safe dish. Cover with plastic wrap.

When chicken is cooked, place beans in oven to cook on HIGH for 6–8 minutes or until tender.

Drain pasta and place on a large serving plate. Serve chicken on bed of pasta with beans served separately.

Stir-fried Thai Chicken

500 g (1 lb) chicken thigh fillets, thinly sliced
1 tbspn peanut oil
1 tspn finely chopped garlic
2 tspns grated fresh ginger
½ cup sliced water chestnuts
2 red chillies, seeded and cut into thin strips

● *From top:* Stir-fried Thai Chicken; Chicken Wings with Thai Peanut Sauce

1 tbspn fish sauce
½ cup (125 ml/4 fl oz) thick coconut milk
1 tspn brown sugar

SERVES 4

Heat oil in a large microwave-safe casserole on HIGH (100%) for 30 seconds. Add garlic and ginger and cook for 1 minute on HIGH. Add chicken and cook on MEDIUM HIGH (70%) for 3–4 minutes, stirring several times. Add remaining ingredients and cook on MEDIUM (50%) for 5–6 minutes or until chicken is tender.

Serve with boiled rice or noodles.

NOTE Some people have an allergic reaction to chillies — handle with rubber gloves and avoid touching face or eyes.

Do not use wire twists to close microwave-safe plastic bags as they may cause arcing (blue sparks) or may ignite, damaging the microwave. Use either the strips of plastic supplied with the bags or the squares of plastic on bags of bread.

Chicken Wings with Thai Peanut Sauce

1 kg (2 lb) chicken wings
2 tspns oil
⅓ cup sliced spring onions including some green tops
1 tbspn Thai curry paste
1 cup (250 ml/8 fl oz) coconut milk
⅓ cup (90 g/3 oz) crunchy peanut butter
1 tbspn lime or lemon juice
1 tbspn palm or brown sugar

SERVES 4

Heat oil in a large frying pan on HIGH (100%) for 30 seconds. Add spring onions and curry paste and cook on HIGH for 2 minutes. Add chicken wings and stir. Cook on HIGH for 3–4 minutes. Add remaining ingredients, stir well and reduce power to MEDIUM HIGH (70%). Continue to cook for 20 minutes or until chicken is cooked, stirring regularly and adding a little water if sauce becomes too thick.

Serve with boiled rice.

Chicken Suprême

A true cordon bleu classic! Give this dish the presentation it deserves, by garnishing each Suprême with fresh tarragon leaves.

4 chicken breasts, skinned and boned
½ cup (125 ml/4 fl oz) good chicken stock (home-made if possible)
1 tbspn (20 g/¾ oz) butter
1 tbspn plain flour
⅔ cup (185 ml/6 fl oz) milk
pinch mustard powder
white pepper to taste
1 tspn lemon juice
2 egg yolks
fresh tarragon leaves for garnish

SERVES 4

Place chicken in a shallow microwave-safe casserole with stock. Cover with a well-fitting lid or plastic wrap. Lightly poach chicken on MEDIUM (50%) for 5 minutes turning meat over halfway through cooking time. Test to see if meat is cooked. Meat juices should be clear when meat is tested with a sharp knife.

Transfer meat to a warmed serving plate. Cover while sauce is being prepared.

Combine cooking juices and stock and make up to ⅔ cup (185 ml/6 fl oz) with water. Place butter in a 1 l (1 qt) microwave-safe dish and cook on HIGH (100%) for 30 seconds. Add flour and stir. Cook for a further 30 seconds on HIGH. Stir in combined stock, milk, mustard powder, pepper and lemon juice and cook on HIGH for 5–6 minutes, stirring every minute until sauce boils and thickens. Allow sauce to continue boiling for 1 minute. Add egg yolks and whisk to combine.

Serve chicken breasts coated with sauce and garnished with tarragon leaves.

Chicken Rosé

2 tspns plain flour
black pepper to taste
720 g (1¼ lb) chicken pieces, skinned*
1 small onion, finely chopped
2 tspns cooking oil
1 clove garlic, crushed
1 green capsicum, seeded and cut into 2.5 cm (1 in) dice

● Chicken Suprême

1 cup (90 g/3 oz) button mushrooms, wiped
and quartered
½ cup (60 g/2 oz) canned tomatoes
¼ cup (60 ml/2 fl oz) rosé wine
¼ tspn dried thyme leaves

SERVES 2

On a sheet of greaseproof paper, or a flat plate, combine flour and pepper, dredge chicken pieces in flour mixture until well coated.

Mix onion, oil and garlic in a shallow microwave-safe dish. Cook on MEDIUM HIGH (70%) for 2 minutes, add chicken and green capsicum. Cook on MEDIUM HIGH for 5 minutes. Stir mixture well then add mushrooms, tomatoes, wine and thyme, cover with a well-fitting lid or plastic wrap and cook on MEDIUM HIGH for 20 minutes, stirring occasionally during cooking. Uncover and cook on MEDIUM HIGH for approximately 5 minutes, until chicken is tender.

*NOTE These chicken pieces will yield approximately 250 g (8 oz) cooked meat. For a serving for four, double recipe. Cook chicken on MEDIUM HIGH for 10 minutes before adding remaining ingredients.

Chicken à l'Orange

finely grated rind and juice of 1 orange
1 tspn raw sugar
1 tspn mustard
2 tspns stock powder
1 kg (2 lb) chicken thighs, skinned and boned
3 tspns cornflour

SERVES 4

Combine orange rind and juice, sugar, mustard and stock powder. Preheat a microwave-safe browning dish on HIGH (100%) for 6 minutes. To brown chicken, toss quickly in browning dish until sizzling stops.

Pour orange sauce over chicken. Cook covered on HIGH for 15 minutes, turn chicken pieces over and baste with juice after 5 and 10 minutes.

Transfer chicken to a warmed serving plate, cover with a piece of aluminium foil and set aside. Mix cornflour with a little cold water and stir into orange sauce in cooking dish. Cook for 3–4 minutes, stirring after 2 minutes, until sauce thickens.

Serve chicken with orange sauce poured over.

Roast Turkey

1 × size 35 turkey (approx. 3.5 kg/7 lb)
2 tbspns (45 g/1½ oz) melted butter
1 tspn microwave browning sauce
STUFFING
¼ cup (60 g/2 oz) butter or margarine
1 medium onion, finely chopped
2 rashers bacon, chopped
250 g (8 oz) sausage mince
1 cup (60 g/2 oz) fresh white breadcrumbs
1 cup (60 g/2 oz) fresh brown breadcrumbs
1 tbspn chopped fresh herbs
grated rind of 1 orange
freshly ground black pepper to taste
1 large egg, beaten
1 tbspn dry sherry

SERVES 6–8

*R*inse the turkey inside and out and pat dry with kitchen paper. Combine butter with browning sauce and set aside.

To prepare stuffing: Place butter, onion and bacon in a large microwave-safe bowl and cook on HIGH (100%) for 2 minutes. Add mince and break up with a fork to prevent it becoming compacted during cooking. Cook on HIGH for a further 3 minutes. Add remaining ingredients and stir well. Pack the stuffing loosely into the body and breast of the turkey and secure openings, legs and wings with thin wooden satay skewers, or by tying. Cover the thinner sections — leg ends and wings — with aluminium foil to shield against overcooking. Brush all over with combined butter and microwave browning sauce.

Place the turkey on a microwave rack in a microwave-safe roasting pan, breast down, and cook on HIGH for 5 minutes, reduce to MEDIUM (50%) and cook for 30 minutes. Turn the turkey onto one side, brush again with butter mixture and cook for a further 20 minutes. Turn on to the other side, baste again and cook for a further 20 minutes. Turn breast uppermost and brush with butter. At this stage, if the turkey is self-basting, prick the skin all over to release the oil under the skin. This helps to keep the flesh moist.

Remove aluminium foil from turkey and cook for a further 30 minutes until the flesh is cooked and the leg joint can be moved easily in its socket. Remove from oven, cover with a 'tent' of aluminium foil and allow to stand 15 minutes before carving. Gravy may be made from the pan drippings. (See photo pages 82–83.)

Austrian Stuffing

This unusual stuffing originated in Austria. Its piquant flavour goes well with all poultry.

2 tbspns cooking oil
1 onion, finely chopped
200 g (6½ oz) chicken livers, chopped
200 g (6½ oz) sausage meat
2 tbspns finely chopped fresh parsley
4 anchovy fillets, finely chopped
2 eggs
juice of ½ lemon
½ tspn dried thyme
½ tspn dried marjoram
freshly ground black pepper to taste
¾ cup cooked long-grain rice (approx. ¼ cup/45 g/ 1½ oz raw)

*H*eat the oil in a 1–2 l (1–2 qt) microwave-safe dish or jug on HIGH (100%) for 2 minutes. Add the onion and chicken livers and stir well to coat in oil. Cover dish with a well-fitting lid or plastic wrap and cook on HIGH for 3–4 minutes, until onion is softened and chicken livers have turned pink.

Stir in sausage meat and continue cooking on HIGH for 2 minutes. Stir in remaining ingredients and use as poultry stuffing.

Apple and Sausage Stuffing

FOR SIZE 30 (3 kg/6 lb) CHICKEN

1 tbspn (20 g/¾ oz) butter
1 large onion, chopped
250 g (8 oz) sausage meat
1 large apple, peeled, cored and chopped
1 stick celery, chopped
grated rind and juice of 1 lemon
1 tspn mixed herbs
½ cup (60 g/2 oz) cornflake crumbs
1 egg, lightly beaten

*P*lace butter and onion in a medium-sized microwave-safe bowl, cover and cook on HIGH (100%) for 2 minutes, stir in sausage meat and continue cooking on HIGH for 5 minutes. Stir in remaining ingredients.

Creamy Turkey, Cheese and Mushroom Casserole

2 tbspns (45 g/1½ oz) butter or margarine
2 tbspns plain flour
1 chicken stock cube, crumbled
black pepper to taste
½ cup (125 ml/4 fl oz) water
1½ cups (375 g/12 oz) thickened cream
3 cups (470 g/15 oz) cooked and well-drained pasta shells
2 cups (250 g/8 oz) cooked and diced turkey meat
125 g (4 oz) mushrooms, wiped and sliced
1 tbspn chopped fresh parsley
2 tbspns sherry
2 tbspns grated Parmesan cheese
2 tbspns grated Cheddar cheese

SERVES 4

*P*lace butter or margarine in a 1–2 l (1–2 qt) microwave-safe dish or casserole. Heat on HIGH (100%) for 1 minute, until melted. Blend in the flour, crumbled stock cube and pepper. Gradually stir in the water and cream. Cook mixture on HIGH for 5–6 minutes. Stir frequently during cooking until sauce boils and thickens.

Stir in pasta, turkey, mushrooms, parsley and sherry. Sprinkle top with mixed grated cheeses. Return to oven and continue cooking on MEDIUM HIGH (70%) for 8–10 minutes, until cheese melts and casserole is thoroughly heated through.

Turkey and Salmon Roll

2 cups (500 g/1 lb) cream cheese
2 × 200 g (6½ oz) cans red salmon, drained with bones removed
2 tbspns tomato paste
2 tbspns gelatine
⅓ cup (90 ml/3 fl oz) chicken stock
1 kg (2 lb) smoked turkey breast roll
⅓ cup (60 g/2 oz) peppercorns, roughly chopped
¾ cup chopped fresh parsley

SERVES 12

Soften cream cheese on MEDIUM (50%) for 1½ minutes. Combine salmon and tomato paste with cheese until mixture is smooth.

Sprinkle gelatine over chicken stock in a microwave-safe jug. Warm on MEDIUM for 1 minute and stir thoroughly to dissolve gelatine. Stir into salmon mixture. Refrigerate while preparing meat.

Cut smoked turkey breast roll into 5 horizontal slices. Sandwich the slices together with salmon, using two-thirds of the mixture. Wrap in aluminium foil and chill for 3–4 hours or overnight in the refrigerator.

Mix peppercorns with chopped parsley. Unwrap roll, soften remainder of salmon mix in the microwave and spread over outside of roll. Roll in parsley and peppercorns.

Serve whole or sliced with crusty bread.

Roast Duckling with Cherry Sauce

If available, choose morello cherries for the sauce. Their somewhat tart flavour is a good foil for the rich flesh of the duck. Use canned or bottled cherries if fresh ones are out of season. Bottled morello cherries are available in many supermarkets and delicatessens.

500 g (1 lb) fresh cherries, stoned
2 tbspns sugar
pinch cinnamon (optional)
juice of 1 orange
1 tspn grated orange rind
⅓ cup (90 ml/3 fl oz) port wine
¼ cup (60 ml/2 fl oz) redcurrant jelly
2 kg (4 lb) duckling
1 orange, cut into quarters
1 medium onion, cut in quarters

SERVES 5–6

Turkey and Salmon Roll

To prepare the sauce, place stoned cherries in a medium-sized microwave-safe casserole, sprinkle with sugar and add a pinch of cinnamon if desired. Cover with unvented plastic wrap and cook on HIGH (100%) for 4–5 minutes. Stand, covered, for 5 minutes. Add orange juice and rind, port wine and redcurrant jelly. Heat, uncovered, on HIGH only until jelly melts, stirring every 30 seconds. Cover and set aside while cooking duckling.

Before cooking duckling, prick skin in a number of places and position on a microwave roasting rack, breast up, in a casserole. Cook on HIGH for 5–6 minutes. Allow to stand in oven for 5 minutes. Drain off any fat and juices from dish and reserve. Draw neck skin over back of duck and secure in place with wooden cocktail sticks. Turn breast up on roasting rack in casserole. Lift wing tips and tuck behind the bird. Place orange and onion quarters in duck cavity and cook on MEDIUM (50%) for 20 minutes. Drain off any accumulated fat and juices and add to those already reserved. Brush duckling with cherry sauce and cook for a further 20 minutes on MEDIUM. Stand, covered, with tented aluminium foil for 10–15 minutes. Check to see if done. When pricked with a fork in the thickest part of the thigh, juices should run clear and temperature in thickest part should be at least 85°C.

Add any pan drippings to reserved juices. Skim off fat and add juices to sauce. Reheat sauce on HIGH until just bubbling and serve with duckling. (See photo page 101.)

Roast Duck with Walnut and Apricot Stuffing

It is important not to overcook duck. Check the bird 5–10 minutes before the end of the estimated cooking time so that the meat does not overcook. Never let the duck sit in fat during cooking.
Duck contains a lot of fat, so, prior to cooking, pierce the bird all over with a fork to allow the fat under the skin to be released during the cooking cycle. Drain this fat away during cooking so that the skin has a chance to crisp.

2.5 kg (5 lb) duck
1 large onion, chopped
1 stick celery, sliced
1 tbspn (20 g/¾ oz) butter
1 cup (125 g/4 oz) walnuts, roughly chopped
½ cup (60 g/2 oz) dried apricots, quartered
½ cup (90 g/3 oz) raisins
black pepper to taste
2 tbspns lemon juice

1 egg, beaten
½ cup (60 g/2 oz) cornflake crumbs
2 tbspns each soy sauce, honey and warm water (optional)

SERVES 5–6

Wash and thoroughly dry duck with kitchen paper. Set aside.

Place onion, celery and butter in a 1–2 l (1–2 qt) microwave-safe dish or casserole. Cover with a well-fitting lid or plastic wrap and cook on HIGH (100%) for 2 minutes. Stir in remaining ingredients and pack into cavity of duck. Secure stuffing inside bird, if necessary using toothpicks to hold skin together at either end.

Like all poultry, duck cooks very well in the microwave. The cooking time is greatly reduced and because of the cooking technique involved the finished result is moist, tasty and not at all greasy. As duck contains a lot of fat which runs off during cooking, it will brown in the microwave, and this browning can be enhanced by brushing on an equal mixture of soy sauce, honey and warm water.

Place the duck, breast side down, on a roasting rack or upturned saucer. Brush with soy sauce and honey mixture if used. Prick skin all over with a fork. Set in oven and cook on HIGH for 10 minutes. Continue cooking on MEDIUM (50%) for 8 minutes per 500 g (1 lb). Total cooking time should be approximately 40 minutes. Turn duck over, breast side uppermost. Halfway through cooking time, prick skin on top of bird all over with a fork and drain off all excess fat.

Cooking time is completed when a sharp knife or skewer inserted into the thickest part of the thigh joint releases juices that run clear.

Remove bird from cooking rack. Wrap in aluminium foil and leave to sand for 10–15 minutes while gravy and vegetables are cooked.

To warm dinner plates, place a wet paper towel or 1–2 tablespoons of water between each plate and heat, elevated, on HIGH (100%) for ½–1 minute (for 2–3 plates).

Muscat Quails

8 quails
black pepper to taste
1 cup (185 g/6 oz) seeded red or white grapes
2 tbspns (45 g/1½ oz) butter
½ cup (125 ml/4 fl oz) chicken stock
¼ cup (60 ml/2 fl oz) dry white wine
2 tspns soy sauce
¼ cup (60 ml/2 fl oz) Muscatel wine
2 tbspns cream

SERVES 4

Season quails inside and out with pepper. Place three or four grapes in the cavity of each and tie legs together. Melt butter in a frying pan on top of stove. When bubbling, add quails and brown birds quickly on all sides in the butter. Place birds breast side up into a floured plastic oven bag set in a shallow microwave-safe baking dish. Add stock, half of the white wine, and soy sauce to bag. Secure with a piece of string or an elastic band. Cook on HIGH (100%) for 5–6 minutes until quails are tender. Transfer birds to a serving dish, cover with aluminium foil and allow to stand.

Place juices from bag with remaining white wine and Muscatel into a 2 cup (500 ml/16 fl oz) microwave-safe jug. Cook on HIGH for 5 minutes. Stir in remaining grapes and cream. Heat through on MEDIUM HIGH for 1 minute. Adjust seasonings to taste if necessary.

Serve quails with sauce spooned over.

Poussins with Mushroom Sauce

These tiny chickens weigh about 500 g (1 lb) and are 'spatch-cocked' or split down the back and flattened before cooking. A poussin makes a small meal for two, or a more substantial serving for one.

2 × 500 g (1 lb) poussins
2 tbspns (45 g/1½ oz) butter
3 tbspns (60 ml/2 fl oz) grapeseed oil
1 tbspn (20 g/¾ oz) extra butter (for making the mushroom sauce)
2 tbspns plain flour
⅓ cup (90 g/3 oz) button mushrooms, sliced
¾ cup (185 ml/6 fl oz) chicken stock
¼ cup (60 ml/2 fl oz) cream
1 egg yolk
salt and pepper to taste
fresh herbs for garnish

SERVES 2 or 4

Using poultry shears or kitchen scissors, cut down the backbone of each poussin and open out flat. If preferred, cut the breast section as well, dividing each bird into two parts. Place the birds skin side up and cover with plastic wrap. Flatten with five or six strokes from a rolling pin or meat mallet.

Keep the birds as flat as possible by threading a thin wooden satay skewer through the wing and breast, and another through the leg and lower breast. Preheat a microwave-safe dish for 8 minutes. Put half the butter and half the oil into dish. Swirl quickly and place one of the poussins, skin side down. Press down briefly until sizzling stops and cook, uncovered, on HIGH (100%) for 1 minute. Turn the bird with tongs and cook on HIGH for 1 minute. Move poussin to a heated microwave-safe dish and cover.

Wipe out browning dish with kitchen paper and reheat for 4 minutes. Add remaining butter and oil, and cook second bird in the same way. Remove bird and cover to keep warm.

Wipe out the dish. Add the extra 1 tablespoon of butter and heat on HIGH for 1 minute. Stir in flour and cook uncovered for 1 minute, stirring several times. Stir in stock and cook, uncovered, on HIGH until just boiling, stirring several times. Return poussins to dish and spoon stock over. Add mushrooms. Cover with a well-fitting lid or vented plastic wrap and cook on MEDIUM (50%) for 10 minutes, or until chicken is cooked. Place birds on serving dish and cover with aluminium foil.

Combine cream and egg yolk. Pour into sauce and cook on MEDIUM until thickened slightly and almost boiling. Return poussins to dish. Spoon sauce over and reheat on MEDIUM for 1–2 minutes without allowing to boil, or until birds are at serving temperature.

Place birds on heated serving dish. Spoon sauce over and garnish with fresh herbs. Serve with vegetables of your choice.

Rabbit Bouillabaisse

1 rabbit, jointed
2 small heads fennel, quartered
pinch saffron or turmeric
finely grated rind and juice of 1 lemon
black pepper to taste
2 small onions, chopped
2 cloves garlic, crushed
4 tomatoes, chopped
2 tbspns finely chopped fresh parsley
½ cup (125 ml/4 fl oz) chicken stock

SERVES 4

Soak rabbit in salted lukewarm water for 30 minutes. Remove, pat dry and place in a shallow 2 l (2 qt) microwave-safe casserole with fennel.

Mix saffron or turmeric with the lemon juice and rind, pepper, onions, garlic, tomatoes and parsley. Pour over the rabbit and leave to stand for 30 minutes, or overnight in the refrigerator.

Add stock to the dish and cover with a well-fitting lid or plastic wrap. Cook on REHEAT (80%) for 30–40 minutes until meat is tender.

Meat

It has been said that the microwave oven is unsuitable for cooking meat. Many owners of microwave ovens know that this is not true but there are some who still need convincing.

One of the main reasons for disappointing results for new cooks has been their handling of roasts. Early failures have been wrongly attributed to the microwave oven itself. In fact, the failures have been a result of incorrect cooking technique or use of the wrong cooking equipment.

While it is true that in the microwave oven some of the less tender cuts of meat take just as long to cook as they would if cooked conventionally, there is still one advantage — the considerable saving of power.

To obtain the best results when cooking meat one has to understand both the character of meat and just how microwaves operate in its cooking. As already explained, microwaves cause moisture molecules in food to vibrate at an incredible speed. This friction produces the heat that cooks the food. In one sense, meat, because of its relatively high moisture content, is a good agent for microwaves to operate on, but another consideration must be taken into account. Meat has both connective tissue and muscle fibres which react to heat in different ways. Connective tissue softens during cooking but excessive heat toughens muscle fibres. Once this happens to the muscle fibres, no degree of added heat, low power or otherwise, will undo the damage already done.

It is now accepted that continued cooking on full power of even tender cuts will toughen the meat and cause excessive moisture loss. It is interesting to note that this emphasis on the desirability of lower power levels for cooking meat not only applies to meats cooked by microwave.

● *Previous pages, from left to right:* Spinach and Smoked Salmon Roulade (page 70); Pork Fillet with Mango Chilli Sauce (page 128); White Mousseline with Raspberry Coulis (page 169)

Conventionally cooked meat roasts are found to have a greater weight loss and a lower moisture content when cooked on the high temperatures formerly recommended, when compared with the same roasts cooked at a more moderate temperature. This is but one of the factors you should take into account if you wish to get the best possible results when cooking meat.

BASIC POINTS FOR COOKING MEAT BY MICROWAVE

FAT
Remove excess fat but retain some to provide juice and flavour and assist browning. Cut away remainder after cooking.

SALT
Don't use salt directly on meat surfaces prior to cooking. It draws out moisture, leaving tough, unpleasant-tasting areas. A little salt may be added to meat loaves and casseroles.

HERBS
Use sparingly as they retain a stronger flavour when cooked by microwave.

BROWNING
If you plan to cook roasts, acquire a browning grill or browning dish. These will bring results closer to conventionally baked roasts (see Browning Dishes, page 17).

BROWNING AIDS
If desired, use liquid or powdered commercial browning agents or a home-made glaze or sauce to enhance colour.

MEAT SHAPES
Uniformly shaped joints cook more evenly than large, thick or odd-shaped ones. If necessary, tie with string to keep a compact shape.

ALUMINIUM FOIL
During roasting, thinner sections of meat should be covered with pieces of foil for part of the cooking time to avoid overcooking — for example, the sec-

tion of meat around the shank end of a leg of lamb. (See also page 15.)

WEIGHT

If you don't own kitchen scales, ask the butcher to write the weight of a roast on the package to ensure you give it the correct cooking time (see Meat Roasting Guide, opposite).

MEAT THERMOMETER

To ensure correct cooking results, use a meat thermometer when cooking roasts. (Not very expensive items, these are available in kitchenware departments. Make sure that it is safe to use in a microwave. If using a conventional meat thermometer, it must never be left in the meat while the oven is in operation.) The Meat Roasting Guide opposite, indicates the ideal internal temperature of meats. You will notice the rise in temperature between the time the meat is taken out of the oven and after it has been left standing. This illustrates well the fact that foods, particularly large or dense amounts, continue to cook for some time after the source of heat has been removed.

To ensure a correct thermometer reading, it is important that the tip of the meat thermometer is not touching a bone or a section of fat when checking internal temperature.

BULB BASTER

A bulb baster — available in good kitchenware departments — will help remove unwanted fat and juices which may accumulate during the roasting of meat. Use as a syringe to draw meat juices from the pan. These may be reserved for later use, skimmed of fat, in gravy or sauces. If these juices are not removed, the steam from the liquid will give the meat a 'braised' flavour — one of the reasons microwave roasting has been criticised. However, the use of the browning grill or dish will largely solve that problem as these dishes help evaporate meat juices in much the same way as a baking dish in a conventional oven. (See also entry in Glossary of Terms, page 236.)

STANDING TIME

Standing time following the cooking of roasts does not apply only to microwave cooking — conventionally cooked roasts should also be covered and allowed to stand before carving. This standing period — from 10 to 20 minutes, depending on the size of the roast — allows the internal heat to equalise, juices to settle and flesh to become firm, for easier carving.

During standing time the meat should be *loosely* covered with a 'tent' of foil. When standing time is completed, the meat should be covered *closely* with foil to insulate the roast and keep it hot if there is any delay before carving.

MICROWAVE COOKING METHOD FOR MEAT

ROASTING

There are four methods of roasting:

1. Place roast, fat side down, on a microwave roasting rack in a suitable roasting dish. The rack keeps the meat above the fat and juices that collect and improves its flavour and appearance. The pan drippings should be removed (preferably with a bulb baster) as the cooking proceeds to achieve a less 'braised' flavour and to reduce spattering of oven walls. A sheet of kitchen paper towel may be used to cover the meat loosely to prevent spattering.

Turn the roast one to three times during cooking, depending on size and thickness. Brush several times during cooking with commercial or home-prepared browning mix or glaze to encourage additional browning.

2. Use a preheated browning dish (following manufacturer's directions) to seal or sear meat on all sides, using HIGH (100%), then reduce to recommended power level and complete cooking, turning the meat at least once. While the meat is standing, the browning dish may be used to cook vegetables and to make gravy. (See recipe for Roast Beef, page 112.)

3. To combine the microwave speed and the conventional oven's 'brown and crisp' result, use a combination of both. Sear the meat well in a pan on the stove-top and complete cooking by microwave, *or* cook initially by Methods 1 or 2 (see table on page opposite for cooking times) and finish in a preheated conventional oven for 10–15 minutes — not quite as economical as Method 1 but possibly more acceptable to some tastes.

4. Oven bags may be used for roasting but the results would more closely resemble the moistness of pot roasting. Brown all surfaces on the stove-top and brush with a microwave browning agent if desired.

Though pork may be roasted by any of the first three methods mentioned, best results are achieved if special attention is paid to the skin or rind which is usually preferred as crisp 'crackling'. For this

MICROWAVE MEAT ROASTING GUIDE

CUT OF MEAT	POWER LEVEL	TOTAL TIME— MINUTES PER 500 G (1 LB)	DEGREE OF COOKING	INTERNAL TEMPERATURE OUT OF OVEN	INTERNAL TEMPERATURE ON STANDING
Lamb					
Leg; boned and rolled leg; butterfly leg; saddle (boned, rolled double loin)	HIGH (100%) first 5 mins then MEDIUM (50%)	11–12 14–15	Medium Well done	55°C 65°C	65–70°C 75–80°C
Mid loin, bone in or boned and rolled; racks	HIGH first 2 mins then MEDIUM	4 6	Medium Well done	60°C 70°C	62–63°C 73–75°C
Crown roast, with or without stuffing	HIGH first 2 mins then MEDIUM	10 12	Medium Well done	60°C 65°C	65–68°C 70–73°C
Shoulder or forequarter, bone in or boned and rolled	HIGH first 5 mins then MEDIUM	15–17	Well done	70°C	75–80°C
Beef					
Slender roasts: Fillet; rib eye; rolled skirt	HIGH first 3 mins then MEDIUM	7 8 10	Rare Medium Well done	50°C 55°C 65°C	55°C 60°C 70°C
Thick roasts: Rump; sirloin plate; topside rib (bone in); blade; rib eye (from large beef)	HIGH first 5 mins up to 2 kg (4 lb); 10 mins over 2 kg then MEDIUM	12 13 15	Rare Medium Well done	50°C 55°C 65°C	55–60°C 60–65°C 70–75°C
Over 1 kg (2 lb) with surrounding fat: Rolled rib or beef roast; rolled sirloin	HIGH first 5 mins up to 2 kg (4 lb); 10 mins over 2 kg then MEDIUM	16 17 19	Rare Medium Well done	50°C 55°C 60°C	55–60°C 60–70°C 65–75°C
Veal					
Leg, bone in or boned; shoulder, bone in or boned and rolled	HIGH first 5 mins then MEDIUM	16–17	Well done	70°C	75–80°C
Loin, boned and rolled; loin rack	HIGH first 5 mins then MEDIUM	18	Well done	70°C	75°C
Pork					
Leg; loin; shoulder boned or bone in — up to 1.5 kg (3 lb)	HIGH first 5 mins then MEDIUM	12–13	Well done	82–85°C	87–90°C

method refer to Roast Pork on page 126.

Gravy for roasts Skim off fat from meat juices reserved after roasting, add extra stock if required and thicken with cornflour. Cook on HIGH until boiling and thickened.

GRILLING

A browning grill or dish will give reasonably good results for small quantities of meat, but will not sufficiently brown more than two or three steaks or chops at once. When one takes into account that the large microwave grill takes 8 minutes to heat, it becomes obvious that a conventional grill will handle cooking for a crowd much more satisfactorily. If, however, you are grilling for a family with staggered meal times, a satisfactory alternative could be to quickly seal all the meat on both sides in a well-heated pan on the stove-top, cover

and refrigerate until required. Microwave each covered serve on a dinner plate for 1–3 minutes, depending on size of meal. While beef steaks give good results following this method, more delicate cuts such as veal leg steaks are much better when cooked conventionally as there is no appreciable time-saving if cooked by microwave.

PAN-FRIED MEAT

For method and cooking chart for pan-frying meat see page 110.

POT ROASTING

There will be no time saving for this method of cooking. The meat must be cooked in a container only just large enough to take it and with the minimum amount of liquid. A deep, round dish and a neatly fitting roast would be the ideal combin-

MEAT	QUANTITY AND THICKNESS	COOKING TIME	STANDING TIME IN MINUTES
Steaks, beef	2 x 2 cm (1 in)	1½ minutes, turn, 2½–3 minutes	½–1
Steaks, ham	2 x 1 cm (½ in)	1½ minutes, turn, 2–3 minutes	½–1
Chops, lamb and veal	2 x 1.5 cm (¾ in)	1½–2 minutes, turn, 2½–3 minutes	1
Chops, pork	2 x 1.5 cm (¾ in)	1½–2 minutes, turn, 3–3½ minutes	1–1½
Sausages	4 thin	2–2½ minutes, turn, 1½–2 minutes	1
Sausages	4 thick	2–2½ minutes, turn, 2–2½ minutes	1½
Beefburgers and rissoles	4 x 1.5 cm (¾ in)	1½–2 minutes, turn, 2–2½ minutes	1–1½

ation. The lid must be a very close fit to prevent as little steam escaping as possible. A topside roast of 1.5 kg (3 lb) will require up to 2 hours' cooking. Rub the meat all over with flour seasoned with pepper and brown in a little butter or oil on all sides in a hot pan on the stove-top before placing in casserole. Add some chopped vegetables and for moisture a 425 g (14½ oz) can of tomatoes with juice. Cook on HIGH (100%) for 10 minutes and approximately 2 hours on DEFROST (30%) or until tender. The meat should be turned over halfway through cooking time. Pot roasts may also be cooked in an oven bag.

CASSEROLE COOKING — BEEF

Some of the more economical beef cuts usually bought for casseroles are not recommended for this method when cooked by microwave. Choose round, topside or blade steak. Not recommended are chuck, shin or brisket which have a large amount of connective tissue.

Method 1 There will be no time saving involved with this cooking method as the recommended cooking power for the entire operation is DEFROST (30%). Meat for this method should be cut into uniform pieces. Marinating the meat overnight may help tenderise it. During cooking great care must be taken to ensure that meat pieces are completely immersed in the cooking liquid. If not, they will dry out and toughen. Place a piece of baking paper over the surface of the casserole mixture, pushing down the meat so it is not exposed. Stir occasionally to ensure even cooking.

Method 2 This method involves cutting the steak into very thin strips, no more than 5 mm (¼ in) thick, and tenderising it. Combine 500 g (1 lb) of one of the recommended steak cuts (cut in strips as suggested) and mix with ½ teaspoon of bicarbonate of soda, 1 tablespoon dry sherry and 2 teaspoons cornflour. Leave for 30 minutes. Mean-

while, select one of your favourite casserole recipes, assemble the ingredients, less the meat, of course, and reduce the liquid normally used by about one-third — this is because there will be less evaporation since the cooking time will be shorter than for your original recipe. Set aside the meat, cook the other ingredients, onions first in a little oil for a minute or two on HIGH (100%), other chopped vegetables and stock for about 5–6 minutes or until almost tender, stirring at least once. Finally, add the meat, stir well and cook, covered, for 6 minutes, stirring several times. If necessary, thicken with a little more cornflour blended with water. Check that the meat is cooked, cover and stand 3 minutes. Serve with boiled rice.

CASSEROLE COOKING — LAMB AND VEAL

Lamb neck, shank and breast and veal shin (knuckle) and breast can be cooked by casserole but will take as long or longer than conventional cooking as low power needs to be used for an acceptable result. As a general rule these cuts should begin very briefly on MEDIUM (50%) and cooking completed on DEFROST (30%). High power levels risk dehydration of the meat.

CORNED MEATS

Some time saving can be achieved with corned meat providing, like pot roasting, the minimum amount of liquid is used. This could provide a problem unless the meat has been freshly pumped — in other words, not very salty. If the meat is a little too salty it may need to have the water changed halfway through the cooking period.

As with pot roasting, the cooking container should be just large enough to hold the meat, therefore requiring the minimum of cooking liquid. Otherwise an oven bag may be used, but only if the meat is lightly salted.

Corned silverside and lamb leg can be cooked successfully but corned brisket is not suitable.

PROCESSED AND MISCELLANEOUS MEATS

Processed meats in casings Use only MEDIUM (50%) to MEDIUM HIGH (70%) power levels for cooking these meats. This should ensure that moistness is retained and prevent splitting of casings and skins.

Bacon rashers and sausages These are best cooked in a browning grill or dish, but if you are in too much of a hurry to heat these dishes, cook the meats on a plate between several sheets of absorbent kitchen paper towel. To a large extent this avoids having the meat cooking in its own fat and also prevents spattering of the oven walls.

Liver (lamb's fry) and kidneys Slice very thinly for best results and cook only briefly — no more than one minute on each side — to ensure tenderness. Use a browning dish if available. Pierce kidneys (if using whole) and chicken livers (or any membranes or casings) to prevent 'popping'.

Brains Pierce in several places with a fork, place in a very small container, covered with unvented plastic wrap and cook briefly until no longer pink. Proceed as recipe requires.

Mince When cooking mince it is very important to ensure an even texture by breaking up the meat with a fork regularly until it is no longer pink. Otherwise the meat forms into small, hard clumps.

Pan-fried Meat

For successful pan frying of steak, chops and sausages it is essential to use a microwave browning dish. The browning dish lightly browns and seals meat surfaces in much the same way as stove-top frying. Without a browning dish this popular method of cooking small meat cuts would be quite unsatisfactory in the microwave oven.

For best results cook only two or three steaks or chops, or four sausages at a time, wiping out and reheating the browning dish between batches. Choose from fillet, scotch fillet or rib eye, sirloin or T-bone steaks approximately 2 cm (1 in) thick, and lamb and pork chops normally chosen for grilling.

Preheat a microwave-safe browning dish for 6–8 minutes (or time recommended in manufacturer's instructions) on HIGH (100%) for first batch. For further batches, after wiping out with crumpled kitchen paper, reheat browning dish for 3–4 minutes. Steak and chops with an outside skin tend to curl up during cooking. This could cause uneven browning where meat is not contacting the surface of the browning dish. Cut away skin and excess fat and snip through just into the meat to ensure this doesn't happen. When meat is placed in the heated browning dish hold down lightly with the back of an egg slice briefly to assist browning; repeat after turning the meat.

All suggested cooking times are approximate, according to taste, quantity of meat and its thickness.

Roast Beef

1.5 kg (3 lb) rolled rib roast
2–3 large potatoes, peeled and cut into pieces
4–6 pieces pumpkin, peeled
1 tbspn plain flour

SERVES 4 (With beef left-overs)

*H*eat a microwave-safe browning dish on HIGH (100%) for 8 minutes. Add meat, fat side down and cook for a further 3 or 4 minutes on HIGH turning the meat several times to brown surfaces. Reduce to MEDIUM HIGH (70%) and cook for 22–24 minutes for medium (15–18 minutes for rare or 27–30 minutes for well-done), turning several times.

Remove meat to a hot serving dish and cover loosely with aluminium foil for 10–14 minutes' standing time.

Leave approximately a tablespoon of meat drippings in browning dish. Heat on HIGH for 3 minutes. Add prepared vegetables and cook on HIGH for about 14 minutes or until just tender, turning several times during cooking. The vegetables will not be crisp but they will be lightly browned and have a 'roasted' flavour. Remove vegetables, cover and keep hot.

Drain and reserve all liquid from browning dish. Heat 1 tablespoon of reserved fat in the browning dish for about 1 minute on HIGH. Sprinkle in flour, stir and heat for 1 minute or until bubbling. Add water to reserved meat stock to make 1 cup (250 ml/8 fl oz). Pour into browning dish and stir. Cook, stirring frequently, until gravy is smooth and thickened. Reheat potatoes and pumpkin for a few seconds if required.

NOTE If you don't have a microwave-safe browning dish, place meat on a microwave roasting rack in a suitable microwave-safe baking dish and proceed as above, removing accumulated pan juices with a bulb baster several times during cooking. The vegetables could be cooked by microwave but need to be browned in a pan on the top of stove.

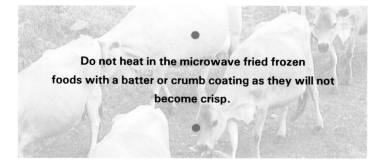

Do not heat in the microwave fried frozen foods with a batter or crumb coating as they will not become crisp.

Corned Beef

2 kg (4 lb) corned silverside
2 cups (500 ml/16 fl oz) water
1 tbspn vinegar
1 onion, cut into quarters
6 cloves
2 tbspns brown sugar
1 tspn cinnamon

SERVES 8–10

*P*lace corned beef in a plastic oven bag in a microwave-safe dish. Add remaining ingredients to bag. Tie bag with string or an elastic band. Make several holes in the bag, close to where it is tied, so that water cannot escape.

Cook meat, fat side up, on HIGH (100%) for 10 minutes. Reduce to LOW (10%) and cook for 30 minutes per 500 g (1 lb). Leave to stand in bag for 30 minutes before carving. Serve with White Parsley Sauce.

Burgundy Beef

2 large onions, sliced
1 clove garlic, crushed
2 tbspns (45 g/1½ oz) butter
600 g (1¼ lb) round, blade or topside steak, diced
2 tbspns seasoned, plain flour
1 cup (250 ml/8 fl oz) burgundy (red wine)
1 cup (250 ml/8 fl oz) beef stock
1 tspn dried tarragon
1 tspn peppercorns
2 carrots, peeled and evenly sliced
125 g (4 oz) small button mushrooms, wiped
2 slices of bread, toasted and cut into small triangles

SERVES 4

*P*lace the onions, garlic and butter in a 3 l (3 qt) microwave-safe dish or casserole. Cover with a well-fitting lid or plastic wrap. Cook on HIGH (100%) for 2 minutes.

While onion is cooking, toss diced beef in the flour. Add beef to onion and stir well to toss meat in butter. Stir in wine, beef stock, tarragon, peppercorns and carrots. Re-cover dish and cook on DEFROST (30%) for 1 hour, stirring after 20 and 40 minutes.

Adjust seasoning, stir in mushrooms and continue cooking on MEDIUM (50%) for 5 minutes.

Serve hot, garnished with triangles of hot toast.

● Corned Beef with White Parsley Sauce (page 219)

Hearty Beef Casserole

2 tbspns seasoned, plain flour
1 tbspn gravy powder
freshly ground black pepper to taste
750 g (1½ lb) round or topside steak, cut into 2 cm (¾ in) cubes
1 potato, peeled and cut into 2 cm (¾ in) pieces
1 carrot, evenly sliced
1 large onion, diced
425 g (13½ oz) can tomatoes
1 tbspn tomato paste
1 tbspn Worcestershire sauce
½ tspn Vegemite (optional)
1 cup (250 ml/8 fl oz) strong beef stock (or stock cubes and water)
1 small swede, peeled and cut into 2 cm (¾ in) pieces
1 small parsnip, peeled and cut into 2 cm (¾ in) pieces
⅓ cup (45 g/1½ oz) frozen peas
90 g (3 oz) mushrooms, wiped and sliced

SERVES 4

In a 3 l (3 qt) microwave-safe casserole, combine the flour, gravy powder and black pepper. Add the meat and toss until well coated with the flour. Add the remaining ingredients, except peas and mushrooms. Cover dish and cook on DEFROST (30%) for 2 hours. Stir occasionally during cooking. Stir in peas and mushrooms, re-cover and cook for a further 5 minutes. Allow to stand for 5–10 minutes before serving.

Serve in large soup bowls as a complete meal.

Beef Stroganoff

2 tbspns (45 g/1½ oz) butter
750 g (1½ lb) fillet, rump or minute beef-steak, cut into thin strips
1 tbspn seasoned, plain flour
2 medium onions, thinly sliced
200 g (6½ oz) button mushrooms, wiped and sliced
1 cup (250 ml/8 fl oz) sour cream
2 tspns prepared French mustard
freshly ground black pepper to taste
chopped fresh parsley for garnish

SERVES 4

*M*elt butter in a 3 l (3 qt) microwave-safe dish or casserole on HIGH (100%) for 1–2 minutes until hot and bubbly.

While butter is heating toss meat in flour. Quickly add meat to butter and stir well to coat. Cover dish with a well-fitting lid or plastic wrap and cook on HIGH for 2 minutes. Stir well then stir in onions. Continue cooking, covered, on HIGH for 3–4 minutes, until meat is almost tender. Stir in mushrooms and cook, uncovered, on HIGH for a further 2 minutes.

In a small bowl, combine sour cream, mustard and seasoning. Stir into beef, re-cover dish and cook on MEDIUM (50%) for 2–3 minutes until cream is heated through.

Serve hot on a bed of rice, garnished with chopped parsley.

Beef with Snow Peas and Mushrooms

¼ cup (60 ml/2 fl oz) soy sauce
1 tbspn sweet sherry
1 tbspn cornflour
1–2 tspns finely shredded fresh ginger
1 clove garlic, crushed
500 g (1 lb) sirloin or rump steak, finely sliced into thin strips
¼ cup (60 ml/2 fl oz) boiling water
90 g (3 oz) mushrooms, wiped and sliced
200 g (6½ oz) fresh snow peas, washed and trimmed

SERVES 4

Combine soy sauce, sherry, cornflour, ginger and crushed garlic in a medium-sized bowl. Add thinly sliced beef and leave, covered, to marinate for approximately 30 minutes.

Preheat a microwave-safe browning dish in the microwave on HIGH (100%) for 6 minutes until hot. Quickly add meat to browning dish and stir briskly until sizzling stops. Quickly add the boiling water to deglaze juices in dish. Stir in mushrooms and snow peas. Cover dish and cook on HIGH for 6 minutes until meat is cooked and vegetables are just tender.

Chilli con Carne

375 g (12 oz) lean minced beef
1 large onion, sliced
1 green capsicum, seeded and sliced
2 cloves garlic, crushed
½–1 tspn chilli powder (or to taste)
425 g (13½ oz) can tomatoes
2 tbspns tomato paste
½ tspn dried oregano
315 g (10 oz) can red kidney beans, washed and drained

SERVES 4

Preheat a microwave-safe browning dish on HIGH (100%) for 6 minutes, until hot. Add the minced beef and stir quickly until sizzling stops. Stir in onion, capsicum, garlic and chilli powder to taste. Cover dish and cook on HIGH for 5 minutes. Stir in tomatoes, tomato paste, oregano and kidney beans. Cook on MEDIUM (50%) for 20 minutes, until meat is cooked. Adjust seasoning if desired with additional chilli powder.

Serve hot on a bed of cooked macaroni or with corn chips.

● Chilli con Carne

Mexican-style Beef

2 tspns paprika
1 cup (250 ml/8 fl oz) beef stock (or stock cube
and water)
½ cup (90 g/3 oz) dried butter beans, soaked in water
overnight in refrigerator, then drained
750 g (1½ lb) chuck steak, cubed
1 large onion, chopped
1 large red capsicum, seeded and sliced
90 g (3 oz) salami, coarsely chopped
315 g (10 oz) can sweetcorn kernels, drained
black pepper to taste
2 cloves garlic, crushed

SERVES 4

Combine the paprika and stock. Put remaining ingredients into a plastic roasting bag. Hold bag closed and gently shake to mix all ingredients evenly. Place bag in a shallow baking dish or large plate and pour in stock. Secure bag with a piece of string or an elastic band. Pierce bag near tie to allow some steam to escape during cooking. Cook on HIGH (100%) for 5 minutes. Reduce power and cook on DEFROST (30%) for 60 minutes. Carefully turn bag over after 30 minutes, wearing oven mitts. Allow to stand for 10 minutes before serving.

Beef and Cheese Roll-up

500 g (1 lb) minced beef
1 onion, finely chopped
1 clove garlic, crushed
2 tbspns chopped fresh parsley
1 egg, beaten
black pepper to taste
1½ cups (185 g/6 oz) grated strong Cheddar cheese

SERVES 4-6

Mix all ingredients (except cheese) in a large bowl until well combined.

Place a large sheet of greaseproof or baking paper on work surface. Place meat mixture on paper and press or roll out firmly to measure approximately 35 × 25 cm (14 × 10 in). (The width should be the size of your microwave-safe loaf pan, and be able to sit evenly on the oven turntable.)

Sprinkle cheese over meat mixture, leaving a 2 cm (¾ in) border around all sides. Tightly roll up meat, using greaseproof paper as a lift and guide.

● Mexican-style Beef

Place in loaf pan and cook on HIGH (100%) for 15–16 minutes until an internal temperature of 70°C is reached, or until meat juices run clear. Drain off excess fat and juices.

Cover dish with aluminium foil and leave to stand for 10 minutes before turning out and slicing.

Cook potatoes and a green vegetable while meat is standing.

NOTE If meat in the corners of the microwave-safe loaf pan begins to cook before the rest of the loaf, protect these areas with small pieces of aluminium foil for half of the cooking time.

To speed up cooking when barbecuing for a crowd, partly cook sausages and hamburgers in advance in the microwave. Then, after a few minutes on the barbecue they will become crisp and brown.

Shepherd's Pie

This is a great way to stretch leftover beef or lamb, and although this recipe is of ancient origin it always remains a family favourite.

4 medium-sized potatoes
250 g (8 oz) cooked corned or roast beef, cut into pieces
1 medium onion, chopped
¼ cup (60 ml/2 fl oz) water
2 tbspns fruit chutney or tomato sauce
1 tbspn chopped fresh parsley
½ cup (60 g/2 oz) grated cheese

SERVES 4-6

Cook potatoes in their jackets on HIGH (100%) for 12 minutes or until they can be just pierced with a fine metal cake tester. Let stand, wrapped in aluminium foil, for at least 5 minutes before peeling and mashing.

Put meat, onion, water, chutney and parsley in a food processor (or chop very finely) and process until evenly chopped. Place meat mixture in a medium-sized microwave-safe casserole and cook on MEDIUM HIGH (70%) for 7 minutes or until heated through, stirring several times. Pile on the mashed potatoes and top with grated cheese. Reheat on MEDIUM HIGH for 2–3 minutes or until cheese melts. For a browned top, heat for a short time under a heated grill. Serve with vegetables.

Beef Madeira

1 tbspn vegetable oil
2 tbspns plain flour
750 g (1½ lb) blade or round steak, cubed
1 large onion, sliced
1 green capsicum, seeded and sliced
1 clove garlic, crushed
½ cup (125 ml/4 fl oz) beef stock
½ cup (125 ml/4 fl oz) Madeira or sherry
½ tspn paprika
2 carrots, evenly sliced
345 g (11 oz) French beans, washed and sliced

SERVES 4

*H*eat the oil in a 2–3 l (2–3 qt) microwave-safe casserole, on HIGH (100%) for 2 minutes. Meanwhile,
toss together the flour and beef until well coated.
Add the floured meat to the hot oil and stir quickly
to coat with oil. Stir in the onion, capsicum and
garlic. Cover dish and cook on HIGH for 5 minutes.
Stir in beef stock, Madeira or sherry, paprika and
carrots. Continue cooking on DEFROST (30%) for 40
minutes. Add prepared green beans to dish, re-
cover and continue cooking for 10 minutes on
DEFROST or until beans are tender.

Serve hot with buttered pasta.

Beef and Mushroom Olives with Mixed Vegetables

750 g (1½ lb) topside steak, thinly sliced
8–12 small potatoes, peeled and cut into
even-sized pieces
500 g (1 lb) broccoli, washed and divided into florets
12 small carrots, peeled and cut into even-sized pieces

STUFFING

4 spring onions, finely chopped
1 tbspn (20 g/¾ oz) butter, softened
90 g (3 oz) mushrooms, wiped and chopped
2 tspns lemon juice
1½ cups (90 g/3 oz) soft breadcrumbs
1 tbspn chopped fresh parsley
black pepper to taste
1 egg, beaten
1 tbspn seasoned, plain flour
1 tbspn oil
½ cup (125 ml/4 fl oz) beef stock
1 large onion, finely sliced
45 g (1¾ oz) mushrooms, wiped and sliced
2 tspns gravy powder

SERVES 4

*U*sing a meat mallet, flatten the steak between two
sheets of greaseproof paper. Cut into eight pieces.

Place prepared vegetables in a shallow
microwave-safe dish. Cover with a well-fitting lid
or plastic wrap. Set aside to cook after meat dish.

Combine stuffing ingredients (up to and including beaten egg) in a large mixing bowl, until well
mixed. Divide stuffing between each piece of meat.
Roll up the beef and secure with a cocktail stick.
Roll each in a little of the seasoned flour.

Heat oil in a shallow microwave-safe dish on
HIGH (100%) for 1 minute. Quickly add beef and
toss gently in the oil. Cook, uncovered, on HIGH,
for 5 minutes. Turn meat over in dish. Add stock
and onion. Cover dish and cook on MEDIUM (50%)
for 15–20 minutes until beef is tender, gently
redistributing meat after 10 minutes.

Transfer beef olives to a warmed plate. Cover
with aluminium foil. Stir sliced mushrooms and
gravy powder, blended with a little cold water,
into meat juices. Heat on HIGH for 2–3 minutes until
gravy thickens. Stir well. Cover and set aside.

Cook vegetables on HIGH for 8–10 minutes.
Meanwhile, pour sauce into sauceboat and reheat
at last moment.

Serve meat garnished with vegetables.

● Beef Madeira

● Beef and Mushroom Olives with Mixed Vegetables

Cheese and Chutney Stuffed Sausages

8 thick beef sausages
⅓ cup (125 g/4 oz) fruit chutney
½ cup finely chopped onion (or spring onion)
¾ cup (90 g/3 oz) grated Cheddar cheese
2 cups (500 ml/16 fl oz) commercial tomato-based pasta sauce
1 tspn brown sugar
2 tbspns chopped fresh parsley or garlic chives

SERVES 4

*H*eat a microwave-safe browning dish for 6 minutes on HIGH (100%). Add four sausages to the browning dish. Press down lightly to assist browning and when sizzling stops cover dish lightly with kitchen paper to avoid spattering. Cook on HIGH for 2–2½ minutes. Turn sausages and cook on HIGH for a further 1½–2 minutes or until cooked. Transfer sausages to a heated plate and cover with aluminium foil. Cook remaining four sausages in the same manner after wiping out the browning dish carefully with crumpled absorbent kitchen paper towel. Reheat for about 4 minutes.

With a sharp knife, split sausages lengthways about two-thirds through. Into each sausage spread 2 teaspoons of chutney and approximately 3 teaspoons chopped onion. Divide grated cheese evenly between the sausages and return to browning dish — no need to heat dish. Heat on HIGH for 2–3 minutes or until cheese melts to your liking. Transfer to heated serving dish and cover to keep warm.

Add pasta sauce and brown sugar to browning dish and heat on HIGH for 4–5 minutes or until just beginning to bubble, stirring several times. Stir in chopped parsley or chives.

Serve sausages with tomato sauce, creamy mashed potatoes and beans or peas.

Steak and Kidney Pudding

1 tbspn (20 g/¾ oz) butter
600 g (1¼ lb) blade steak, fat removed and cut into 2.5 cm (1 in) cubes
6 lamb's kidneys, membranes removed, quartered and cored
2 large onions, sliced
2 cups (500 ml/16 fl oz) beef stock
black pepper to taste
1 tspn mixed herbs
1 tbspn gravy powder
1 tbspn Worcestershire sauce
200 g (6½ oz) mushrooms, wiped and sliced
DUMPLING TOPPING
1 cup (125 g/4 oz) self-raising flour
black pepper to taste
2 tspns mixed herbs
1 tbspn chopped fresh or dried parsley
1½ tbspns (30 g/1 oz) butter or margarine
1 egg and ¼ cup (60 ml/2 fl oz) milk combined

SERVES 6

*P*reheat a microwave-safe browning dish on HIGH (100%) for 6 minutes, until hot. Quickly add the butter, meat and kidneys and press down to sear edges and seal meat. Cook, uncovered, on HIGH for 2 minutes. Turn meat over and continue cooking on HIGH for 2 minutes. Stir in onions, beef stock, seasoning, herbs, gravy powder and Worcestershire sauce. Stir well to de-glaze dish. Cover dish with a well-fitting lid or plastic wrap. Cook on HIGH for 5 minutes. Stir well then reduce power and cook on DEFROST (30%) for 1 hour or until meat is tender. Stir occasionally during cooking. Stir in mushrooms.

While meat is cooking, prepare dumpling topping: Place the flour, seasoning and herbs in a large mixing bowl. Rub the butter or margarine through the flour until the mixture resembles fine breadcrumbs. Add enough of the egg and milk mixture to form a soft dough. Form dough into 16 small dumplings. Place these on top of meat, around the edge of the dish for more even cooking. Cook on HIGH for 7–10 minutes, until dumplings are cooked through. Serve hot.

Beef in Beer

750 g (1½ lb) round or blade steak, cubed
2 tbspns seasoned, plain flour
1 tbspn cooking oil
1 large red capsicum, seeded and cut into 1 cm (½ in)
cubes
¾ cup (185 ml/6 fl oz) strong beer
¾ cup (185 ml/6 fl oz) water
45 g (1½ oz) pkt French onion soup mix
1 French breadstick, sliced
approx. 2 tbspns (45 g/1½ oz)
mustard-flavoured butter

SERVES 4–5

Coat the beef in the flour.

Heat the oil in a 3 l (3 qt) microwave-safe dish or casserole on HIGH (100%) for 1 minute. Add the beef and quickly toss to coat in the oil. Cook on HIGH, uncovered, for 3–4 minutes, stirring well halfway through cooking time.

Stir remaining ingredients into casserole. Cover with a well-fitting lid or plastic wrap and cook on HIGH for 5 minutes. Stir well and continue cooking on DEFROST (30%) for 45 minutes or until meat is tender, stirring once during cooking.

To make the topping, toast slices of bread, spread with a little mustard-flavoured butter.

Transfer beef to a serving dish and serve topped with toast.

Meatballs in Cream Sauce

¾ cup (185 ml/6 fl oz) milk
3 slices bread, cubed
500 g (1 lb) beef, minced
1 egg, lightly beaten
1 small onion, grated
2 tbspns finely chopped fresh parsley
freshly ground black pepper to taste
¼ cup (30 g/1 oz) plain flour
1½ cups (375 ml/12 fl oz) beef stock
1 tbspn tomato paste
¼ tspn paprika
⅓ cup (90 ml/3 fl oz) sour cream

SERVES 4

Pour milk into a large microwave-safe mixing bowl. Heat on MEDIUM HIGH (70%) for 1 minute or just long enough to warm the milk. Add bread cubes and mix until all the milk is absorbed by the bread. Stir in the beef, egg, onion, parsley and pepper. Blend well, then form mixture into 3 cm (1¼ in) balls.

Arrange meatballs in a shallow microwave-safe dish. Cook, covered with a well-fitting lid or plastic wrap, on HIGH (100%) for 3 minutes. Turn meatballs over, re-cover dish and cook for a further 2 minutes on HIGH. Drain off any fat and liquid.

Stir together flour and beef stock to make a smooth liquid. Stir in tomato paste and paprika. Pour mixture over top of meatballs. Re-cover dish and cook on MEDIUM HIGH (70%) for 5 minutes, stirring occasionally.

Top meatballs with sour cream and stir lightly. Re-cover dish and cook on DEFROST (30%) for 8–10 minutes, until sauce is heated through.

Serve with cooked rice or pasta.

Egg Meatloaf Slice

2 carrots, sliced
2 zucchini, sliced
1 onion, chopped
345 g (11 oz) minced beef
155 g (5 oz) sausage mince
¼ cup chopped fresh parsley
1 cup (60 g/2 oz) soft wholemeal breadcrumbs
salt and pepper to taste
2 tbspns tomato sauce
2 eggs
3 hardboiled eggs, shelled
2 tbspns barbecue sauce

SERVES 4

Cook carrots, zucchini and onion in a covered microwave-safe casserole on HIGH (100%) for 2–3 minutes. While the vegetables are cooking, combine the remaining ingredients, excluding the hardboiled eggs and barbecue sauce. Drain any moisture from the cooked vegetables and gently fold vegetables into the meat mixture.

Place half the meat mixture into a microwave-safe loaf dish. Make three indentations on top of the meat for the eggs. Place the hardboiled eggs in the indentations and place the remaining meat mixture over the eggs, pressing down gently.

Cover with plastic wrap and cook on MEDIUM (50%) for 10–12 minutes. Remove the plastic wrap and be careful of steam. Brush the top with barbecue sauce and cook on DEFROST (30%) for 4–6 minutes. Allow to cool slightly in the cooking dish before turning out.

● Beef in Beer

Roast Seasoned Veal

Veal has little fat so it's important to keep its cut surfaces moistened with a little oil or pan juices during cooking.

2 kg (4 lb) boned leg of veal
1 tbspn oil
SEASONING
2 rashers bacon, chopped
1 small onion, finely chopped
1½ cups (90 g/3 oz) soft white breadcrumbs
freshly ground pepper to taste
1 tspn dried thyme or marjoram
1 tbspn (20 g/¾ oz) melted butter

SERVES 6

First prepare seasoning. Heat a microwave-safe browning dish for 6 minutes on HIGH (100%). Add bacon and cook on HIGH for 2–3 minutes, stirring once. Remove bacon pieces with a slotted spoon and place on a paper towel-lined plate. Add chopped onion to pan drippings and cook on HIGH for 2 minutes. Remove onion and combine with all other seasoning ingredients.

Open out veal, place seasoning in the centre and roll up. Tie into a neat shape with string. Brush all over with oil.

Reheat browning dish on HIGH for 3–4 minutes. Add veal and press down onto hot surface until sizzling stops. Cover lightly with kitchen paper towel and cook on HIGH (100%) for 10 minutes, turning several times during cooking. Reduce to MEDIUM (50%) and cook for a further 60 minutes, or until meat is cooked, brushing with pan juices several times and turning meat over halfway through cooking time.

Pan juices may be removed during cooking with a bulb baster to avoid having the meat develop a braised flavour from excess steam.

Cover loosely with aluminium foil and let stand for 10–14 minutes. If meat is not to be served immediately after standing time, wrap tightly with aluminium foil to keep warm until required. Gravy may be made by thickening the pan juices with a little cornflour blended in cold water.

NOTE If you don't own a microwave-safe browning dish, place meat on a microwave roasting rack in a suitable microwave-safe baking dish.

Veal and Pineapple Casserole

2 tbspns plain flour
1 tspn mixed herbs
1 tspn chicken stock powder
1 tspn dried basil
black pepper to taste
750 g (1½ lb) veal steak, diced
4 rashers bacon, chopped
2 onions, sliced
440 g (14 oz) can pineapple pieces, drained
2 tbspns finely chopped fresh parsley
1 cup (250 ml/8 fl oz) tomato sauce

SERVES 4

Mix the flour, mixed herbs, stock powder, dried basil and black pepper in a 3 l (3 qt) microwave-safe casserole. Add the veal and toss to coat in the seasonings. Stir in remaining ingredients.

Cover dish and cook on MEDIUM (50%) for 40 minutes. Stir well after 20 minutes.

Serve hot with rice.

Veal Parmigiana

500 g (1 lb) veal escalopes
1 tbspn seasoned, plain flour
1 egg, lightly beaten
1 cup (125 g/4 oz) dry breadcrumbs
2 tbspns cooking oil
250 g (8 oz) mozzarella cheese, grated or thinly sliced
2 tbspns grated Parmesan cheese
TOMATO SAUCE
1 tbspn cooking oil
1 onion, chopped
1 clove garlic, crushed
425 g (13½ oz) can tomatoes and juice
½ tspn dried oregano
pinch dried basil leaves
black pepper to taste

SERVES 4

Wipe meat with kitchen paper and pound with a meat mallet until very thin. Coat in a little flour, then in egg and breadcrumbs. Set aside while preparing tomato sauce.

Heat the oil for the sauce in a 1–2 l (1–2 qt) microwave-safe dish or casserole on HIGH (100%) for 2 minutes. Add the onion and cover dish with a well-fitting lid or plastic wrap and cook on HIGH for 2 minutes. Stir in remaining ingredients. Cook, uncovered, on HIGH for 2 minutes. Reduce the power and cook on MEDIUM (50%) for 5 minutes. Allow to stand for 5 minutes, then push mixture through a sieve or process in a food processor until well blended.

Heat a microwave-safe browning dish on HIGH for 7 minutes, until very hot. Add the cooking oil to the pan and quickly add escalopes. Press meat down to brown the edges and seal the meat. Cook on HIGH for 2 minutes. Turn meat over and cook for a further 1½–2 minutes on HIGH until meat is cooked through.

Place half the cooked veal in the base of a shallow microwave-safe dish or casserole. Cover with half the tomato sauce. Top with the remaining veal, tomato sauce then mozzarella cheese and Parmesan. Cook on MEDIUM for 10–15 minutes, until heated through and cheese is melted.

Creamy Veal

250 g (8 oz) boneless veal, cut into thin strips
1 tbspn gravy powder
2 tspns butter or margarine
6 spring onions, sliced
1 tspn seeded mustard (optional)
freshly ground pepper to taste
¼ cup (60 ml/2 fl oz) sour cream
½ red capsicum, cut into strips

SERVES 2

Combine the veal, gravy powder and butter or margarine in a microwave-safe casserole and cook on MEDIUM HIGH (70%) for 4 minutes. Stir in the remaining ingredients and cook on MEDIUM HIGH for a further 2–3 minutes. Stir well.

Serve with cooked pasta if desired.

To make dry breadcrumbs, scatter 1½–2 cups of cubed bread over a microwave-safe plate covered with a paper towel. Cook on HIGH (100%) for 2–3 minutes, rearranging the bread 2 or 3 times. Cool and crumble the cubes as required.

Indian Spiced Veal

600 g (1¼ lb) veal escalopes
black pepper to taste
pinch curry powder
425 g (13½ oz) can sliced peaches, well drained
1 tbspn (20 g/¾ oz) butter
CURRY SAUCE
1 tbspn (20 g/¾ oz) butter
1 large onion, finely sliced
1 tbspn curry powder or to taste
1 apple, peeled, cored and sliced
1 banana, sliced
½ cup (90 g/3 oz) raisins
½ cup (155g/5 oz) fruit chutney
1 tbspn plain flour
1½ cups (375 ml/12 fl oz) chicken stock
½ cup (125 ml/4 fl oz) dry white wine
⅔ cup (30 g/1 oz) shredded coconut
½ orange, sliced (reserve remaining half, sliced,
for garnish)

SERVES 4–6

Pound veal until very thin and cut into pieces approximately 8 × 6 cm (3 × 2½ in). Season each side of the meat with pepper and a little curry powder.

Place one peach slice onto each piece of meat. Roll up and secure with toothpicks. Set aside while curry sauce is made.

Melt butter for sauce in a 2–3 l (2–3 qt) microwave-safe dish or casserole on HIGH (100%) for 45 seconds. Stir in onion, curry powder, apple,

banana and raisins. Cover dish and cook on HIGH for 4 minutes, stirring well after 2 minutes. Add chutney, flour, stock and wine, stir well again. Continue cooking, uncovered, on HIGH for 5 minutes. Stir in the shredded coconut and orange slices and cook for 3–4 minutes until orange is broken down. Strain and set aside.

Melt the butter for the veal in a shallow microwave-safe dish on HIGH for 1 minute until bubbling. Add the veal rolls and toss to coat in butter. Cook on HIGH for 2 minutes. Turn meat over in dish and pour strained curry sauce over meat. Cover dish with a well-fitting lid or plastic wrap. Cook on MEDIUM (50%) for 10 minutes, until meat is tender.

Lift the meat onto a serving plate, remove the toothpicks and serve with curry sauce poured over and garnished with remaining orange slices.

Peach-glazed Veal

1.5 kg (3 lb) leg or loin of veal
1 tbspn (20 g/¾ oz) butter, softened
paprika to taste
2 tbspns honey
½ cup (125 ml/4 fl oz) puréed peaches
1 tbspn soy sauce
1 tbspn cornflour
½ cup (125 ml/4 fl oz) water
fresh peach, halved, for garnish
sprigs of cress for garnish

SERVES 4

Brush the veal with butter and dust with a little paprika. Place veal in a microwave-safe casserole on a microwave roasting rack or upturned saucer. Cook in the microwave on HIGH (100%) for 5 minutes. Turn veal over and cook on MEDIUM (50%) for 20 minutes, basting occasionally with meat juices.

Combine honey, peaches and soy sauce. Spread over meat and cook on MEDIUM for 10 minutes. Turn meat again, basting with meat juices and peach glaze. Cook on MEDIUM for a further 20 minutes. Remove meat from pan, cover with aluminium foil and allow to stand for 15 minutes.

Stir cornflour into water and add to pan juices. Cook on HIGH for 4 minutes, until sauce boils and thickens. Stir after 2 minutes, to ensure sauce is smooth.

Serve veal sliced with a little sauce poured over and remainder in a sauce boat. Garnish with peach halves and cress. (See photo page 129.)

● Pork and Veal Terrine

Pork and Veal Terrine

6–8 rashers bacon
1 kg (2 lb) pork and veal mince
1 egg
2–3 tspns mixed herbs to taste
1 tbspn chopped fresh parsley
1 onion, finely chopped
1 tspn onion salt
freshly ground black pepper to taste

SERVES 6

Line a 23 × 10 cm (9 × 4 in) microwave-safe terrine dish with the bacon rashers, allowing them to hang over the sides of dish.

Combine remaining ingredients thoroughly in a large mixing bowl. Firmly pack meat mixture into bacon-lined dish. Fold bacon rashers over top of meat. Cover loosely with plastic wrap. Cook on MEDIUM HIGH (70%) for 20–22 minutes, until meat is cooked and juices run clear.

Allow to cool slightly; pour off excess liquid. Re-cover and cool with a heavy weight on top so that terrine forms a compact, solid shape, draining off any additional juice that forms as meat cools.

Serve cold.

NOTE For extra effect and added flavour, place bay leaves in dish on top of bacon before cooking.

Roast Pork

A pork roast cooks well by microwave, but if its main attraction for you is the crisp crackling, you will need to make a slight alteration to the usual cooking procedure. If the skin is left on the pork for the duration of its cooking in the microwave oven it becomes rather hard instead of crisp. To achieve a crisp result ask the butcher to remove the skin — though you could, of course, remove it yourself with the careful use of a sharp knife. Trim excess fat from both the pork itself and the skin. This is not just good microwave advice — in the interests of good nutrition, trimming excess fat is strongly recommended for roasts of all kinds.

There are two methods for acquiring crisp crackling after the skin is removed. The first is by *microwave*: Rub the rind with lemon juice and sprinkle with salt. Cut the skin into portions about 5 cm (2 in) square after cutting away some of the fat layer. Place between double layers of absorbent kitchen paper on a plate in the microwave oven. Cook on HIGH (100%) for 6 minutes, using fresh kitchen paper after 3 minutes for extra fat absorption.

The second method uses the *griller of a conventional stove*: Cut the skin into fairly narrow strips and place, fat side up, across the rungs of a grilling pan. Cook under a preheated griller until the fat is almost transparent, turn and cook the rind until crisp and very lightly browned.

The following recipe offers a third alternative for achieving crisp crackling by removing the rind half-way through the cooking time.

1 leg of pork (about 2.5 kg/5 lb)
SAUCE
½ cup (125 ml/4 fl oz) dry white wine
2 tbspns redcurrant jelly
¾ cup (185 ml/6 fl oz) cream

SERVES 7–8

Place pork, fat side down, on a microwave rack in a microwave-safe baking dish. Cook on HIGH (100%) for 10 minutes. Reduce power to MEDIUM (50%) and allow 10 minutes per 500 g (1 lb) — about 50 minutes.

Turn pork over halfway during cooking and, using a sharp knife, cut away the rind in one piece. Place rind on a sheet of aluminium foil and just before you serve the pork, place the rind under a hot griller. This will crisp up crackling. If left on the pork for the whole of the cooking time it will become hard instead of light and crunchy.

Wrap pork in aluminium foil and let stand for 15–20 minutes while preparing vegetables.

To prepare sauce: Skim fat from pan drippings, add white wine and redcurrant jelly and heat on HIGH (100%) until jelly melts, stirring every 20 seconds. Stir in cream and heat on MEDIUM (50%) until almost boiling.

Serve with pork.

Fruity Roast Pork with Orange Sauce

2 tbspns brandy or sherry
90 g (3 oz) prunes, seeded and roughly chopped
½ cup (75 g/2½ oz) roughly chopped dried apricots
1–1.5 kg (2–3 lb) loin of pork, boned and rind scored through to fat
salt for rubbing into rind

SAUCE
2 tbspns cornflour
½ cup (125 ml/4 fl oz) chicken stock (or a stock cube and water)
2 tbspns brandy or sherry
2 tbspns plum jam
juice and finely grated rind of 1 orange

SERVES 4–6

Combine brandy or sherry with prunes and apricots. Leave to marinate for as long as possible — at least 1 hour. Heat a microwave-safe browning dish on HIGH (100%) for 6 minutes, until hot. Meanwhile, place pork flat, rind side down. Place stuffing (prunes and apricots) down centre of pork. Roll up and tie securely. Rub salt into scored rind.

Put pork, rind side down, onto heated browning dish. Place a piece of absorbent kitchen paper on top. Cook on HIGH for 10 minutes. Turn meat over, cook on MEDIUM (50%) for 16–18 minutes. Turn meat over again and baste with meat juices. Cook for 8–10 minutes. Insert a knife into meat to ensure juices are clear. Cover meat with aluminium foil. Leave to stand for 15 minutes.

To prepare sauce: Combine cornflour and stock. Mix well and stir in brandy or sherry, plum jam and orange juice and rind, including any juices from the meat that are not greasy. Cook sauce on HIGH for 4 minutes, stirring after 2 minutes, until mixture boils and thickens.

Serve pork sliced, with a little sauce poured over and remainder in a sauce boat.

NOTE For crisp crackling, rind should be removed from loin before stuffing and excess fat cut away from meat.

Stir-fry Pork in Black Bean Sauce

1 tbspn cooking oil
600 g (1¼ lb) pork schnitzels or leg steaks, cut into thin strips
1 clove garlic, crushed
1 large onion, cut into wedges
½ cup (125 ml/4 fl oz) commercially prepared black bean sauce
½ cup (125 ml/4 fl oz) chicken stock
½ tspn chilli sauce (or to taste)

GARNISH
4 spring onions, cut into 10 cm (4 in) lengths
1 small carrot, peeled
4 radishes, thoroughly washed

SERVES 4

Heat a microwave-safe browning dish on HIGH (100%) for 7 minutes until very hot. Quickly add oil, then pork, and press down so that edges of meat seal and brown. Cook on HIGH for 2 minutes. Stir in garlic and onion and continue cooking on HIGH for a further 2 minutes. Stir in black bean sauce, stock and chilli sauce. Cook, uncovered, on HIGH for 2–3 minutes until meat is tender and sauce boils and thickens slightly. Serve with boiled rice and dress with vegetable garnish.

To prepare garnish: Trim spring onions to 10 cm (4 in) lengths (including green stems if necessary). Using a sharp knife, make three or four vertical cuts (about 8 cm (3 in) long) along each spring onion, stopping just short of end of white bulb. Soak in a bowl of iced water. Make wafer-thin slices of carrot by peeling with a vegetable peeler. Add to iced water. Cut the radish three or four times from the top towards base, and be careful not to cut right through base. Place in iced water. After 5–10 minutes the vegetables will curl up into decorative shapes. Drain well.

Honeyed Pork Spare Ribs with Redcurrant Sauce

1 large onion, finely chopped
2 cloves garlic, crushed
¾ cup (250 g/8 oz) redcurrant jelly
¼ cup (90 ml/3 fl oz) honey
¼ cup (60 ml/2 fl oz) soy sauce
¼ cup (60 ml/2 fl oz) wine vinegar
½–1 tspn chilli sauce to taste
black pepper to taste
1 kg (2 lb) pork spare ribs
1 tbspn cornflour

SERVES 4

Combine the onion, garlic, redcurrant jelly, honey, soy sauce and vinegar in a large bowl. Stir in chilli sauce and black pepper to taste. Add the spare ribs and stir well to coat with the marinade. Cover dish and leave overnight in the refrigerator, or for at least 30 minutes, so that the meat can absorb the flavours.

Remove spare ribs from bowl (reserving marinade). Place ribs in a single layer in a shallow microwave-safe dish. Cook, uncovered, on HIGH (100%) for 5 minutes. Turn ribs over and continue cooking on MEDIUM (50%) for 25–30 minutes, or until ribs are tender, turning ribs over once during cooking.

Blend cornflour with a little cold water and stir into reserved marinade. Pour sauce over spare ribs. Cook on HIGH for 5 minutes, basting ribs after 2 and 3 minutes until they are well coated and the sauce thickens slightly.

Serve hot.

Pork Fillet with Mango Chilli Sauce

This is the perfect main course for a dinner for two. Serve with tiny new potatoes and sliced French beans with toasted slivered almonds. Follow with White Mousseline with Raspberry Coulis.

1 whole pork fillet (approx. 250 g/8 oz)
1 small lime, juiced
½ tspn fresh chilli, seeded and finely sliced (reserve a few slices for garnish)
1 tspn soy sauce
2 tbspns chicken stock
1 large ripe mango, halved, cut into slices and remaining flesh mashed or puréed
1 tspn cornflour
2 tspns honey

SERVES 2

Slice pork into 3 cm (1 in) medallions. Cut each medallion almost in half again, without cutting right through. Open out to give a butterfly shape. Place meat in-between sheets of greaseproof paper and lightly flatten each one with a meat mallet or rolling pin. Place in a suitable shallow microwave-safe dish. Add lime juice, chilli slices, soy sauce, chicken stock and puréed mango. Toss meat in marinade. Cover with plastic wrap and leave to marinate in the refrigerator for at least 30 minutes, or overnight.

Stir meat and juices well. Re-cover dish with a well-fitting lid or plastic wrap. Cook on HIGH (100%) for 3 minutes, turning each piece of meat over and stirring well after 2 minutes. Test to see if meat is cooked. If not, cook for another minute, until tender. Remove meat from dish, arrange on warmed plates and garnish with mango slices.

Blend cornflour with 2 tablespoons of water and stir into meat juices and marinade ingredients together with honey. Heat on HIGH for 2 minutes, stirring well after 1 minute until liquid boils and thickens. Strain sauce into a small jug.

Serve dish with a little sauce drizzled over meat and mango, and garnished with reserved chilli slices.

NOTE Some people have an allergic reaction to chillies. Handle with rubber gloves and avoid touching face or eyes. (See photo pages 104–105.)

● *From left:* **Peach-glazed Veal (page 124); Honeyed Pork Spare Ribs with Redcurrant Sauce**

Pork Roll-ups

8 pork leg steaks or schnitzels
approx. 2 tspns prepared mustard
8 strips processed cheese
4 heads chicory, halved lengthways,
or 8 asparagus spears
4 rashers bacon, halved
1 tbspn (20 g/ ¾ oz) butter

SERVES 4

*U*sing a meat mallet, flatten each pork steak between two sheets of greaseproof paper until thin. Spread each one lightly with mustard. Lay a strip of cheese along the meat, then half a piece of chicory or an asparagus spear. Roll up each piece of pork, then roll a piece of bacon round each one. Secure with a wooden cocktail stick.

Preheat a microwave-safe browning dish on HIGH (100%) for 8 minutes, until hot. Quickly add the butter and pork roll-ups. Press meat down gently to sear each piece. Cook, uncovered, on HIGH for 5 minutes. Turn meat over and continue cooking, uncovered, on HIGH for 4–5 minutes or until tender.

Transfer meat to a warmed serving plate. Serve meat juices separately in a sauce boat.

● Pork Roll-ups

Peppered Pork Chops

4 pork loin chops, trimmed of excess fat
juice of ½ lemon
freshly ground black pepper to taste
¼ cup (60 ml/2 fl oz) dry white wine
1 tbspn seasoned, plain flour
1 tspn whole peppercorns
2 tbspns cream

SERVES 4

*P*reheat a microwave-safe browning dish on HIGH (100%) for 7 minutes, until very hot.

Meanwhile, rub the chops with lemon juice and black pepper. Carefully remove dish from oven and quickly add chops; press down lightly so that the meat sears and browns.

Return dish to oven and cook on HIGH for 4 minutes. Turn meat over in dish, cover dish with a well-fitting lid and cook on MEDIUM HIGH (70%) for 5–6 minutes until tender. Remove chops and place them on a warmed serving plate on a piece of absorbent kitchen paper to absorb any excess fat.

De-glaze dish with the wine and stir well. Stir in the flour and peppercorns. Continue cooking on HIGH for 2 minutes, stirring well after 1 minute, until liquid boils and thickens. Stir in the cream.

Serve chops with a little of the sauce drizzled over and remainder in a sauce boat.

Glazed Christmas Ham

If the ham is to be served as part of a cold buffet, prepare it at least the day before. Decorating the ham is a simple matter, though it does involve a little time. Have the butcher or delicatessen skin the ham for you. It should be done carefully, leaving a relatively smooth surface on the fat beneath. You could attempt to remove some of the fat, but this usually spoils the even surface and consequently the diamond-patterned decoration.

3 kg (6 lb) leg-end joint of cooked ham
¾ cup (185 ml/6 fl oz) pineapple juice
½ cup (90 g/3 oz) brown sugar
1 tspn mustard powder
1 tspn ground cinnamon
cloves

SERVES 12

Cover the thinner bone-end of the ham with a piece of aluminium foil.

Combine pineapple juice, sugar, mustard and cinnamon in a small microwave-safe bowl and heat on HIGH (100%) for 1 minute or until mixture boils. Stir well to dissolve sugar.

Place ham, fat side up, on a roasting rack in a shallow microwave-safe casserole. Brush liberally with glaze and heat on MEDIUM (50%) for 20 minutes, brushing with additional glaze every 6–7 minutes. Remove from oven and score the fat of the ham with diagonal cuts about 2–3 cm (1 in) apart, first in one direction and then in the other to form a diamond pattern. Cut only about 5 mm (¼ in) deep into the fat. Brush liberally again with glaze and place a clove in the centre of each of the 'diamonds' of fat. Reheat on MEDIUM for a further 10 to 15 minutes.

VARIATION Leave skin on ham but do not score. Cook and glaze as above and serve decorated with canned pineapple slices studded with maraschino cherries. (See photo pages 82–83.)

Ham Steaks Cranberry

4 ham steaks
1 tbspn (20 g/¾ oz) butter, melted
SAUCE
1 bacon stock cube
¾ cup (185 ml/6 fl oz) orange juice
1 tspn grated orange rind
¼ cup (90 ml/3 fl oz) cranberry sauce
freshly ground pepper to taste

SERVES 4

Heat a microwave-safe browning dish for 6 minutes on HIGH (100%). Meanwhile, brush steaks with melted butter. Add two steaks to heated browning dish, pressing down to allow steaks to brown a little. When sizzling stops, cook, uncovered, on HIGH for 1½–2 minutes. Turn steaks and cook, uncovered, on HIGH for a further 2–3 minutes. Remove to a heated serving dish, cover and keep warm. Quickly wipe out browning dish with crumpled kitchen paper towel and reheat dish 2–3 minutes on HIGH. Cook remaining steaks in the same way. Keep them warm while preparing sauce.

To prepare sauce: Add the crumbled bacon stock cube to the browning dish with orange juice and stir to incorporate any pan drippings. Add orange rind and cranberry sauce, stir and cook, uncovered, on HIGH for 2 minutes, or until sauce is smooth and hot. Season with pepper — the added bacon stock cube may make it unnecessary to add salt.

Return steaks to sauce and reheat on HIGH for about 30 seconds.

Heat a microwave-safe browning dish on HIGH for 7 minutes until hot. Meanwhile weigh meat to calculate cooking time (10–12 minutes per 500 g (1 lb) weight). Rub inside and out of meat with lemon juice. Pack stuffing loosely into centre of meat.

Carefully place crown roast on hot browning dish, lifting it with an egg slice to ensure that stuffing does not dislodge. Cook on HIGH for 2 minutes, then MEDIUM (50%) for remainder of cooking time.

When cooked, remove roast to a warmed serving plate. Cover loosely with aluminium foil and leave to stand for 10–15 minutes. Spoon off excess fat from browning dish and discard. Deglaze dish with stock and redcurrant jelly. Heat on HIGH for 2 minutes. Meanwhile, mix cornflour with a little cold water and stir into hot sauce. Reheat on HIGH for 2–3 minutes until sauce boils and thickens. Brush a little of the sauce over meat to give a good sheen.

Serve remainder of sauce in a gravy boat to accompany meat.

● Crown Roast with Pinenut Stuffing

Crown Roast with Pinenut Stuffing

STUFFING

1 tbspn (20 g/ ¾ oz) butter
2 rashers bacon, chopped
3 spring onions, finely chopped
½ cup (30 g/1 oz) fresh breadcrumbs
50 pinenuts
2 tbspns chopped fresh parsley
1 egg, beaten
1 crown roast of lamb with 16 ribs
juice of 1 lemon
½ cup (125 ml/4 fl oz) chicken stock
2 tbspns redcurrant jelly
1 tbspn cornflour

SERVES 4–5

*T*o make the stuffing, melt butter in a shallow microwave-safe dish on HIGH (100%) for 1 minute. Add bacon and cook on HIGH for 2 minutes, until crisp. Stir in spring onions, breadcrumbs, nuts, parsley and egg.

Lamb Bourguignonne

2 tbspns cooking oil
650 g (1¼ lb) lean lamb, cut into 2 cm (¾ in) cubes
1 large onion, sliced
1 large carrot, sliced
½ cup (125 ml/4 fl oz) red wine
¼ cup (60 ml/2 fl oz) stock, or stock cube and water
1 tbspn tomato purée or paste
1 tbspn plain flour
1 tspn mixed herbs
freshly ground black pepper to taste
90 g (3 oz) mushrooms, wiped and sliced

SERVES 4

*P*our the oil into a shallow 2 l (2 qt) microwave-safe casserole. Heat in the microwave on HIGH (100%) for 2 minutes, until hot. Quickly add the lamb and toss to coat in oil. Stir in the onion and carrot. Cover dish. Cook on HIGH for 5 minutes. Stir in the red wine and cook on MEDIUM (50%) for 8 minutes.

Meanwhile, combine stock, tomato purée, flour, mixed herbs and seasoning. Stir stock mixture into meat. Re-cover and continue cooking on DEFROST (30%) for 15 minutes. Stir in mushrooms, continue cooking for 2 minutes. Leave to stand for 5–10 minutes.

Adjust seasonings to taste just before serving.

Stuffed Loin of Lamb

1.25 kg (2½ lb) loin of lamb, boned
¾ cup cooked rice (approx. ¼ cup/45 g/1½ oz raw)
½ cup (60 g/2 oz) chopped bacon or ham
6 spring onions or 1 small onion, chopped
1 egg, lightly beaten
8 prunes, stoned and chopped
salt and freshly ground pepper to taste
SAUCE
1 cup (250 ml/8 fl oz) orange juice
2 tbspns redcurrant jelly
1 tbspn Galliano (optional)
2 tspns cornflour

SERVES 4–6

Open out loin of lamb and trim any excess fat, taking care not to cut the outer skin which helps to keep the rolled loin in a neat shape. Combine the next five ingredients and season the meat, remembering that the addition of bacon or ham will reduce the need for salt.

Spread the mixture in a fairly consolidated roll shape along the length of the loin. Draw up the thin edge over the filling and lap it over the thick side of the meat to completely enclose the filling. Don't force all the stuffing in if the flap will not cover it entirely — some may be pushed back in after the meat is tied.

Tie the meat into a neat roll with string, making individual ties about 2–3 cm (1–1½ in) apart along the length of the loin. Take care to tie the two ends very securely.

If using a microwave-safe browning dish, heat it for 8 minutes and add meat, fat side down. Cook on HIGH (100%) for 22–24 minutes, turning the meat once or twice during the cooking time to brown more evenly. If your microwave has a browning cycle, follow the manufacturer's instructions to brown the meat either before or after cooking. If no browning cycle or browning dish, use a frying pan on the top of stove to brown the meat before cooking it by microwave. In this case, ensure the meat is on a rack or raised so that it will not sit in the juices that accumulate when cooking meat in a microwave-safe casserole.

Remove meat to a plate or serving dish and cover loosely with aluminium foil. Spoon off as much fat as possible from the dish, leaving any tasty drippings from the meat. Add orange juice, redcurrant jelly, Galliano and cornflour mixed with 1 tablespoon orange juice or water. Cook on HIGH until thickened and bubbly, stirring regularly to incorporate the pan drippings. Pour into sauce boat and cover with aluminium foil to keep warm.

VARIATION If preferred, a conventional gravy may be made in a microwave-safe browning dish in place of the orange sauce. Heat the browning dish with meat drippings for 1–2 minutes, depending on quantity of drippings, and stir in 1 tablespoon of plain flour. Heat on HIGH for 30 seconds. Stir well and add 1 cup (250 ml/8 fl oz) stock. Continue to cook on HIGH, stirring regularly, until gravy thickens. Pour into a jug and reheat later in the microwave if necessary.

Colonial Roast Lamb

1 cup (60 g/2 oz) soft breadcrumbs
1 tspn thyme
black pepper to taste
pinch ground ginger
½ cup (60 g/2 oz) dried apricots, quartered
½ cup (90 g/3 oz) pistachio nuts, chopped
1 onion, finely chopped
1 tbspn (20 g/¾ oz) butter, melted
1 egg, lightly beaten
1.5–2 kg (3–4 lb) leg lamb, boned (weight after boning)
¾ cup (185 ml/6 fl oz) red wine

SERVES 4–6

Mix breadcrumbs with thyme and seasonings in a large mixing bowl. Stir in apricots, nuts, onion and melted butter, and enough egg to bind the mixture to a fairly dry consistency.

Fill the leg cavity of the meat with the stuffing, holding it in place with toothpicks. Carefully place lamb in a shallow microwave-safe roasting dish. Pour wine over lamb. Cook on HIGH (100%) for the first 5 minutes, then reduce the power to MEDIUM (50%) for 14 minutes per 500 g (1 lb) of meat plus stuffing. (Allow approximately 300 g (10 oz) for stuffing.) Meat will take approximately 60 minutes to cook to medium–well done. Baste with meat juices and wine during cooking.

● Colonial Roast Lamb

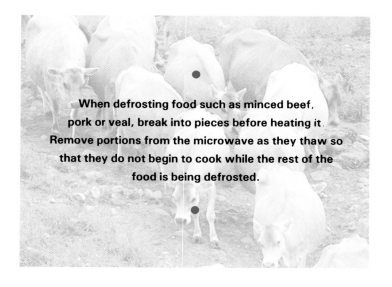

When defrosting food such as minced beef, pork or veal, break into pieces before heating it. Remove portions from the microwave as they thaw so that they do not begin to cook while the rest of the food is being defrosted.

Mild Lamb Curry

This curry has a delicious mild flavour. For a really hot curry use 2–3 teaspoons of hot Madras curry powder.

2 tbspns oil
1 large onion, chopped
1 clove garlic, crushed
2 tspns curry powder
1 stick celery, sliced
1 green apple, cored and chopped
250 g (8 oz) lamb, visible fat removed and meat diced
1 tbspn cornflour
1 cup (250 ml/8 fl oz) chicken stock
1 cup (60 g/2 oz) fruit and bran cereal
1 large tomato, diced

SERVES 4

Heat oil in a 3 l (3 qt) microwave-safe casserole on HIGH (100%) for 2 minutes. Stir in onion, garlic, curry powder, celery and apple. Cook for 2 minutes. Add cubed lamb and cook, covered, on HIGH for 5 minutes, until meat changes colour, stirring well after 2–3 minutes. Stir in cornflour and mix well. Gradually add stock, cook, covered on HIGH for 2–3 minutes, until sauce boils and thickens. Stir in cereal and tomato. Re-cover dish, reduce power to DEFROST (30%) and cook for 10 minutes, or until lamb is tender.

Serve with hot cooked rice or pappadums and non-fat natural yoghurt, mixed with diced fresh cucumber.

Sherried Lamb Noisettes

4 lamb noisettes, 3 cm (1¼ in) thick (ask your butcher
to roll and tie them separately)
4 spring onions, chopped
200 g (6½ oz) button mushrooms, wiped and sliced
1 tbspn chopped fresh tarragon
¼ cup (60 ml/2 fl oz) dry sherry

SERVES 2–4

Heat a microwave-safe browning dish on HIGH
(100%) for 7 minutes, until very hot. Quickly add
the lamb and press meat down to seal and brown
the edges. Cook on HIGH for 2 minutes. Turn meat
over and continue cooking on MEDIUM HIGH (70%)
for 3–4 minutes until meat is tender. Remove meat
from dish and set aside.

Add spring onions, mushrooms, tarragon and
sherry to dish. Stir well and cook, uncovered, on
HIGH for 2 minutes. Return meat to pan. Toss in
sherry sauce. Heat through on HIGH for 1 minute.

Serve hot with creamed potatoes and carrots.

Kashmiri Lamb Kofta

500 g (1 lb) lean minced lamb
1 tspn finely shredded fresh ginger
1 fresh chilli, finely chopped
1 tspn chopped fresh coriander
½ tspn chilli powder (or to taste)
2 tspns garam masala
½ cup (125 ml/4 fl oz) natural yoghurt
1 tbspn (20 g/¾ oz) ghee or butter
1 tbspn dried whole milk powder
1 tspn sugar
½ cup (125 ml/4 fl oz) boiling water
1 tbspn tamarind sauce or 2 tspns tamarind paste
¼ tspn ground cardamom seeds for garnish

SERVES 8

Place the lamb in a mixing bowl with the ginger,
chilli, coriander, chilli powder, 1 teaspoon of the
garam masala and 1 tablespoon of the yoghurt.
Mix well and form into small balls, approximately
3–4 cm (1¼–1½ in) in diameter.

Heat the ghee or butter in a 3 l (3 qt) microwave-safe casserole or dish on HIGH (100%) for 1
minute. Add the dried milk, remaining garam
masala, sugar and yoghurt. Heat on HIGH for 2 minutes and stir in boiling water. Carefully add koftas
to dish. Cook on MEDIUM (50%) for 20 minutes,
turning meatballs over after 10 minutes. Remove
meat from liquid and leave to drain on a piece of

absorbent kitchen paper. Carefully drain off and
discard any excess fat from remaining liquid, and
strain into a small ovenproof bowl. Stir in tamarind sauce or paste. Reheat sauce on HIGH for 1–1½
minutes. Transfer meat to a serving dish. Pour
sauce over and serve sprinkled with ground cardamom. (See photo page 162.)

Pappadums

Buy deep-golden pappadums rather than pale-
yellow ones.

Place three pappadums at a time on the turntable or glass base plate of the microwave. Make
sure they do not overlap. Cook on HIGH (100%) for
45–60 seconds, until they are light and puffy.
There will be no change in the colour. Remove
from the oven and cool on a wire rack. They crisp
as they cool. Continue cooking desired quantity in
the same way. (See photo page 162.)

● Dolmades

Dolmades

You can use pickled vine leaves in place of cabbage leaves in this recipe if you prefer (available from delicatessens, tinned or in bulk). You will end up with more dolmades as vine leaves need less filling.

1 large onion, finely chopped
1 tbspn cooking oil
500 g (1 lb) lamb, minced
⅓ cup (60 g/2 oz) rice
1 tomato, peeled and chopped
2 tbspns chopped fresh parsley
1 tspn chopped fresh dill or mint
pinch ground cinnamon
20 cabbage leaves, washed
1 cup (250 ml/8 fl oz) chicken stock, hot
1 tbspn (20 g/¾ oz) butter
freshly ground black pepper to taste
2 tspns cornflour
2 eggs, separated
juice of 1 lemon
sprigs of fresh dill for garnish

SERVES 4–6

Place the onion and cooking oil in a 3 l (3 qt) microwave-safe dish or casserole. Cover with a well-fitting lid or plastic wrap and cook on HIGH (100%) for 2 minutes, until tender. Stir in the next six ingredients for the stuffing mixture. Set aside.

Separate the cabbage leaves and place them in a large bowl. Cover closely with plastic wrap and cook on HIGH for 3–4 minutes, until leaves are just soft but not soggy. If necessary, remove outer leaves as they cook and continue cooking on HIGH until all leaves are tender. Cut out thick centre of large leaves and if very large, cut in half.

Place spoonfuls of stuffing mixture on base of each leaf. Turn up base, fold in sides and wrap firmly into small parcels.

Pack rolls close together, seam side down, in a single layer in a shallow microwave-safe dish. Pour over the stock. Top each dolmade with a dot of butter and a sprinkle of black pepper. Cover dish with a well-fitting lid or plastic wrap. Cook on MEDIUM HIGH (70%) for 25 minutes. Test a dolmade from the centre of the dish to check whether rice and meat are cooked. If not, continue cooking at 1 minute intervals on MEDIUM HIGH.

Carefully drain off cooking liquor into a small microwave-safe dish. Cover dolmades with a piece of aluminium foil and set aside.

Stir cornflour into cooking liquor. Heat on HIGH for 2–3 minutes, stirring well after 1 minute, until sauce boils and thickens.

Beat egg whites in a large microwave-safe bowl until stiff but not dry. Continuing to whisk, adding the egg yolks, then the lemon juice and finally the hot thickened stock. Return to oven and cook on MEDIUM (50%) for 3–4 minutes, stirring every minute until egg thickens sauce slightly, but does not reach boiling point.

Serve dolmades with a little of the sauce poured over and garnished with sprigs of fresh dill. Serve remaining sauce separately in a sauce boat.

Lamb's Fry with Vegetables

4 potatoes, peeled and cut into ⅛
3–4 carrots, peeled and evenly sliced
2 cups (315 g/10 oz) frozen peas
4 rashers bacon, each cut into 3 pieces
410 g (13 oz) lamb's fry, washed and thinly sliced
2 tbspns plain flour
black pepper to taste
1 cup (250 ml/8 fl oz) beef stock
1 extra tbspn plain flour
1 tspn Worcestershire sauce
1 tbspn fruit chutney
2 tspns butter (optional)
chopped fresh parsley for garnish

SERVES 4

Place potatoes into a 1–2 l (1–2 qt) microwave-safe dish. Cover with a well-fitting lid or plastic wrap. Cook on HIGH (100%) for 6–7 minutes until just tender. Leave to stand.

Place carrots in a 1 l (1 qt) microwave-safe dish. Cover with a well-fitting lid or plastic wrap. Cook on HIGH for 5 minutes. Stir in frozen peas and set aside.

Preheat a microwave-safe browning dish on HIGH for 6 minutes until hot. Carefully add bacon and cook, uncovered, on HIGH for 2 minutes, turning bacon over after 1 minute.

Remove bacon and keep warm. Reheat browning dish on HIGH for 1 minute. Meanwhile toss lamb's fry in combined flour and pepper, and add to browning dish, pressing down to seal surface and brown. Cook on MEDIUM (50%) for 5 minutes, turning meat over after 2 minutes.

Remove lamb's fry from dish and keep warm with bacon. Add stock blended with extra flour, Worcestershire sauce and chutney to browning dish. Cook on MEDIUM for 2–3 minutes, stirring well after 1 minute, until sauce boils and thickens.

Cream potatoes with butter.

When lamb's fry is completed, return peas and carrots to oven and heat on HIGH for 1–1½ minutes.

Serve lamb's fry with gravy, garnished with a little chopped parsley, accompanied by the cooked vegetables.

Irish Stew

This enduring favourite is best made a day in advance. When cold, remove any fat from the surface and reheat on DEFROST (30%).

750 g (1½ lb) best neck lamb chops, excess fat removed and cut meat into chunks
2 tbspns seasoned, plain flour
1 kg (2 lb) potatoes, peeled and sliced
2 tbspns chopped fresh parsley
freshly ground black pepper to taste
1 tspn dried thyme
2 onions, sliced
2 cups (500 ml/16 fl oz) dark beef broth, hot
extra chopped fresh parsley for garnish

SERVES 4

Toss the meat in the flour.

Grease a 2–3 l (2–3 qt) microwave-safe dish or casserole. Place a layer of the sliced potatoes in the base. Follow with a layer of the meat. Sprinkle with a little of the chopped parsley, pepper and thyme.

Cover with a layer of onion. Repeat layers until all ingredients are used, finishing with a layer of potato. Pour in beef stock.

Cook, uncovered, on HIGH (100%) for 10 minutes, then reduce power and cook, covered, on DEFROST (30%) for 1 hour or until tender.

Serve sprinkled with a little chopped parsley.

Vegetables

If the microwave oven was only used to cook vegetables, it would still justify its place in the kitchen. Cooking vegetables is a sheer delight. Most cook without the addition of water, the vegetables cooking literally in their own juices. Do not add salt during cooking — it dehydrates the vegetables. Without the addition of water and salt the vegetables retain their natural salts and the flavour is heightened, so always test before adding salt when serving.

Vegetables should be cooked in containers just large enough to hold them — excess space allows a certain amount of drying out, especially on the surface of cut vegetables.

A very successful alternative to a container is to make a parcel of the vegetable with microwave-safe plastic wrap or plastic bags. These need not be vented if the plastic wrap is folded over on to itself, excluding as much air as possible, and tucked under the 'parcel' of vegetables. In the same way, extract as much air as possible when using a plastic bag, twist the end and tuck it under the vegetables.

Vegetables cooked in their own skin, such as potatoes, should be pricked with a fork in several places to prevent small explosions. Cooking time seems to shorten if, in addition, each potato is wrapped in a small piece of plastic wrap — the trapped steam helps to hasten the cooking.

Unsatisfactory results with the cooking of vegetables almost invariably arise because the air space around them has not been kept to a minimum, or, of course, because of overcooking.

All vegetables will cook more quickly if cut into small pieces rather than large chunks. For example, whole large carrots take a great deal longer to cook than thin 'sticks' of carrot and the flavour and colour of the 'sticks' are far superior to the whole carrots. A variety of vegetables, cut into

● *From top:* Ratatouille (page 161); Stir-fry Spinach with Hazelnuts (page 160)

similar sized pieces, can be cooked all bundled together in a plastic wrap 'parcel'. At least once during the cooking period, give the vegetables a shake or two to assist even cooking.

Vegetables of an uneven shape such as cauliflower and broccoli florets or asparagus spears will cook more evenly if the thicker, or stalk ends, are at the outer edge of the cooking container. Trim any woody ends of the asparagus before cooking and cut up into the stalks of cauliflower and broccoli several times to assist even cooking.

Warning Dishes of just-cooked vegetables do not look hot — even handles on the cooking container may not be hot, but beware — there is steam inside the dish, especially if it is covered with plastic wrap. Use tongs or wear oven-mitts and always lift the lid or edge of the plastic wrap away from you on the far side of the dish — never towards you.

All vegetables cook on HIGH (100%). Try cooking them without water wherever possible. It is essential to have them cooking with as little air space around them as possible for best results. Cook always for the minimum time recommended. Unlike conventional cooking, overcooking by microwave does not oversoften vegetables. On the contrary, it dehydrates and toughens them. Be particularly careful when cooking jacket potatoes. Test with a fine metal cake tester and if it can be passed through the potato with just a little resistance, remove them from the oven, wrap in foil and let stand for 2–4 minutes. In this time the cooking will be completed but if by chance they are not quite done, put them back for about 30 seconds longer. Don't check potatoes by the 'squeeze' method (incidentally, a very dangerous operation without wearing an oven-mitt!). If you wait until the flesh 'gives' you will find after a minute or two of standing the potato will be somewhat wrinkled and slightly dried out under the skin.

The microwave oven presents us with vegetables cooked as we are surely meant to eat them — just tender, perhaps a little crisp, with good flavour and great colour.

FROZEN VEGETABLES

These can be taken straight from freezer to microwave oven. Cook either closely covered with unvented plastic wrap or in their own package following the package directions for microwave. If the vegetables are in a mass with some visible ice, cook ice-side up. Make sure you vent the package, and it will be necessary to stir the vegetables at least once during the cooking time. Vegetables, like fish, do not need a special period for defrosting before their cooking time commences. Because all vegetables have been blanched before freezing they have, in a sense, been partly cooked, so no additional time is usually needed to cook them beyond the timings given in the vegetable cooking chart.

REHEATING COOKED VEGETABLES

Cooked vegetables regain most of their freshness when covered and reheated in the microwave oven. They heat internally rather than heating and drying out on the surface as conventionally reheated vegetables do. However, reheat briefly or the vegetables *will* dry out. Obviously, in the interests of nutrition, it is preferable to cook vegetables as they are required, but the microwave oven certainly does a far superior job of reheating than any conventional method.

REHEATING PLATED DINNERS WITH VEGETABLES

If the dinner includes a variety of vegetables, place the large pieces around the edge of the plate and the smaller ones nearer to the centre to achieve even reheating. Cover with unvented plastic wrap.

COOKING FOR ONE

If cooking for one, cook your vegetables on the plate from which you'll be eating and save washing-up. Remember, for even cooking, cut the vegetables into pieces of fairly equal size.

WATER — TO ADD OR NOT TO ADD!

In the following cooking chart no water is added to the vegetables during cooking. Not everyone agrees with this method and you may find recipes elsewhere which suggest using up to a tablespoon or two of water for most vegetables.

Try both methods and find the one that suits you best. However, you will probably find that the vegetables that are allowed to cook in their own juices will give the better looking and tastier result.

The only vegetable fancier the microwave oven can't satisfy is the one who likes 'nice soft vegetables' as vegetables cooked by microwave move very quickly from 'just right' to 'dried out'.

VEGETABLE COOKING GUIDE			
VEGETABLE	**COOKING METHOD**	**COOKING TIME ON HIGH (100%)**	**STANDING TIME**
Artichoke	Wrap in plastic wrap.		
1 medium		4–5 mins	2 mins
2 medium	Wrap separately, as above.	6–7 mins	2 mins
3 medium	Wrap separately, as above.	8–9 mins	2 mins
Asparagus, fresh 500 g (1 lb)	Wrap closely in a bundle with plastic wrap, heads facing in alternate directions for more even cooking.		
	Young spears	5–6 mins	1 min
	Older spears	8–10 mins	2 mins
Aubergine (eggplant) 1 medium, sliced, peeled or unpeeled	Place in well-covered shallow dish.	4–5 mins	1 min
Beans, French 500 g (1 lb)	Slice, place in well-covered container or in plastic wrap or bag.	8–10 mins	1 min
1 cup (155 g/5 oz), sliced	Place in small, well-covered container or in plastic wrap.	2½–3 mins	None
1 cup (155 g/5 oz), frozen	Place in small, well-covered container or in plastic wrap, stir or shake at least once during cooking time.	3–5 mins	1 min

VEGETABLE COOKING GUIDE

VEGETABLE	COOKING METHOD	COOKING TIME ON HIGH (100%)	STANDING TIME
Beans, broad			
fresh, 1 cup (155 g/5 oz)	Must be well covered in small container or enclosed in plastic wrap.	3–4 mins	1 min
frozen, 375 g (12 oz) pack	Cook in commercial pack, piercing bag 3 or 4 times with a fork and shaking at least once during cooking.	7–8 mins	2 mins
frozen, 1 cup (155 g/5 oz)	Place in small covered container and stir halfway through cooking time.	3 mins	30 secs
Beetroot, 4 medium, unpeeled	In casserole with ½ cup (125 ml/4 fl oz) water.	15–16 mins	5–6 mins
Broccoli, fresh			
500 g (1 lb)	In small well-covered container or wrapped in plastic wrap. Cut deep cross in thick stalk end.	7–8 mins	1 min
250 g (8 oz)	In small well-covered container or wrapped in plastic wrap. Cut deep cross in thick stalk end.	3–4 mins	30 secs
frozen, 375 g (12 oz) pack	In plastic pack, pierced 3 or 4 times with a fork, shaking at least once during cooking.	5–6 mins	1 min
Brussels sprouts			
fresh, 500 g (1 lb)	In well-covered container or plastic bag or wrap, stirring or shaking once during cooking. Cut deep cross through thick stalk end.	6–7 mins	2 mins
fresh, 250 g (8 oz)	In well-covered container or plastic bag or wrap, stirring or shaking once during cooking. Cut deep cross through thick stalk end.	4 mins	1 min
frozen, 375 g (12 oz) pack	In plastic pack, pierced 3 or 4 times with a fork, shaking at least once during cooking.	4–5 mins	2 mins
Cabbage ½ medium, shredded	Choose smallest casserole into which washed cabbage can be pressed, with only water left on leaves after rinsing.	5–6 mins	1 min
Carrots			
small, whole 250 g (8 oz)	Wrap in plastic wrap, alternating thick ends with thin ends for more even cooking, or use smallest container which will hold them. Cover closely with plastic wrap.	4–5 mins	1 min
cut in sticks 250g (8 oz)	Wrap closely in plastic wrap.	2-3 mins	None
frozen, 375 g (12 oz), whole	In plastic pack, pierced 3 or 4 times with fork, shaking at least once during cooking.	6–7 mins	2–3 mins
Cauliflower			
1 medium	Cut out most of the central core, cutting a cross in remaining core, cover with plastic wrap and place in dish.	9–13 mins	5 mins
cut in florets, 250 g (8 oz)	Place in dish just large enough to hold florets and cover closely or wrap in plastic wrap. Cut deep cross in stalks.	2½–3 mins	30 secs
frozen, 375 g (12 oz) pack	Place in closely covered dish, stirring halfway through cooking time.	7 mins	2 mins
Celery 2 cups (220 g/7 oz), sliced	Place in small well-covered dish or wrap in plastic wrap.	2 mins	None
Corn, young, fresh			
1 cob	Remove husk and silk, wrap in plastic wrap.	2–2½ mins	2 mins
2 cobs	Remove husk and silk, wrap in plastic wrap.	3–4 mins	2 mins
4 cobs	Remove husk and silk, wrap in plastic wrap.	6–7 mins	2 mins
frozen, 1 cob	Wrap in plastic wrap.	7–9 mins	4 mins
Kumara (sweet potato/yam)			
unpeeled, 1 medium	Place on paper towel in oven, prick several times with fork.	3–4 mins	2 mins
2 medium	Place on paper towel in oven, prick several times with fork.	7 mins	2 mins
4 medium	Place on paper towel in oven, prick several times with fork.	12 mins	2 mins

VEGETABLE COOKING GUIDE

VEGETABLE	COOKING METHOD	COOKING TIME ON HIGH (100%)	STANDING TIME
Mushrooms, cultivated 125 g (4 oz), whole	Wipe or brush caps, trim stalks, cook in shallow container in single layer covered closely with plastic wrap (in this time they should be just tender but keep their shape).	2 mins	30 secs
125 g (4 oz), sliced	Place in small container, covered closely with plastic wrap, stir once.	2 mins	30 secs
Onions 2 large	Peel and quarter, place in plastic bag or cover closely in small container.	3 mins	1 min
6 small	Cover closely in small container.	6 mins	2 mins
Parsnips, young, 3 medium, sliced	Wrap in plastic wrap or place in small dish with closely fitting lid or plastic wrap.	3–5 mins	2 mins
Peas 500 g (1 lb)	Shell, place in dish just large enough to hold them, stirring at least once.	6–8 mins	1–2 mins
1 cup (155 g/5 oz), frozen	Place in small covered dish, stirring once.	2½–3 mins	30 secs
Potatoes 1 medium	Pierce skin in several places with a skewer. Place on paper towel. (Wrapping individually in plastic wrap will shorten cooking time a little.) Turn twice.	3½–4 mins	2 mins
2 medium	Pierce skin in several places with a skewer. Place on paper towel. (Wrapping individually in plastic wrap will shorten cooking time a little.) Turn twice.	6½–7 mins	2 mins
4 medium	Pierce skin in several places with a skewer. Place on paper towel. (Wrapping individually in plastic wrap will shorten cooking time a little.) Turn twice.	10–12 mins	2 mins
small new potatoes 500 g (1 lb)	Pierce with skewer, place in closely covered dish. (Wrap together loosely in plastic wrap to shorten cooking time a little.) Rearrange twice.	10–12 mins	2 mins
peeled for mashing 500 g (1 lb)	Cut into pieces, wrap closely in plastic wrap, place in container and shake halfway through cooking time.	7–8 mins	2 mins
Pumpkin 500 g (1 lb)	Peel (optional), cut into pieces, place in a covered container just large enough to take them, or wrap in plastic wrap. Rearrange once.	8–10 mins	2 mins
Snow peas 250 g (8 oz)	Nip off short stem; string the pods. Wrap in a close bundle in plastic wrap and place in shallow container.	3 mins	30 secs
Spinach, 500 g (1 lb) stems removed	After removing white stems (which can be cooked as a separate vegetable if desired), wash very carefully and shake well. Press into the smallest container that will just hold it and cover closely *or* place in an oven bag, extracting most of the air — twist open end of bag and tuck under when placed in cooking container.	5–6 mins	1 min
Squash, baby 1 kg (2 lb)	Prick skin several times; place on kitchen paper. Arrange twice. After cooking, wrap during standing time.	8–10 mins	5 mins
Tomatoes, 4 medium	Halve tomatoes and remove any hard core, place around edge of container; cover.	3–5 mins	1 min
Zucchini whole baby, 500 g (1 lb)	Place in shallow dish or wrap loosely in plastic wrap, pierce skin in several places. Rearrange twice.	5–7 mins	1–2 mins
sliced, 500 g (1 lb)	Place in dish just large enough to hold them and cover closely with plastic wrap; stir once.	5–7 mins	1–2 mins

Artichokes with French Dressing

Serve these as an entrée. Pull artichoke leaves off, dip into dressing, then eat the fleshy part at the base of each leaf. Young artichokes will have a succulent heart which can be eaten. Older artichokes have a hairy 'choke' on top of the heart which must be discarded before eating.

4 artichokes
FRENCH DRESSING
¼ cup (60 ml/2 fl oz) olive oil
1 tbspn white wine vinegar
½ tspn dry mustard
pinch salt
freshly ground black pepper to taste
1 clove garlic, crushed

SERVES 4

Rinse artichokes in cold water and cut stems off close to base. Remove any small, loose or discoloured leaves at the bottom. Cut off about 2 cm (¾ in) from the top of each artichoke and trim the outside leaves, cutting the sharp tips off each leaf with scissors.

Wrap each artichoke in plastic wrap and place in oven on the outer edge of turntable. Cook on HIGH (100%) for 16–20 minutes, or until tender and outside leaves pull away easily. Refresh in iced water, then drain well.

To prepare dressing: Place all ingredients in a screw-top jar and shake well until the ingredients are evenly mixed.

To serve, place French dressing in four individual bowls and the artichokes on individual plates.

Asparagus with Mustard Cream

1 kg (2 lb) asparagus spears, trimmed and well washed
SAUCE
½ cup (125 ml/4 fl oz) cream, lightly whipped
2 tspns prepared French mustard
1 tbspn white vinegar
1 tbspn mayonnaise
pepper to taste
GARNISH
2 hardboiled eggs
finely chopped fresh parsley

SERVES 4

*P*lace the prepared asparagus in a shallow microwave-safe dish, in a single layer for thick spears, or a double layer for thin spears. Cover dish with a well-fitting lid or plastic wrap and cook on HIGH (100%) for 5–7 minutes until just tender. Remove from oven and dip asparagus into cold water. Drain well and set aside on a piece of absorbent kitchen paper to cool completely.

● Green Beans Almondine

Prepare sauce by combining the cream, mustard, vinegar and mayonnaise in a small bowl. Adjust seasoning to taste. Arrange asparagus on a large serving plate. Spread sauce over the stalks.

Cut the hardboiled eggs in half, finely chop the whites and push the yolks through a fine nylon sieve. Arrange a layer of egg white, then yolk and a sprinkling of parsley on top of sauce for garnish. (See photo page 153.)

Green Beans Almondine

500 g (1 lb) green beans, topped and tailed
2 tbspns water
2 tbspns (45 g/1½ oz) butter
¼ cup (30 g/1 oz) slivered almonds, blanched

SERVES 4

*P*lace beans in a microwave-safe dish with 2 tablespoons water. Cover and cook in microwave on HIGH (100%) for 8 minutes. Stir to re-distribute beans. Re-cover and leave to stand for a few moments.

Meanwhile melt butter in a small bowl on HIGH for 30 seconds. Stir in almonds and cook on HIGH for 1 minute. Cover beans with melted butter and almonds. Re-cover dish and cook on HIGH for 2 minutes.

Leave to stand for 2 minutes before serving.

Piquant Beans

500 g (1 lb) fresh green beans, topped and tailed
2 anchovy fillets, chopped
1 clove garlic, crushed
few sprigs fresh parsley, finely chopped
2 tbspns olive oil
2 tbspns lemon juice
pepper to taste

SERVES 4

*P*lace the beans in a medium-sized microwave-safe dish or casserole. Cover with a well-fitting lid or plastic wrap and cook on HIGH (100%) for 8 minutes until just tender, giving dish a good shake or stir halfway through cooking time.

While beans are cooking combine anchovies with garlic and parsley in a small bowl. Stir in the olive oil and lemon juice. Season.

Drain beans and place in a serving dish. Serve with piquant sauce poured over. Serve hot or cold. (See photo pages 82–83.)

Broccoli with Piquant Topping

250 g (8 oz) broccoli, washed and broken into florets
2 tspns margarine cut into small pieces
TOPPING
200 ml (7 /fl oz) carton natural yoghurt
1 cup (125 g/4 oz) grated Cheddar cheese
1 egg
pinch nutmeg
black pepper to taste
1 tbspn finely grated Parmesan cheese

SERVES 4

*P*lace broccoli in a shallow microwave-safe dish. Scatter margarine over broccoli, cover dish with a well-fitting lid or plastic wrap and cook on HIGH (100%) for 3 minutes.

While broccoli is cooking, prepare topping by combining yoghurt, Cheddar cheese, egg, nutmeg and pepper in a small bowl.

Spoon yoghurt topping over broccoli and sprinkle with Parmesan cheese.

Cook on MEDIUM (50%) for 8–10 minutes. Serve broccoli immediately with cooked chicken, pork, lamb or fish.

Broccoli and Ham with Mustard Sauce

300 g (10 oz) broccoli florets, washed
1 tbspn (20 g/ ¾ oz) butter, softened
2 tbspns plain flour
2 tspns prepared horseradish sauce
2 tspns prepared mustard
½ tspn Worcestershire sauce
440 g (14 oz) can pineapple slices (juice reserved)
½ cup (125 ml/4 fl oz) milk
1 egg, lightly beaten
4 slices Swiss cheese
90 g (3 oz) ham, thinly sliced

SERVES 4

*P*lace broccoli in a shallow microwave-safe dish or casserole. Cover with a well-fitting lid or plastic wrap and cook on HIGH (100%) for 5–6 minutes until tender. Set aside in serving dish.

Place butter in a 1 l (1 qt) microwave-safe jug. Stir in the flour and cook on HIGH for 30 seconds. Add horseradish, mustard and Worcestershire sauce. Stir until well combined, then stir in the pineapple juice reserved from the can, together with the milk and beaten egg. Cook on HIGH for 4–5 minutes, stirring every minute until the mixture boils and thickens.

Cover broccoli with cheese slices, then slices of ham. Pour half of the sauce over ham. Top with pineapple rings and remaining sauce. Return dish to oven and cook on MEDIUM HIGH (70%) for 2–3 minutes, until cheese melts and sauce bubbles.

Brussels Sprouts with Hazelnut Butter

½ cup (60 g/2 oz) hazelnuts
1 onion, finely chopped
2 tbspns (45 g/1½ oz) butter
black pepper to taste
500 g (1 lb) small Brussels sprouts, trimmed

SERVES 4

Spread the hazelnuts on a large, flat microwave-safe plate. Cook on HIGH (100%) for 3–4 minutes until the skins pop. Using a clean tea-towel, rub away the skins then chop the nuts finely.

Place the onion and butter into a 1–2 l (1–2 qt) microwave-safe dish. Cover with a well-fitting lid or plastic wrap and cook on HIGH for 3 minutes until onion is softened. Stir in the hazelnuts and pepper. Cook, covered, on HIGH for 1 minute. Stir in the Brussels sprouts. Re-cover dish and cook on HIGH for 5–6 minutes, giving dish a good shake or stir halfway through cooking time. Serve hot.

Stuffed Capsicums

4 rashers bacon
2 red and 2 green capsicums, washed, seeded and with tops removed
1 tbspn (20 g/¾ oz) butter or margarine
1 onion, finely chopped
½ cup (75 g/2½ oz) currants
½ cup (125 ml/4 fl oz) tomato sauce
2 cups (250 g/8 oz) dry breadcrumbs
2 tbspns chopped fresh parsley

SERVES 4

Place a triple layer of absorbent kitchen paper on the glass turntable in the microwave. Place bacon on paper and cover with another sheet of kitchen paper.

Cook on HIGH (100%) for 3 minutes, until bacon is crisp. Allow to stand for 2 minutes, discard paper and chop bacon coarsely. Meanwhile, pre-pare capsicums and stand them in a shallow microwave-safe dish.

Melt butter or margarine in a medium-sized microwave-safe bowl on HIGH for 1 minute. Add onion to dish, cover with plastic wrap and cook for 2 minutes. Stir in remaining ingredients and chopped bacon. Use to fill capsicums. Cover dish with plastic wrap and cook on HIGH for 6–8 minutes, until capsicums are tender and filling is heated.

Sweet and Sour Red Cabbage

½ small red cabbage, washed and finely sliced
1 green apple, washed and finely diced
1 medium onion, finely chopped
½ cup (90 g/3 oz) unsweetened, canned pineapple pieces
2 tbspns pineapple juice from can
¼ cup (60 ml/2 fl oz) wine vinegar

SERVES 6

Place all ingredients in a large 1.5–2 l (1½–2 qt) microwave-safe casserole. Cook in microwave, covered, on HIGH (100%) for 3 minutes. Stir to redistribute ingredients, cover again and cook on HIGH for 3 minutes. Stand for 2–3 minutes before serving.

Carrot and Parsnip Loaf

The vegetables in this tasty vegetarian main course are blended in a food processor. If a food processor is not available, simply mash the vegetables with a potato masher.

500 g (1 lb) carrots, peeled and finely sliced
375 g (12 oz) parsnips, peeled and finely sliced
½ cup (125 ml/4 fl oz) water
1 clove garlic, crushed
2 tbspns (45 g/1½ oz) butter or margarine
3 eggs, beaten
1 cup (125 g/4 oz) grated Gruyère or Emmental cheese
salt and pepper to taste
1 tbspn chopped fresh parsley

SERVES 6

Place carrots, parsnips, water, garlic and butter or margarine in a shallow microwave-safe casserole. Cook, covered, on HIGH (100%) for 16–17 minutes, or until vegetables are tender. Allow to cool for about 10 minutes, then process in a food processor until smooth. Pour into a bowl and stir in the remaining ingredients.

Pour the mixture into a lightly greased microwave-safe loaf or ring dish. Carefully smooth the surface with a spatula. Cook, covered, on HIGH for 13–15 minutes, or until mixture is set. Allow loaf to stand for 5 minutes before turning out.

Serve with steamed green vegetables and potatoes in their jackets.

Carrot and Mushroom Ring

¼ cup (60 g/2 oz) butter or margarine
2 cloves garlic, crushed
1 onion, chopped
500 g (1 lb) mushrooms, wiped and chopped
4½ cups (500 g/1 lb) grated carrot
4 eggs, beaten
1 cup (60 g/2 oz) fresh wholemeal breadcrumbs
1 cup (125 g/4 oz) grated Cheddar cheese
¼ cup finely chopped fresh coriander or parsley
¼ tspn basil
¼ tspn thyme
freshly ground black pepper to taste

SERVES 4–6

Melt butter in a large bowl on HIGH (100%) for 30 seconds. Add garlic, onion and mushrooms. Cook, covered, on HIGH for 2 minutes or until tender. Stir in remaining ingredients, but use only three-quarters each of breadcrumbs and cheese.

Mix well. Place mixture in a buttered microwave-safe ring pan or rectangular baking dish. Sprinkle with remaining breadcrumbs and cheese. Cook on MEDIUM HIGH (70%) for 9–11 minutes until tender.

Allow to stand for 5 minutes before serving.

Herbed Corn and Cauliflower Salad

In this recipe the cauliflower may be cooked in advance and the salad assembled just prior to serving.

1 large head cauliflower, washed and divided into florets
¼ cup (60 ml/2 fl oz) water
315 g (10 oz) can sweetcorn, drained
1 large head celery, washed and thinly sliced
½ cup (60 g/2 oz) walnut pieces
3 red apples, washed and diced
juice of 1 lemon
2 tbspns chopped fresh chives
2 tbspns chopped fresh parsley
1¼ cups (315 ml/10 fl oz) Italian dressing

SERVES 12

Place cauliflower in a large microwave-safe casserole with 3 tablespoons water. Cover with a well-fitting lid or plastic wrap. Cook on HIGH (100%) for 4 minutes, shaking or stirring well after 2 minutes. Drain off any liquid and leave to cool. Stir in sweetcorn, celery, walnuts and apple.

Mix lemon juice, herbs and Italian dressing together. Add to salad and toss well to coat vegetables in dressing. Arrange in a large salad bowl and chill until required.

ITALIAN DRESSING

Combine 3 tablespoons oil, 1 tablespoon vinegar, salt and pepper and chopped fresh herbs in a jar with a lid. Cover jar and shake before use.

Creamy Fennel with Parmesan

4 heads of fennel, washed and quartered
¼ cup (60 ml/2 fl oz) chicken stock (or stock cube and water)
juice of ½ lemon
½ cup (125 ml/4 fl oz) cream
1 tbspn caraway seeds
⅓ cup (30 g/1 oz) grated Parmesan cheese

SERVES 4–6

Place the fennel into a 1–2 l (1–2 qt) microwave-safe dish with the stock and lemon juice. Cover with a well-fitting lid or plastic wrap and cook on HIGH (100%) for 10–12 minutes until tender.

Pour the cream into a small microwave-safe dish or jug. Stir in the caraway seeds and most of the cheese. Heat on HIGH for 2–3 minutes until the cheese melts.

Place the fennel into a microwave-safe serving dish and pour on the cream. Top with remaining grated cheese. Cook on HIGH for 3–4 minutes until cheese bubbles. If desired, brown under a hot grill. (See photo page 153.)

Stuffed Kohlrabi

4 kohlrabi
1 tbspn (20 g/¾ oz) butter
2 slices bread, soaked in milk, squeezed, and crumbled
1 egg yolk, lightly beaten
2 tbspns chopped chives
⅓ cup (90 ml/3 fl oz) natural yoghurt or sour cream
freshly ground black pepper to taste
1 apple, cored, peeled and grated

SERVES 4

Wash and trim kohlrabi and wrap individually in plastic wrap. Place on the outer edge of turntable. Cook on HIGH (100%) for 15 minutes or until tender.

Melt butter in a frying pan and gently fry bread until light and golden in colour. Stir in egg yolk, chives, half the yoghurt or sour cream, pepper and the apple.

Hollow out each kohlrabi. Finely chop the scooped-out flesh and add to the bread mixture. Fill the kohlrabi with the stuffing and place in a shallow microwave-safe dish.

Top with remaining yoghurt and sprinkle with a little freshly ground black pepper. Cook on HIGH for 1–2 minutes to heat through.

Herbed Leeks

6 medium-sized leeks
1 tbspn chopped fresh tarragon or 1 tspn dried tarragon
1 tbspn finely chopped parsley
small pinch thyme
1 tbspn lemon juice
freshly ground black pepper to taste
¼ cup (60 ml/2 fl oz) water
1 tomato, skinned and sliced

SERVES 6

Cut tops off leeks, leaving 5 cm (2 in) of green tops. Cut diagonally through leaves to within 6 cm (2½ in) of bulb end. Spread leaves slightly and thoroughly wash to remove any grit. Place leeks in a shallow microwave-safe dish, sprinkle with the herbs, lemon juice, black pepper and water.

Cover dish with a well-fitting lid or plastic wrap. Cook in the microwave on HIGH (100%) for 3 minutes. Turn leeks over in dish. Arrange tomato slices on top. Continue cooking on HIGH for 2–3 minutes, until just slightly tender when tested with a sharp knife.

Leave, covered, in dish to stand for 5 minutes before serving.

Lentil and Mushroom Pie

A colourful vegetable mixture that is well flavoured and appetising.

500 g (1 lb) kumara (sweet potato), peeled and finely sliced
¼ cup (60 ml/2 fl oz) water
1 cup (185 g/6 oz) split red lentils
2 tbspns (45 g/1½ oz) butter or margarine
1 red or green capsicum, seeded and cut into thin strips
1 medium onion, chopped
315 g (10 oz) can corn kernels, drained
220 g (7 oz) fresh button mushrooms, sliced
425 g (13½ oz) can whole tomatoes, drained
salt and pepper to taste

SERVES 4–6

Place the kumara and water into a large microwave-safe casserole and cook, covered, on HIGH (100%) for 10–12 minutes, or until soft. Keep covered while preparing the remaining ingredients.

Place the lentils in a large microwave-safe casserole and add boiling water to cover the lentils by about 2–3 cm (¾–1¼ in). Cook, covered, on HIGH for 6–8 minutes. Allow to stand covered for about 10 minutes.

Combine half the butter or margarine, capsicum and onion in a bowl or microwave-safe casserole and cook on HIGH for 2 minutes. Stir in the corn and mushrooms and cook for a further 2–3 minutes.

Drain off any excess water from the lentils and stir in the vegetables, tomatoes and season to taste with salt and pepper. Spoon into a greased deep microwave-safe pie plate.

Mash the kumara with the remaining butter or margarine until soft and fluffy (a food processor is ideal). Spoon over the pie, fluffing with a fork. Cook on MEDIUM HIGH (70%) for 4–6 minutes, or until heated through.

Serve with a tossed salad and crusty bread.

Dhal

1 cup (185 g/6 oz) red lentils, washed
1½ tbspns (30 g/1 oz) ghee or butter
1 tspn mustard seeds
1 large onion, sliced
2 cloves garlic, crushed
2 tspns fresh ginger, finely diced
2 curry leaves (optional)
½ tspn turmeric
1 tspn garam masala
2 cups (500 ml/16 fl oz) water, boiling

SERVES 8

Soak lentils in water while remaining ingredients are prepared.

Heat ghee or butter in a 1–2 l (1–2 qt) microwave-safe dish or casserole for 30 seconds. Stir in the mustard seeds and cover with a well-fitting lid or plastic wrap. Cook on HIGH (100%) for 1 minute.

Stir in onion, garlic, ginger and curry leaves and cook on HIGH for 2 minutes. Stir in turmeric, garam masala and well-drained lentils. Cook for 2 minutes, stir in boiling water and continue cooking, uncovered, on MEDIUM (50%) for 15–20 minutes until lentils are soft and pulpy. Stir occasionally during cooking. Serve hot. (See photo page 162.)

● *From top:* Asparagus with Mustard Cream (page 146); Herbed Leeks; Creamy Fennel with Parmesan (page 151)

Greek-style Mushrooms

2 tbspns olive oil
1 onion, finely chopped
2 cloves garlic, crushed
⅓ cup (90 ml/3 fl oz) tomato purée
1 tspn chopped mixed fresh herbs
1 cup (250 ml/8 fl oz) chicken stock, hot
freshly ground black pepper to taste
500 g (1 lb) small button mushrooms, wiped
chopped fresh parsley for garnish

SERVES 4

*P*lace the olive oil, onion and garlic in a 2 l (2 qt) microwave-safe dish. Cover with a well-fitting lid or plastic wrap and cook on HIGH (100%) for 4 minutes, until onion is tender. Stir once during cooking.

Stir in tomato purée, herbs, stock, seasoning and mushrooms. Re-cover dish and cook on HIGH for 6–8 minutes, stirring after 2 and 4 minutes, until mushrooms are heated through.

Spoon the mushrooms and cooking liquor into a warm serving dish.

Serve hot or cold garnished with parsley.

● Greek-style Mushrooms

Mushroom Moussaka

3 small eggplants (total 1 kg/2 lb), sliced 1.5 cm (½ in) thick
500 g (1 lb) fresh mushrooms, sliced
1 onion, chopped
¼ cup (30 g/1 oz) plain flour
1 clove garlic, crushed
425 g (13½ oz) can whole tomatoes, drained
2 tbspns tomato paste
1 tspn dried oregano or basil
300 g (10 oz) carton sour cream
3 eggs
salt and pepper to taste
¼ cup (30 g/1 oz) grated Parmesan cheese

SERVES 6

*P*lace the eggplant slices in a 25 cm (10 in) square, microwave-safe casserole and cook, covered, on HIGH (100%) for 4–6 minutes. Allow to stand, covered, while preparing the remaining ingredients.

In another large microwave-safe casserole, combine the mushrooms, onion, flour and garlic and cook on HIGH for 2–3 minutes. Stir in tomatoes, tomato paste and herbs and cook on HIGH for a further 3–4 minutes.

Spread a layer of eggplant on the base of the 25 cm casserole. Pour over the mushroom sauce and top with the remaining eggplant.

In a bowl, combine the remaining ingredients and evenly pour over the eggplant. Cook on MEDIUM HIGH (70%) for 8–10 minutes or until topping has set.

Stuffed Mushrooms with Camembert

Although this recipe calls for Camembert, any cheese may be substituted as a topping and sprinkled with paprika for added colour.

1 tspn butter or margarine
1 rasher bacon, chopped
2 spring onions or ½ small onion, finely chopped
1 tbspn dry breadcrumbs
freshly ground black pepper to taste
pinch dried oregano or 1 tspn chopped fresh oregano
2–3 large, open mushrooms, wiped, with stalks removed
2 tbspns Camembert, finely sliced
pinch of paprika

SERVES 1

Melt the butter in a small microwave-safe dish on HIGH (100%) for 30 seconds. Stir in bacon and spring onions or onion and cook, uncovered, on HIGH for 2 minutes. Stir in breadcrumbs and seasonings.

Place mushrooms, stalk side uppermost, on a flat microwave-safe plate. Divide stuffing mixture between each mushroom and cover with slices of cheese. Sprinkle with paprika. Cook on HIGH for 1–1½ minutes, until stuffing is hot and cheese is melted.

Onions in Cheese Sauce

2 large onions
2 tbspns (45 g/1½ oz) butter
¼ cup (30 g/1 oz) slivered almonds
2 tbspns plain flour
1 cup (250 ml/8 fl oz) milk
¼ cup (30 g/1 oz) grated cheese

salt and pepper to taste
chopped fresh parsley for garnish

SERVES 4

Quarter onions and cook on HIGH (100%) in a microwave-safe plastic bag or small covered dish for 3 minutes, then let stand, leaving covered. Heat half the butter in a bowl and add slivered almonds. Cook on HIGH until lightly browned; remove almonds with slotted spoon and set aside. Add remaining butter and flour to bowl, stir and cook about 1 minute on HIGH. Stir in milk and cheese. Cook on HIGH, uncovered, for about 3 minutes, stirring every 30 seconds or until sauce is smooth and thickened. Turn onions into serving dish, coat with sauce and sprinkle with almonds and parsley. (See photo pages 82–83.)

Dried and concentrated herbs, spices and seasonings are generally more powerful in microwave recipes as the quicker cooking time does not always allow them to be completely dehydrated, diluted and absorbed.

Ham, Cheese and Chive Stuffed Potatoes

4 medium potatoes
100 g (3½ oz) ham, finely diced
¼ cup chopped fresh chives
2 tbspns (45 g/1½ oz) butter
½ cup (60 g/2 oz) grated Cheddar cheese
freshly ground black pepper to taste

SERVES 4

Wash and scrub potatoes well. Prick skins three or four times with a sharp knife and place on a piece of absorbent kitchen paper set on turntable.

Cook potatoes on HIGH (100%) for 10–14 minutes, until tender.

Cut tops of potatoes and scoop out pulp from centres, leaving 1–2 cm (½–¾ in) in shell. Mash potato pulp and combine with remaining ingredients. Spoon filling back into potatoes and replace lid. Place potatoes into a large, shallow ovenproof dish. Cook on HIGH 2–3 minutes, until cheese has melted. Serve hot.

Swiss Potato Casserole

750 g (1½ lb) pontiac (red) potatoes
2 medium carrots, sliced
2 medium zucchini, sliced
1 cup (125 g/4 oz) grated Swiss cheese
¼ cup finely sliced spring onions
1 tbspn chopped fresh basil or parsley
salt and pepper to taste
1 tbspn (20 g/¾ oz) butter or margarine
¾ cup (185 ml/6 fl oz) tomato juice
extra ½ cup (60 g/2 oz) grated Swiss cheese

SERVES 4

Wash potatoes (do not peel) and slice very thinly. Scrub carrots and slice thinly. Slice zucchini.

Place one-third of potato slices in a greased 20 cm (8 in) microwave-safe dish and top with half

From left: Swiss Potato Casserole; Tomato and Fennel Fettucine (page 48)

the carrot and zucchini slices. Sprinkle half of the cheese, spring onions and herbs over vegetables and sprinkle with salt and pepper. Repeat this entire procedure. Top with remaining one-third of potatoes. Melt the butter or margarine in a small dish on HIGH (100%) for 30–60 seconds and brush over the top potato slices. Gently pour tomato juice over vegetables and allow juice to run through vegetables.

Cover dish and cook on HIGH for 16–18 minutes, or until potatoes are tender. Sprinkle extra cheese on top of potatoes, cover and cook on HIGH for another 1 minute.

Allow covered potatoes to stand for 5 minutes before serving.

Golden Nuggets Filled with Spiced Vegetables

4 small, golden nugget pumpkins (about 315 g/10 oz each)
2 tbspns water
1 large onion, roughly chopped
1 tbspn (20 g/¾ oz) butter or margarine
1 tspn curry powder, or to taste
1 tbspn natural yoghurt
410 g (13 oz) mixed, raw chopped vegetables
(e.g. cauliflower, eggplant, beans, capsicum, tomato, broccoli)
salt and pepper to taste

SERVES 4

*T*rim the bases of the pumpkins so that they stand securely. Cut off the pumpkin tops, scoop out seeds, leaving the shell intact. Place pumpkins in a shallow microwave-safe casserole with water. Cook, covered, on HIGH (100%) for 8–10 minutes, or until tender when pierced with a knife. Keep covered and set aside.

Place onion, butter or margarine and curry powder in a microwave-safe dish and cook, covered, on HIGH for 3 minutes. Add yoghurt and mixed vegetables and stir well. Cook, covered, on HIGH a further 4–5 minutes. Season vegetables with salt and pepper.

Drain pumpkins and fill each with the cooked vegetable mixture. Place on a plate and heat on HIGH for 2–3 minutes before serving.

Serve hot with buttered noodles.

● Golden Nuggets Filled with Spiced Vegetables

● Herbed Tomatoes

Herbed Tomatoes

8–10 small, even-sized tomatoes
3 tbspns (60 g/2 oz) butter
4 spring onions, finely chopped
1 stick celery, finely chopped
1 clove garlic, crushed
freshly ground black pepper to taste
2 tbspns chopped fresh chives
2 tbspns chopped fresh parsley
1 tbspn chopped fresh oregano or ¼ tspn dried oregano

SERVES 4–5

Place tomatoes in a large bowl and cover with boiling water. Prick skins and leave to soak for 1 minute. Remove tomatoes from water and peel.

Melt butter in a shallow microwave-safe dish, covered with a well-fitting lid or plastic wrap, on HIGH (100%) for 2 minutes. Stir in spring onions, celery, garlic and pepper. Re-cover dish and continue cooking on HIGH for 2 minutes, until celery is soft. Stir in herbs, then gently add tomatoes, tossing them in the butter. Re-cover dish and cook on HIGH for 2–3 minutes until tomatoes are soft. Allow to stand for 3–4 minutes.

Just before serving, baste tomatoes again with a little of the herbed butter.

Souffléd Tomatoes

This dish is suitable for a first course and can be partly prepared the day before, up to the step where the egg yolks are added.

4 medium-sized tomatoes
2 tbspns (45 g/1½ oz) butter or margarine
1 tbspn plain flour
⅔ cup (140 ml/5 fl oz) milk
½ cup (60 g/2 oz) grated Cheddar cheese
2 tbspns grated Parmesan cheese
¼ tspn dried thyme
1 tbspn chopped fresh parsley
3 eggs, separated
½ tspn cream of tartar

SERVES 4

Cut the tops off the tomatoes and carefully scoop out and reserve the pulp. Invert the tomatoes to drain.

Place the butter or margarine in a bowl and melt on HIGH (100%) for 30–60 seconds. Stir in flour. Gradually stir in the milk and mix until smooth. Cook on HIGH for 3–4 minutes, stirring once during cooking and at the end of cooking. Stir in cheeses, herbs, reserved tomato pulp, and egg yolks.

In a clean bowl beat the egg whites and cream of tartar together until soft peaks form. Fold 1 tablespoon of egg white into the sauce mixture, then lightly fold in the remaining egg whites into the sauce.

Carefully spoon the mixture into the tomato cases. Place on a flat round plate and cook on MEDIUM (50%) for 5–7 minutes or until the surface of the soufflé is just moist.

Serve immediately with extra chopped parsley if desired.

NOTE Not all the mixture will fit into the tomato cases so spoon into a greased 20–23 cm (8–9 in) microwave-safe pie plate and cook on MEDIUM HIGH (70%) for 4–6 minutes and serve sliced with Souffléd Tomatoes.

The sequence for food preparation and microwave cooking should be planned according to the foods that can be cooked beforehand and quickly reheated, and the cooking time and standing time required. Vegetables are usually cooked last.

Stir-fry Chinese Vegetables

500 g (1 lb) mixed vegetables (e.g. sliced capsicum, carrot, celery, spring onions or onions, bean sprouts and snow peas)
1 tbspn green ginger wine
2 tbspns plum sauce

SERVES 4

*P*lace prepared vegetables in a shallow casserole dish and add ginger wine. Cook, covered, on HIGH (100%) for 4 minutes. Stir through plum sauce and cook a further 2–3 minutes on HIGH.

Serve with buttered pasta or rice.

Herbed Cheese and Vegetable Casserole

1½ cups (345 g/11 oz) firm ricotta cheese, cubed
2 tbspns vegetable oil
2 onions, thinly sliced
2 cloves garlic, crushed
2 tspns fresh ginger, finely chopped
2 tbspns chopped fresh coriander
1 tspn cummin
¼ tspn turmeric
½ tspn chilli powder
1 cup (200 g/6½ oz) fresh or frozen peas
2 tomatoes, diced
1 cup (250 ml/8 fl oz) chicken stock
1 cup (60 g/2 oz) cornflakes with sultanas
freshly ground black pepper to taste
3 tbspns chopped fresh parsley for garnish

SERVES 4

*L*eave cubed cheese on a piece of kitchen paper to absorb excess moisture. Meanwhile, heat oil in a 2 l (2 qt) microwave-safe casserole on HIGH (100%) for 2 minutes. Add onions and garlic, cook, covered, for 2 minutes. Stir in remaining ingredients except fresh parsley. Re-cover dish and cook on MEDIUM HIGH (70%) for 10 minutes. Adjust seasonings to taste if necessary.

Sprinkle with parsley and serve with boiled rice and a tossed salad.

● Stir-fry Chinese Vegetables

Snow Peas and Mango Salad

500 g (1 lb) snow peas, washed and trimmed
1 large mango, peeled and thinly sliced
2 tbspns pinenuts
2 tbspns lemon juice
⅓ cup (90 ml/3 fl oz) salad dressing
1 mignonette lettuce, washed

SERVES 4–6

*T*op, tail and string the snow peas. Arrange in a flat layer in an microwave-safe bag. Twist neck of bag, fold underneath and place on turntable. Alternatively, place snow peas in a shallow microwave-safe dish and cover with a well-fitting lid or plastic wrap. Cook on HIGH (100%) for 3–4 minutes, until tender-crisp to taste.

Gently toss snow peas together with mango slices, pinenuts, lemon juice and French dressing.

Divide lettuce leaves between four to six individual serving dishes. Top with snow peas and mango mixture. Serve well chilled.

SALAD DRESSING

Combine 3 tablespoons oil, 1 tablespoon vinegar, salt and pepper to taste, in a jar with a screw-top lid. Cover jar and shake before use.

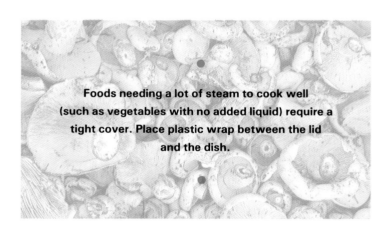

Foods needing a lot of steam to cook well (such as vegetables with no added liquid) require a tight cover. Place plastic wrap between the lid and the dish.

Braised Baby Squash

2 tbspns olive oil
1 clove garlic, crushed
500 g (1 lb) baby squash (if possible use a blend of yellow and green to give extra colour)
1 tbspn chopped fresh basil leaves
freshly ground black pepper to taste

SERVES 4

*P*lace the oil and garlic in a 2–3 l (2–3 qt) microwave-safe dish or casserole. Cover with a well-fitting lid or plastic wrap and cook on HIGH (100%) for 2 minutes, until oil is really hot. Add the squash and toss quickly to coat in the oil. Re-cover dish and cook on HIGH for 5–6 minutes, until almost tender, tossing dish or stirring squash occasionally.

Stir in basil 2 minutes before the end of cooking time. Leave to stand for 5 minutes.

Sprinkle with black pepper before serving.

Stir-fry Spinach with Hazelnuts

2 tbspns (45 g/1½ oz) butter
2 cloves garlic, crushed
1 large bunch spinach, washed, trimmed and torn into pieces
½ tspn ground nutmeg
freshly ground black pepper to taste
2 tbspns chopped hazelnuts

SERVES 4

*P*lace butter in a 3 l (3 qt) microwave-safe dish or casserole. Melt on HIGH (100%) for 1 minute. Add the garlic and stir well. Cover with a well-fitting lid or plastic wrap and cook on HIGH for 1 minute. Stir in the spinach. Re-cover dish and cook on HIGH for 3–4 minutes, until tender. Drain off any excess liquid.

Stir in nutmeg, pepper and hazelnuts. Heat on MEDIUM (50%), uncovered, for 1–2 minutes to allow steam to escape. (See photo page 146.)

Kumara with Sherried Orange Sauce

3 medium-sized kumara (sweet potatoes), well scrubbed
10 fresh or canned apricot or peach halves
3 tbspns raw sugar
1 tbspn cornflour
¼ tspn cinnamon
pinch ground cumin
¼ cup (60 ml/2 fl oz) orange juice
¼ cup (60 ml/2 fl oz) sherry or port
1 tbspn grated orange rind

SERVES 4–6

*P*lace kumara in a shallow microwave-safe dish and cover with a well-fitting lid or plastic wrap. Alternatively, place in a microwave-safe bag, twist end to seal and place on turntable of oven. Cook on HIGH (100%) for 10–12 minutes until just tender.

Peel and cut kumara in half lengthways. Place in a round, shallow microwave-safe dish in a single layer and arrange apricots or peaches on top.

In a small microwave-safe bowl, mix together sugar, cornflour, cinnamon, cumin and orange juice. Cook on HIGH for 2–3 minutes, stirring frequently until mixture boils and thickens. Stir in sherry or port, and orange rind. Spoon glaze over apricots and kumara and cook on MEDIUM HIGH (70%) until well glazed, basting occasionally. Serve hot with pork or ham. (See photo pages 82–83.)

Sweet Potato Dauphinoise

1 clove garlic, peeled and halved
1 tbspn (20 g/ ¾ oz) butter
500 g (1 lb) sweet potato (kumara), peeled and thinly sliced
freshly ground black pepper to taste
1 cup (125 g/4 oz) grated Cheddar cheese
1 tbspn caraway seeds
1 egg, lightly beaten
1 cup (250 ml/8 fl oz) milk
½ cup (125 ml/4 fl oz) cream

SERVES 4–6

*R*ub the cut garlic halves over the surface of a shallow microwave-safe dish and grease with a little of the butter. Arrange half the slices of sweet potato in the bottom of the dish, and sprinkle with freshly ground black pepper, half the grated cheese and ½ tablespoon of the caraway seeds. Repeat these layers with remaining sweet potato, pepper, cheese and caraway seeds.

In a small microwave-safe bowl, beat egg, milk and cream and pour over the sweet potato mixture, dot with remaining butter. Cook on HIGH (100%) for 2 minutes, then on MEDIUM (50%) for 10 minutes until tender.

Ratatouille

1 medium eggplant
1 tbspn salt
1 tbspn butter
1 large onion, finely chopped
1 small red and 1 small green capsicum, washed, seeded and finely sliced
2 zucchini, washed and sliced
1 clove garlic, crushed
2 tomatoes, peeled and quartered

freshly ground black pepper to taste
chopped fresh parsley
fresh sorrel leaves for garnish

SERVES 4

*W*ipe eggplant and cut into slices 1 cm (½ in) thick. If time permits soak in a little water and sprinkle liberally with salt; this helps remove the bitter flavour. After soaking, rinse well and pat dry with paper towels.

Melt the butter in a 2 l (2 qt) microwave-safe casserole on HIGH (100%) for 30 seconds. Stir in the finely chopped onion and cook on HIGH for 1 minute. Stir in the sliced capsicums, cook, covered, on HIGH for 2 minutes. Add the sliced zucchini, crushed garlic, quartered tomatoes, a little freshly ground black pepper and chopped parsley, together with eggplant. Cover and cook on HIGH for 10 minutes, stir well after 5 minutes.

Stand for 5 minutes and garnish with sorrel leaves before serving. (See photo page 146.)

Burmese Vegetable Curry

Two shrimp or prawn products are used in the vegetable curry. Blachan is dried shrimp paste, while prawn powder is simply a powder ground from fresh prawns that have been sun-dried. For the mixed vegetables in this curry choose from peas or beans, florets of cauliflower, capsicum, eggplant, pumpkin or other vegetables that, when cut into fairly small pieces, should cook in about the same time.

500 g (1 lb) mixed vegetables
⅓ cup (90 ml/3 fl oz) oil
3 large onions, finely sliced
2 cloves garlic, very finely chopped
1 fresh chilli (optional)
2 tspns prawn paste (blachan)
60 g (2 oz) prawn powder
2 cups (500 ml/16 fl oz) chicken stock, hot

SERVES 3

Cut all vegetables into bitesized small pieces. If using the chilli, discard seeds for less 'heat' and slice the chilli very thinly. Chop blachan into small pieces. Heat the oil in a large microwave-safe casserole on HIGH (100%) for 1 minute. Add onions and garlic and cook on HIGH for 4–5 minutes or until onions are transparent and colouring slightly, stirring 3 or 4 times. Add chilli, blachan, prawn powder and chicken stock. Cover and cook on HIGH for 3 minutes or until boiling, stirring several times. Reduce to MEDIUM (50%) and continue to cook for 8–10 minutes. Add vegetables and cook on HIGH for 6 minutes or until vegetables are tender–crisp. Check for seasoning — you will probably find the spices have added all the seasoning you need!

NOTE For some, chillies can cause a severe skin irritation. They are best handled with rubber gloves and remember not to touch your face, particularly your eyes, with the gloves.

Dry Vegetable Curry

This would be an ideal dish to serve at a curry party.

2 tbspns (45 g/1½ oz) ghee or butter
1 large onion, chopped
2 tspns fresh ginger, finely diced

● Curry party, *clockwise from top left:* Pappadums (page 135); Chicken Curry (page 93); Dhal (page 152); Fresh Mint Chutney (page 226); Dry Vegetable Curry; Pumpkin and Yoghurt Raita (page 229); Kashmiri Lamb Kofta (page 135); Tomato and Onion Sambal (page 226); Golden Coconut Rice (page 54)

3 large potatoes, cut into 2 cm (¾ in) cubes
½ head cauliflower, divided into florets
100 g (3½ oz) green beans, cut into 5 cm (2 in) lengths
2 tomatoes, chopped
¾ tspn turmeric
½ tspn chilli powder
½ tspn mustard seeds
2 tspns garam masala

SERVES 8

Place ghee or butter, onion and ginger in a 2–3 l (2–3 qt) microwave-safe dish or casserole. Cover with a well-fitting lid or plastic wrap. Cook on HIGH (100%) for 2 minutes, stir in potatoes, re-cover, and cook for a further 2 minutes. Add remaining ingredients, stirring thoroughly, but gently. Re-cover dish and cook on HIGH for 15–20 minutes, until vegetables are tender but still a little crisp. Leave to stand, covered, for 5 minutes before serving.

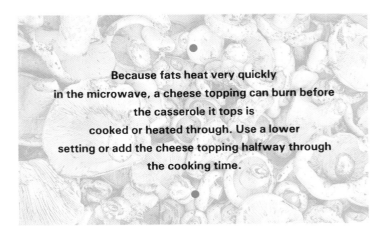

Because fats heat very quickly in the microwave, a cheese topping can burn before the casserole it tops is cooked or heated through. Use a lower setting or add the cheese topping halfway through the cooking time.

Zucchini Sauté

4 medium zucchini, thinly sliced
250 g (8 oz) fresh or frozen peas
2 tbspns (45 g/1½ oz) butter
3 spring onions, chopped
juice of ½ lemon
½ tbspn chopped fresh basil
½ tbspn chopped fresh chives
black pepper to taste
¼ cup (30 g/1 oz) slivered almonds for garnish

SERVES 4

Place all the ingredients except the almonds in a 1–2 l (1–2 qt) microwave-safe dish or casserole. Cover with a well-fitting lid or plastic wrap and cook on HIGH (100%) for 5–6 minutes, stirring well halfway through cooking time. Cook until vegetables are just tender.

Transfer to a serving plate and serve hot, garnished with slivered almonds.

Desserts

It seems that the microwave oven can be held partly responsible for a resurgence of interest in the dessert course. It can only have happened because more and more people are realising that instead of dessert being just another chore that our busy lives have made expendable, it can in fact be a treat whipped together and served in the time it takes to heat the conventional oven.

It is now possible for many desserts, which have been assembled in advance, to be cooked while the main course is being eaten. Fitting into this category are many fruit desserts which taste great when microwaved. Fruit flavours are retained to an extent not possible with any other cooking technique.

Many old favourites are being revived simply because of their speedy cooking. Baked apples are a good example. Before the advent of the microwave oven it took 30 minutes to bake an apple — the microwave can bake one in about 2½ minutes! BM (before microwave, of course) one wouldn't have considered baking an apple just for one person — think of the fuel bill!

Another favourite that should now never go out of fashion is Lemon Sauce Pudding (or lemon delicious) (see page 178). Make it in the microwave oven in a ring mould in 8 minutes — some improvement on 40 minutes in a conventional oven!

Not all desserts can be made by microwave, but it's surprising how many time-consuming steps in our traditional recipes can be cut short by the microwave. Gently but quickly softening butter and chocolate is one task that most of us have now taken for granted as being one for the microwave.

Many winter puddings are a great success when microwaved. Those with moist ingredients such as mashed banana, grated carrot or with oil or sour cream in place of some or all of the shortening do not dry out to the same degree as traditional mixtures. If you are disappointed with the colour of microwaved puddings — they are often pale shadows of their original selves — try adding a few drops of yellow food colouring or parisian essence with the liquid ingredients. Better still, make them chocolate flavoured and no one will complain.

● *Previous pages, middle shelf from left:* Old-fashioned Syrup Pudding (page 173); Lemon Meringue Pie (page 188); Olde English Trifle (page 174); Custard (page 175); *bottom shelf from left:* Baked Custard (page 172); Mocha Mousse (page 170)

● Crème Caramel

Divide custard between ramekin dishes or pour directly over caramel in large dish.

Place individual dishes around outside of turntable in oven. Cook on DEFROST (30%) for 12–15 minutes, until custard sets lightly (it may be still almost liquid in the centre). This will complete cooking on standing.

Place large, whole custard in oven and cook on DEFROST for 20 minutes. Chill for 1 hour.

Turn out custard(s) onto a serving plate, allowing caramel to drizzle down sides.

Chocolate Mousse

Although considered rather exotic, chocolate mousse is really quite simple to make. However, great care must always be taken to heat the chocolate gently and slowly. The problem is that the chocolate can be completely softened but still hold its original shape, hence the need for regular stirring. Overheating can cause the chocolate to scorch and burn.

120 g (4 oz) cooking chocolate
2 eggs, separated
⅔ cup (185 ml/6 fl oz) thickened cream
⅓ cup (90 ml/3 fl oz) thickened cream, whipped
chocolate curls or grated chocolate

SERVES 4

*B*reak the chocolate into a small microwave-safe bowl. Melt on DEFROST (30%) for 1–2 minutes; stir well. If chocolate has not thoroughly melted return to the oven and continue heating on DEFROST for 30 seconds.

Don't be impatient. Overheating will scorch and burn the chocolate. Chocolate melts well in the microwave, but it must be done on a low power setting to avoid any mishaps.

When chocolate is melted, stir in egg yolks. Whisk egg whites until stiff but not dry. Whisk the two-thirds cup cream until thick.

Fold the cream, then the egg whites gently through chocolate mixture. Spoon mixture into individual serving dishes. Allow to set in the refrigerator for 1–2 hours.

To serve, top with the one-third cup whipped cream and chocolate curls or grated chocolate.

CHOCOLATE CURLS

To make good chocolate curls use good quality cooking chocolate. Melt 45 g (1½ oz) chocolate in a small bowl on DEFROST (30%) for 1 minute; test to check for softening by stirring with a spoon, preferably using a microwave-safe spoon (plastic or china) which can be left in the bowl for frequent

Crème Caramel

This delicious dessert may be enriched with the addition of an extra egg yolk in the custard mixture.

½ cup (125 g/4 oz) white sugar
¾ cup (185 ml/6 fl oz) water, boiling
2 cups (500 ml/16 fl oz) milk
2 eggs
2 egg yolks
extra 1 tbspn white sugar
½ tspn vanilla essence

SERVES 6

*P*lace the half cup of sugar and boiling water into a 1–1.5 l (1–1½ qt) microwave-safe dish or casserole. Stir well to dissolve sugar. Cook on HIGH (100%) for 2 minutes. Stir well, ensuring that sugar has completely dissolved. Continue cooking on HIGH for 10–12 minutes, without stirring, until sugar begins to change colour. If leaving caramel in a large container, pour over 1 tablespoon of boiling water. If using six greased individual ramekin dishes, quickly pour caramel into dishes before it sets. (There is no need to add water if using individual dishes.)

Combine remaining ingredients in a mixing bowl or large jug. Whisk gently to blend eggs through mixture but do not allow mixture to become frothy.

stirring. Continue heating on DEFROST at 1 minute intervals and checking until chocolate is evenly softened.

Transfer chocolate to a cool flat surface — a marble slab is perfect, otherwise use a cool kitchen bench. For best results, work the chocolate with the flat of a palette knife in a 'massaging' motion for about half a minute then spread to an even thickness. Allow to almost set. (The perfectionist would melt, work and allow to set 2 or 3 times for best results.)

Use a long, sharp knife and holding it at a slightly slanting angle, shave off thin layers of chocolate which should immediately curl or come away in attractive flakes. Perfect curls take practice, but even small fragmented curls look attractive sprinkled over a cake or dessert.

If the chocolate is too soft, refrigerate for a short time; if too hard, place in a warm position for a few minutes. The curls should be fairly thin and have a crisp look. Lift the curls with the edge of a sharp bladed knife and transfer to baking paper prior to using. Under no circumstances try to handle them.

● Chocolate Mousse

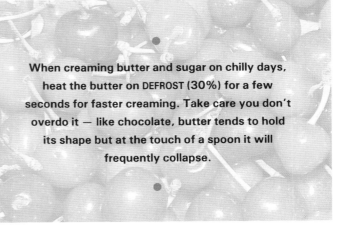

When creaming butter and sugar on chilly days, heat the butter on DEFROST (30%) for a few seconds for faster creaming. Take care you don't overdo it — like chocolate, butter tends to hold its shape but at the touch of a spoon it will frequently collapse.

White Mousseline with Raspberry Coulis

This elegant but simply prepared dessert may be made a day ahead. If fresh berries are out of season, buy frozen or canned berries.

155 g (5 oz) white chocolate
½ cup (125 ml/4 fl oz) milk
2 tbspns (45 ml/1½ fl oz) Baileys Irish Cream liqueur (optional)
2 tspns gelatine
⅔ cup (185 ml/6 fl oz) thickened cream, stiffly whipped
4 egg whites, stiffly beaten
200 g (6½ oz) raspberries or boysenberries, washed and hulled (reserve 12 for decoration)
2 tspns Cassis liqueur (optional)
approx. ⅓ cup (30 g/1 oz) icing sugar, sifted

SERVES 4

*B*reak chocolate into pieces and melt with milk in a small microwave-safe bowl on DEFROST (30%) for 4–6 minutes, stirring regularly until chocolate is melted.

In another small microwave-safe bowl blend Baileys, 2 tablespoons cold water and gelatine. Heat on HIGH (100%) for 45 seconds and stir well to ensure gelatine is thoroughly dissolved. Gently stir into chocolate mixture together with whipped cream. Lastly fold in stiffly beaten egg whites. Pour into four individual moulds. Chill for at least 1 hour or overnight, until set.

Rub the fruit through a fine nylon strainer — do not blend in a liquidiser. Stir in the Cassis and icing sugar a little at a time until a fairly thick purée is made.

To serve, turn the mousses out onto individual serving plates, carefully pour a little of the sauce around their bases. Decorate with reserved fruit or a small mint sprig. Serve with remaining sauce in a sauce boat. (See photo pages 104–105.)

Mocha Mousse

100 g (3½ oz) dark chocolate, chopped
4 eggs, separated
½ cup (125 g/4 oz) caster sugar
1 tbspn coffee powder
2 tbspns brandy or rum
1 cup (250 ml/8 fl oz) cream
whipped cream (optional)
grated chocolate or chocolate curls (see recipe on page 168) (optional)

SERVES 6

Place the chocolate in a small microwave-safe bowl and heat on DEFROST (30%), stirring and testing after 2–3 minutes and then regularly at 2 minute intervals until melted.

Beat egg yolks, sugar, coffee and brandy or rum together. Slowly stir in the melted chocolate and mix well.

Beat the egg whites in a separate bowl until soft peaks form and fold into the chocolate mixture. Beat cream in a clean bowl until it forms soft peaks; fold into the mixture. Pour into individual bowls and chill until ready to serve.

Serve with whipped cream and grated chocolate or chocolate curls if desired. (See photo pages 164–165.)

Chocolate Mousse Torte

2 tbspns cake crumbs
200 g (6½ oz) dark chocolate, broken into pieces
1 tbspn instant coffee granules
⅓ cup (90 ml/3 fl oz) water
4 eggs, separated
½ cup (125 g/4 oz) caster sugar
1 tspn vanilla essence
½ cup (125 ml/4 fl oz) thickened cream, stiffly whipped

SERVES 6

Lightly butter a 20–23 cm (8–9 in) microwave-safe flan dish and coat with the cake crumbs.

Place the chocolate, coffee granules and water into a 1 l (1 qt) microwave-safe dish or bowl. Heat on MEDIUM (50%) for 3–4 minutes, stirring well after 2 minutes, until chocolate dissolves. Stir well until mixture becomes thick, smooth and glossy.

Whisk (preferably with an electric whisk) the egg yolks, caster sugar and vanilla essence together until thick and double in volume. Continue to whisk, slowly adding the chocolate mixture to the egg yolks. Whisk until well combined.

Whisk the egg whites until stiff but not dry. Gently fold into the chocolate mixture. Fill the flan dish with approximately three-quarters of the mixture. Place the remainder in a covered bowl in the refrigerator to chill. Bake the flan on MEDIUM for 5–6 minutes, until the mixture rises and sets. Allow to cool, then chill in refrigerator for 1 hour.

To serve, top the baked chocolate torte with the chilled chocolate mousse mixture. Spread evenly, then finish by spreading the whipped cream on top. Serve well chilled.

Coffee Bavarois

¾ cup (185 ml/6 fl oz) milk
⅓ cup (75 g/2½ oz) white sugar
1 tbspn cornflour
1 tbspn gelatine
1 tbspn instant coffee powder
2 egg yolks
300 ml (10 fl oz) carton thickened cream
1 tspn vanilla essence
extra cream
sprinkle of cocoa
grated chocolate or chocolate curls (see recipe on pages 168)

SERVES 4

Lightly whisk the milk, sugar, cornflour, gelatine, coffee and egg yolks together in a 1 l (1 qt) microwave-safe bowl or jug, until thoroughly combined. Heat on HIGH (100%) for 1 minute, whisk with a fork again until mixture is smooth. Continue heating mixture on MEDIUM (50%) for 3 minutes, whisking well every 1 minute until coffee mixture is smooth, thick and glossy. Put in refrigerator to cool for 10 minutes.

Whisk cream and vanilla essence together in a large mixing bowl until stiff. Place 2 tablespoons of the whipped cream in a piping bag fitted with a star-shaped nozzle. Reserve this for decoration.

Add the cooled coffee mixture to remaining cream in bowl. Continue whisking until well combined. Pour mixture into a large serving dish, individual dishes or a fluted mould. Allow to set in refrigerator for 1 hour.

Serve in serving dish, individual dishes, or turned out onto a serving plate, with cream dusted with cocoa and grated chocolate or chocolate curls. (See photo page 171.)

● *From left:* Hot Citrus Savarin (page 181); Coffee Bavarois

Baked Custard

Delicately flavoured baked custard is so simple to cook in the microwave it's a snap for beginners. You can see exactly what's happening during cooking. Scald the milk in the measuring jug and arrange the finished cups of custard in a ring on oven tray or turntable. With the microwave you don't need the conventional pan of hot water to ensure a good texture in the custard. Just use a medium-high power setting to avoid overcooking the eggs.

1⅓ cups (325 ml/10½ fl oz) milk
3 eggs
¼ cup (60 g/2 oz) sugar
¼ tspn vanilla essence
sprinkle of ground nutmeg

SERVES 4

Heat the milk in a clear 2 cup measuring jug on HIGH (100%) for 2–3 minutes until tiny bubbles appear around the edges.

Combine eggs, sugar and vanilla essence in a 1 l (1 qt) microwave-safe bowl and blend in the milk. Divide mixture between four small ovenproof dishes or cups. Sprinkle each with nutmeg.

Arrange dishes or cups in a ring around outer edge of turntable. Cook on MEDIUM HIGH (70%) for 5–7 minutes until custard resembles soft-set gelatine. Centre will become firm as custard cools.

Serve cold or hot by first allowing custard to stand and cool, then reheating gently on DEFROST (30%) for a few seconds. (See photo pages 164–165.)

Gulab Jamuns

3 cups (345 g/11 oz) full cream instant milk powder
½ cup (60 g/2 oz) self-raising flour
few ground cardamom seeds
approx. ⅔ cup (170 ml/5½ fl oz) thickened cream
oil for frying
SUGAR SYRUP
2 cups (500 ml/16 fl oz) boiling water
1 cup (220 g/7 oz) white or brown sugar
1–2 tbspns rose water to taste

MAKES APPROXIMATELY 40 BALLS

Mix milk powder, flour and cardamom seeds in a large mixing bowl. Add three-quarters of cream and mix with your hand until mixture forms a stiff dough, adding the remainder of the cream a little at a time until the dough is kneadable and smooth.

Take approximately 1 teaspoon of dough and roll it between palms to make a small ball. Continue until all of the dough is used.

Heat approximately 2 cm (¾ in) of cooking oil in a wok or large frying pan until hot. Quickly and carefully add a few of the balls and fry for 2–3 minutes, turning constantly. As soon as balls turn a golden-brown colour, remove and allow to drain on a piece of absorbent kitchen paper. Continue until all balls are cooked.

To prepare syrup: Pour boiling water into a large 2–3 l (2–3 qt) microwave-safe dish. Stir in sugar and heat on HIGH (100%) for 4 minutes, until syrup comes to the boil. Remove from oven. Add rose water and cooked gulab jamuns.

Allow to soak for at least 12 hours, until most of the syrup has been absorbed.

Old-fashioned Syrup Pudding

½ cup (125 g/4 oz) butter or margarine, softened
⅓ cup (90 g/3 oz) caster sugar
3 eggs
½ cup (125 ml/4 fl oz) milk
5 tbspns (50 g/1½ oz) plain flour, sieved
2 tspns baking powder
2–3 tbspns golden syrup to taste
extra golden syrup or prepared custard
orange rind for garnish

SERVES 4–6

Cream the butter or margarine and sugar together until light and fluffy; add the eggs, milk and 1 tablespoon of the flour. Beat well until smooth. Fold in remaining flour and baking powder.

Thoroughly grease a 1–1.5 l (1–1½ qt) microwave-safe pudding basin or jug. Carefully spoon in golden syrup, then pour batter over syrup. Cover top loosely with plastic wrap. Cook on HIGH (100%) for 5–6 minutes, until well risen and spongy to touch. Let stand for 2–3 minutes before turning out to serve.

Serve with more golden syrup poured over or with custard, garnished with orange rind. (See photo pages 164–165.)

Pecan Praline Cream

CARAMEL
½ cup (125 g/4 oz) sugar
¾ cup (185 ml/6 fl oz) boiling water

CUSTARD
3 eggs, at room temperature
¼ cup (60 g/2 oz) caster sugar
1 tspn vanilla essence
¼ cup (30 g/1 oz) full cream milk powder
410 ml (13 fl oz) milk
½ cup (125 ml/4 fl oz) cream

COMPOTE
500 g (1 lb) mixed dried fruits e.g. pears, peaches,
apricots, apple rings, prunes and nectarines
½ cup (90 g/3 oz) sultanas
½ cup (90 g/3 oz) raisins
1 cup (250 ml/8 fl oz) orange juice
¾ cup (185 ml/6 fl oz) orange liqueur or fruit juice
light syrup made from ¾ cup (185 ml/6 fl oz) water
and ¼ cup (60 g/2 oz) sugar

PECAN PRALINE
½ cup (125 g/4 oz) sugar
¼ cup (60 ml/2 fl oz) water
¾ cup (90 g/3 oz) pecans, chopped

TOPPING
whipped cream

SERVES 6

Place sugar and water for caramel in an microwave-safe bowl. Stir well and cook on HIGH (100%) for 2 minutes, stirring well to dissolve sugar. Continue cooking on HIGH for a further 10–12 minutes, or until mixture turns golden brown. Do not stir. Immediately divide mixture between six ovenproof soufflé dishes or teacups. Toffee will set almost immediately.

To prepare custard: Place eggs, sugar, vanilla essence and milk powder into a large bowl. Beat until smooth and creamy. Combine milk and cream in a small microwave-safe jug. Heat on HIGH for 2 minutes, or until hot, but not boiling. Gradually whisk hot milk mixture into eggs. Pour mixture into six caramel-lined dishes. Place dishes around the outer edge of the turntable. Cook on DEFROST (30%) for 15–16 minutes, or until just set. Remove from oven and allow to stand for 10 minutes before placing in refrigerator to chill.

To prepare compote: Mix dried fruit together with orange juice, liqueur or fruit juice, and sugar syrup in a large microwave-safe bowl. Cover and cook on HIGH for 4 minutes. Stir well and allow to stand, covered, for 10–15 minutes.

● Pecan Praline Cream

To prepare pecan praline: Combine sugar and water in a microwave-save bowl and cook on HIGH for 2 minutes. Stir until sugar dissolves. Cook for a further 6–8 minutes, or until mixture is a golden-brown colour. Remove immediately and stir in the pecans. Turn onto a lightly greased oven tray, separating nuts with a fork. Allow to cool, then coarsely chop.

Unmould the custard and decorate with whipped cream and pecan praline. Serve with warm or cold fruit compote.

Custard

1½ cups (375 ml/12 fl oz) milk
1–2 tbspns caster sugar, or to taste
3 eggs
1–2 tspns vanilla essence

MAKES 1½ CUPS

Combine all ingredients in a 1 l (1 qt) microwave-safe jug. Heat on HIGH (100%) for 2 minutes. Stir well, then continue cooking on MEDIUM (50%) for 3–4 minutes. Stir every minute, until the custard coats the back of a spoon, and leaves a trail when a teaspoon is run through the custard.

Olde English Trifle

6 sponge fingers
2–3 tbspns strawberry jam
60 g (2 oz) ratafia or amaretti biscuits
½ cup (125 ml/4 fl oz) fruit juice
2 tbspns sherry
1½ cups prepared custard (see previous recipe)
½ cup (125 ml/4 fl oz) thickened cream, stiffly whipped
6–12 glacé cherries, halved
toasted almonds

SERVES 6

Spread the sponge fingers thickly with the jam and place into a glass serving dish. Add the ratafia or amaretti biscuits and pour the fruit juice and sherry over them.

Spoon over the custard and allow the trifle to stand in the refrigerator — preferably overnight — to allow the sponge fingers to absorb all the moisture. The custard will also thicken enough to take the weight of the cream.

To serve, spoon the stiffly whipped cream over the custard and decorate with the cherries and toasted almonds. (See photo pages 164–165.)

Christmas Pudding

½ cup (75 g/2½ oz) currants
½ cup (90 g/3 oz) sultanas
¾ cup (125 g/4 oz) raisins
¼ cup (45 g/1½ oz) glacé cherries, halved
¼ cup (45 g/1½ oz) mixed peel
¼ cup (60 ml/2 fl oz) brandy, rum, or fruit juice
finely grated rind and juice of 1 orange
1 tbspn black treacle
2 eggs
few drops parisian essence
⅓ cup (75 g/2½ oz) raw sugar
1 tbspn cooking oil
¼ cup (60 g/2 oz) butter, melted
½ cup (30 g/1 oz) fresh brown breadcrumbs
1 cup (125 g/4 oz) roughly chopped almonds
2 tspns mixed spice
⅔ cup (90 g/3 oz) plain flour, sifted
extra brandy

SERVES 6

Grease and line the base and sides of a 1.5 l (1½ qt) microwave-safe pudding basin with baking paper.

Place the fruit in a medium-sized microwave-safe dish or bowl, and stir in brandy or rum or fruit juice with orange juice and rind. Heat on HIGH (100%) for 2 minutes. Stir in black treacle and leave to stand while remaining ingredients are being prepared.

Combine remaining ingredients in a large mixing bowl. Stir in the fruit and transfer mixture to prepared pudding basin. Cover basin loosely with plastic wrap and cook on MEDIUM (50%) for 25–28 minutes. Pudding is cooked when a skewer inserted into the middle comes out clean.

Wrap basin in a tea-towel and let stand 5 minutes before turning out to serve.

For a special effect, heat extra brandy in a small microwave-safe jug on HIGH for 30 seconds, light and pour over pudding.

Serve with Brandy Butter (see recipe below) or Brandy Sauce (see page 221). (See photo pages 82–83.)

NOTE This pudding may be made 4–6 weeks ahead and stored in the freezer. To serve, leave to thaw for two days in refrigerator. (Slow thawing prevents moisture loss and allows the natural fruit flavour to develop.) Reheat pudding on MEDIUM for 5–6 minutes, or sliced into portions in serving dishes for 1½–2 minutes, on MEDIUM. Be careful not to overheat when reheating, for if it starts to cook again the pudding will dry out.

Brandy Butter

250 g (8 oz) unsalted butter
½ cup (75 g/2½ oz) icing sugar
brandy to taste

Soften (but do not melt) unsalted butter in a microwave-safe bowl on MEDIUM (50%) for 1–1½ minutes. Beat in sifted icing sugar and brandy to taste until mixture is smooth.

Basic Steamed Pudding

100 g (3½ oz) butter
½ cup (125 g/4 oz) sugar
2 eggs
1½ cups (185 g/6 oz) self-raising flour
2–4 tbspns milk
prepared custard or cream

SERVES 6–8

Heat butter and sugar on HIGH (100%) 30–45 seconds. Stir to combine. Stir in the eggs, then the flour and milk — the mixture should be fairly stiff.

Pour batter into a 2 l (2 qt) microwave-safe glass or plastic jug, or use a ring mould. Cover and cook, elevated, on HIGH for 4–5 minutes. Allow to stand for 5 minutes, then turn out.

Serve with custard or cream.

VARIATIONS

Chocolate Pudding Add 2 tablespoons cocoa and an extra 2 tablespoons milk.

Coffee Pudding Add 1 tablespoon instant coffee powder.

Fruit Pudding Add ¾ cup (125 g/4 oz) dried mixed fruit that has been soaked in 2 tablespoons brandy. Increase cooking time by 1 minute.

Jam/Honey/Golden Syrup Pudding Line dish with 2 tablespoons of jam, honey or golden syrup before pouring in batter. Drizzle 2 tablespoons of jam, honey or golden syrup over batter before cooking. Jam etc. will sink through the pudding as it cooks, giving streaks of jam through the cooked pudding.

Spice Pudding Add 2 teaspoons mixed spice.

Fruit Pudding 2 Place drained, stewed or canned fruit in dish. Increase cooking time 1–2 minutes.

Choco-Chip Pudding Add half a cup chocolate chips to the plain or chocolate batter.

Individual Puddings Divide batter between six microwave-safe ramekins. If you do not have ramekins, microwave-safe teacups work just as well.

These individual puddings are great to serve as a dessert for a winter dinner party. Choose a sauce or custard to complement the flavour of the pudding — perhaps a rich chocolate or apricot sauce with a chocolate pudding. A liqueur custard or sauce goes well with any of the variations.

Chocolate–Orange Sponge Pudding

½ cup (125 g/4 oz) butter or margarine, softened
½ cup (125 g/4 oz) caster sugar
finely grated rind and juice of 1 orange
3 eggs, beaten
⅓ cup (90 g/3 oz) self-raising flour, sifted with
1 heaped tbspn cocoa, sifted

SERVES 4–6

Cream the butter or margarine, sugar and finely grated rind of orange together in a large mixing bowl, until light and fluffy. Gradually beat in the orange rind, juice and eggs together with 1 tablespoon of the sifted flour and cocoa. Gently fold in remaining flour.

Carefully spoon the mixture into a well-greased 1–1.5 l (1–1½ qt) microwave-safe pudding basin. Cover loosely with plastic wrap and cook on HIGH (100%) for 7–8 minutes until light and spongy to touch. Allow to stand for 5 minutes before turning out of mould. Serve hot.

● Basic Steamed Pudding

Passionfruit Crèmes

250 g (8 oz) cream cheese, softened
2 tbspns caster sugar
2 tspns lemon juice
1 egg, beaten
410 g (13 oz) can or similar weight natural apple,
apricot or peach filling
1 tbspn dry sherry or brandy
125 g (4 oz) can passionfruit pulp in syrup
shredded orange rind

SERVES 4

Beat cream cheese and sugar together until smooth. Add lemon juice and egg, continue beating until thoroughly combined. Combine half the can of apple, apricot or peach filling with cheese mixture. Spoon this equally into four, 1-cup, very lightly oiled microwave-safe ramekins or cups. Smooth over the tops.

Place ramekins evenly around the edge of the turntable. Cook on MEDIUM HIGH (70%) for 5 minutes. Leave in oven and allow ramekins to cool (approx. 30 minutes).

Place remaining fruit filling in a blender or food processor. Add sherry or brandy. Blend to a purée. Stir in passionfruit pulp.

Run the tip of a small, sharp knife around ramekin edge and turn out crèmes onto medium serving plates.

Decorate with purée and orange rind. (See photo page 179.)

Plum Soufflé Omelette

SOUFFLÉ
4 eggs, separated
¼ cup (50 g/1¾ oz) caster sugar
¼ cup (30 g/1 oz) cocoa powder, sifted
1 tbspn brandy or rum
825 g (1¾ lb) can plums, drained, syrup reserved
PLUM SAUCE
reserved plum syrup
1–2 tbspns Cointreau or brandy
1 tbspn cornflour
TOPPING
sifted icing sugar (optional)

SERVES 4–6

Using electric mixer, beat egg yolks until thick and creamy (approx. 8 minutes). Beat egg whites until soft peaks form, adding sugar 1 tablespoon at a time until meringue is glossy. Add cocoa to whites, 1 tablespoon at a time, and continue beating until mixture is stiff but not dry. Fold egg yolk mixture, then brandy or rum into cocoa mixture.

Spoon plums into a 20 cm (8 in) microwave-safe ring dish. Pour cocoa mixture over and smooth top with a spatula. Cook on HIGH (100%) for 3–4 minutes, turning dish each minute, or until just set. Allow to stand, covered, for 5 minutes while making sauce.

To prepare sauce: Combine reserved syrup, Cointreau or brandy and cornflour until smooth. Place in small microwave-safe container. Heat, uncovered, on HIGH for 5 minutes or until just boiling, stirring every minute.

Sprinkle icing sugar over soufflé, if desired, and serve immediately with plum sauce.

Lemon Sauce Pudding

1 tbspn (20 g/¾ oz) butter or margarine
¾ cup (185 g/6 oz) caster sugar
2 tbspns (20 g/½ oz) self-raising flour
juice and grated rind of 2 lemons
1¼ cups (315 ml/10 fl oz) milk
2 eggs, separated
toasted coconut (optional)
whipped cream (optional)

SERVES 4–6

Cream butter and sugar and stir in flour (don't worry if mixture is not smooth). Combine juice and rind of lemons with milk and yolks of eggs. Beat lightly and stir gradually through the first mixture. Beat egg whites until stiff and fold through.

Pour into a microwave-safe ring dish (at least 5 cup capacity) and cook on MEDIUM (50%) for 5 minutes. Reduce to DEFROST (30%) and cook a further 3 minutes or until just set. When cool, decorate with coconut and cream if desired. (See photo page 179.)

NOTE If using a regular-shaped microwave-safe dish the pudding may appear cooked around the edges while the centre is still not set. In this case, allow the pudding to stand for 3 or 4 minutes halfway through the second cooking period for the heat to equalise; then continue to cook until set.

● *From left:* Passionfruit Crèmes; Lemon Sauce Pudding

Strawberry Cream Rice

When cooking the rice for this lovely dessert, add the grated rind of the two oranges which are used in the recipe.

2 punnets ripe strawberries, washed and hulled
1 cup (75 g/2½ oz) skim milk powder
juice of 2 oranges
¾ cup (155 g/5 oz) caster sugar
1 tbspn gelatine
3 cups Calrose rice, cooked (approx. 1 cup/200 g/6½ oz uncooked)
juice of 1 lemon
whipped cream (optional)

SERVES 4–6

*R*eserve eight strawberries for decoration. Place remainder in bowl of food processor or liquidiser, blend until smooth.

Pour 1 cup of the strawberry purée into a bowl, sprinkle over skim milk powder, stir well until dissolved. Chill until required.

Tip remaining purée into a 1 l (1 qt) microwave-safe dish or bowl and add orange juice, sugar and gelatine. Heat on MEDIUM (50%) for 2–3 minutes, until sugar and gelatine are dissolved, stirring well after 1 minute. Pour mixture back into bowl of processor or liquidiser. Blend, adding purée mixed with skim milk powder a little at a time, until the mixture is smooth and creamy. Tip strawberry mixture back into a large bowl and stir in rice and lemon juice. Pour into a 5–6 cup fancy mould. Chill until set.

Unmould dessert onto a large platter. Decorate with reserved strawberries and serve, if desired, with whipped cream.

Almond Pears Hélène

This is a variation of a classic dessert with the very successful combination of the delicate flavour of pears and a rich chocolate sauce.

825 g (1¾ lb) can pear halves in natural juice, drained, juice reserved

FILLING
125 g (4 oz) cream cheese
2 tbspns reserved pear juice
¼ cup (45 g/1½ oz) sultanas
¼ cup (30 g/1 oz) slivered almonds
2 tbspns glacé ginger, chopped

SAUCE
125 g (4 oz) cooking chocolate, roughly chopped
155 ml (5 oz) can evaporated milk
⅓ cup (90 ml/3 fl oz) reserved pear juice
¼ cup (45 g/1½ oz) brown sugar
¼ tspn nutmeg
¼ cup (60 g/2 oz) butter or margarine, chopped

SERVES 4–6

Cut cream cheese into small portions, place in glass bowl and soften, uncovered, on MEDIUM HIGH (70%) for 30 seconds. Beat until smooth. Add reserved pear juice, sultanas, slivered almonds and ginger; stir until combined.

Fill six pear cavities with mixture. Place pear halves onto individual plates or all onto a large platter. Set aside.

To prepare sauce: Place chocolate pieces into a microwave-safe bowl or 1 l (1 qt) jug. Cook on MEDIUM (50%) for 3–4 minutes. Add evaporated milk, reserved pear juice, brown sugar and nutmeg. Stir until combined. Cook on MEDIUM for a further 3–4 minutes, stirring every minute. Whisk in butter or margarine pieces until melted into sauce.

Spoon sauce around base of pear halves and decorate if desired.

Hot Citrus Savarin

CAKE DOUGH
1½ cups (185 g/6 oz) plain flour, sifted
½ cup (45 g/1½ oz) barley flour
2 tbspns (30 g/1 oz) sugar
3 tspns (7 g) pkt dry yeast
½ cup (125 ml/4 fl oz) warm milk
3 eggs
⅓ cup (90 g/3 oz) butter, melted

SYRUP
1¼ cups (280 g/9 oz) sugar
1¼ cups (315 ml/10 fl oz) water
juice of 1 large orange
juice of 1 large lemon
¼ cup (60 ml/2 fl oz) Cointreau (optional)

TOPPING
⅓ cup (90 ml/3 fl oz) marmalade, warmed

DECORATION
orange rind
strawberries

SERVES 6–8

Place the sifted plain and barley flour, 1 tablespoon of the sugar and all the yeast into a large mixing bowl. Make a well in the centre and pour in the warmed milk.

Whisk the eggs, remaining sugar and melted butter together until thick and frothy. Pour into the flour mixture and mix until batter is smooth.

Cover bowl and leave in a warm place for 10 minutes, until the batter has risen a little. Pat the batter with a spatula for 3–4 minutes to redistribute the air bubbles. Transfer mixture to a 2 l (2 qt) greased microwave-safe savarin or gugelhupf mould. Leave in a warm place to rise for 30–40 minutes, until it doubles in volume.

Cook on HIGH (100%) for 5 minutes until cooked through. Cover mould with aluminium foil or plastic wrap and let stand for 5–10 minutes; it will continue to cook a little while standing. Turn out onto a wire rack to cool.

Wash the cooking container, dry thoroughly and return cake to it.

To prepare syrup: Place the sugar and water in a 1 l (1 qt) microwave-safe bowl or jug. Heat on HIGH for 5 minutes until sugar dissolves, boils and thickens slightly. Stir twice during cooking. Allow to cool for 3–4 minutes, then pour in fruit juices and Cointreau if used.

Prick the savarin all over with a fork. Pour syrup over surface and allow to soak until all the syrup is absorbed.

Transfer to a microwave-safe plate and brush outside with warmed marmalade. Return to oven. Heat on HIGH for 1 minute.

Serve decorated with orange rind and strawberries. (See photo page 171.)

Fruit in Rum Syrup

¼ cup (45 g/1½ oz) brown sugar
2 tspns butter
¼ cup (60 ml/2 fl oz) orange juice
2 tbspns rum
1 kiwi fruit, peeled and cut into quarters, lengthways
1 punnet strawberries, washed and hulled
250 g (8 oz) black grapes, washed

SERVES 4

*P*lace brown sugar, butter, orange juice and rum into a 1 l (1 qt) microwave-safe dish. Cook on HIGH (100%) for 2–3 minutes, stirring well after 1½ minutes, to distribute melted butter. Gently stir in prepared fruit and toss gently to cover with syrup. Cook on HIGH for 2 minutes, until fruit has softened.

Berries with Dumplings

For this very simple family dessert, choose a shallow, microwave-safe casserole (approximately 5 cm/2 in deep), no less than 23 cm (9 in) square. This will allow all the dumplings to be arranged around the outer edge of the dish to allow even cooking. The dumplings are quite small when prepared but they more than double their size during cooking. If you have to use a smaller dish, rearrange the dumplings halfway through cooking time as those around the edge will be cooked before those closer to the centre

2 × 420–440 g/13–14 oz) cans raspberries
or boysenberries
DUMPLINGS
½ cup (60 g/2 oz) self-raising flour, sifted
3 tspns butter or margarine
¼ cup (60 ml/2 fl oz) milk

SERVES 4–6

*P*lace the berries in a microwave-safe casserole, cover with vented plastic wrap and cook on HIGH (100%) for 4–5 minutes or until almost boiling.

Meanwhile make dumplings. Sift flour into a bowl, rub in butter evenly and add sufficient milk to form a fairly sticky dough. Turn the mixture out onto a well-floured surface and knead lightly but well, until smooth. Divide the dough into 12 even

> **When adding cream to a sauce, cook on MEDIUM (50%) to prevent the sauce from curdling. Cream mixtures should never be brought to the boil.**

pieces. With floured hands, form into balls and place around the edge of the casserole with the berries. Return to oven and cook on HIGH for 5–6 minutes or until the dumplings are no longer soft — a finger placed lightly on top of a dumpling should not leave a depression.

Baked Lemon Cheesecake

To ensure the cake is easily removed from the pan, take 3 strips of baking paper, folded several times to a width of 5–7 cm (2–2¾ in), long enough to place evenly across the base of the microwave-safe dish. Make sure there is enough paper to come at least 8 cm (3¼ in) above the edge of the dish. Then press a circle of plastic wrap or baking paper into the dish, covering the strips. When cooked and quite cold, lift the cake out using the paper strips as handles.

BASE
150 g (5 oz) butter
200 g (6½ oz) morning coffee or Marie biscuits, crushed
FILLING
250 g (8 oz) cream cheese
250 g (8 oz) cottage cheese
3 eggs, lightly beaten
¾ cup (185 g/6 oz) sugar
1 tbspn cornflour
½ cup (125 ml/4 fl oz) sour cream
grated rind of 1 lemon
¼ cup (60 ml/2 fl oz) lemon juice
¼ cup (60 ml/2 fl oz) Lemon Butter (see recipe on page 225)
twist of lemon

SERVES 8

*M*elt butter in a medium-sized bowl on HIGH (100%) for 1 minute. Stir in biscuit crumbs and mix thoroughly. Press over the base and sides of a 21 cm x 5 cm (8 x 2 in) round microwave-safe dish. Refrigerate while preparing filling.

To prepare filling: Soften cream cheese in a bowl on HIGH for 1 minute, then beat until smooth. Add cottage cheese, eggs, sugar, cornflour, sour cream, lemon rind and 1 tablespoon of lemon juice. Beat mixture until smooth and well blended.

Pour filling onto biscuit crumbs and cook on MEDIUM (50%) for 20 minutes. Allow to cool, then remove cheesecake from dish. Blend remaining lemon juice with Lemon Butter, warm on DEFROST (30%) for 2 minutes and stir well. Pour over top of cheesecake and decorate with lemon twist.

Chill before serving.(See photo pages 184–185.)

● Fruit in Rum Syrup

Gingered Pumpkin Cheesecake

BASE
75 g (2½ oz) butter
125 g (4 oz) ginger nut biscuits, finely crushed

FILLING
315 g (10 oz) pumpkin, peeled and seeded
1½ tbspns ginger in syrup, finely chopped
375 g (12 oz) cream cheese
½ cup (100 g/3½ oz) caster sugar
grated rind of 1 lemon
2 eggs

TOFFEE
1 cup (220 g/7 oz) sugar
¼ cup (60 ml/2 fl oz) water
1 tbspn white vinegar

SERVES 8–10

Melt butter in a medium-sized microwave-safe bowl on HIGH (100%) for 1 minute. Mix with biscuit crumbs. Press into the base of a paper-lined 23 cm (9 in) microwave-safe pie plate. Chill.

To prepare filling: Chop pumpkin into 2 cm (¾ in) cubes, place around the edge of a microwave-safe plate. Sprinkle with water. Cover loosely with plastic wrap and cook on HIGH for 7 minutes, until well cooked. Purée until smooth. Add ginger to pumpkin.

Soften cream cheese on HIGH for 30 seconds. Beat with caster sugar and lemon rind until smooth. Add pumpkin and ginger, together with eggs, until well combined. Pour mixture onto biscuit crumbs and cook on MEDIUM (50%) for 22 minutes. Allow to cool. Chill and decorate with whipped cream and toffee before serving.

To prepare toffee: Combine all ingredients in a large, deep microwave-safe bowl and cook on HIGH for 4 minutes; stir well. Continue cooking on HIGH for another 4 minutes; stir well. Test by dropping a little of the mixture into cold water to see if it forms a hard ball. If not at hard ball stage, cook for a further 2 minutes. Watch carefully to ensure that the toffee does not burn. Warm toffee may be drizzled onto aluminium foil to form a lattice, allowed to set, then placed on top of the cheesecake. Toffee may otherwise be allowed to set, then ground to a powder and used to decorate cheesecake.

● *Clockwise from top:* Banana-Yoghurt Cheesecake (page 186); Choc-Mallow Swirl (page 186); Baked Lemon Cheesecake (page 182); Gingered Pumpkin Cheesecake

Choc–Mallow Swirl

BASE
⅓ cup (90 g/3 oz) butter
200 g (6½ oz) chocolate ripple biscuits, crushed
FILLING
500 g (1 lb) cream cheese
⅓ cup (75 g/2½ oz) sugar
½ cup (125 ml/4 fl oz) cream
vanilla essence to taste
2 tbspns water
1 tbspn gelatine
100 g (3½ oz) cooking chocolate bits
100 g (3½ oz) marshmallows

SERVES 8

Melt butter in a microwave-safe bowl on HIGH (100%) for 1½ minutes and mix with biscuit crumbs. Press crumbs into the base and sides of a well-greased, paper-lined 20 cm (8 in) springform tin; refrigerate while preparing filling.

To prepare filling: Soften cream cheese in a large microwave-safe bowl on MEDIUM (50%) for 1½ minutes. Add sugar, cream and vanilla essence; mix well until smooth. Blend water and gelatine together. Cook on HIGH for 30 seconds until gelatine is dissolved. Add to cheese mixture and blend thoroughly.

Melt chocolate in a small bowl on MEDIUM for 3 minutes, stirring occasionally until melted. Melt marshmallows in a separate bowl and heat on MEDIUM HIGH (70%) for 30 seconds until melted.

Pour cheese filling onto biscuit base, then carefully swirl chocolate and marshmallow mixtures through the filling. Refrigerate for 2 hours until set. (See photo pages 184–185.)

Banana–Yoghurt Cheesecake

BASE
100 g (3½ oz) butter
125 g (4 oz) Marie biscuits, crushed
FILLING
500 g (1 lb) continental-style cottage or ricotta cheese
¾ cup (125 g/4 oz) brown sugar
½ cup (125 ml/4 fl oz) natural yoghurt
2 bananas, mashed
3 eggs
DECORATION
slices of banana dipped in chocolate

SERVES 10–12

Melt butter on HIGH (100%) for 1 minute in a medium-sized bowl, mix with crushed biscuits. Press into the base of a 24 cm microwave-safe (9½ in) flan dish. Chill while preparing filling.

To prepare filling: Beat cottage cheese with brown sugar until smooth. Add yoghurt, bananas and eggs and beat until well combined.

Pour filling mixture into prepared flan dish. Cook on MEDIUM HIGH (70%) for 25 minutes. Remove from microwave and chill. Decorate with banana slices dipped in chocolate. (See photo pages 184–185.)

Chestnut Charlotte Russe

½ pkt lemon jelly crystals
½ cup (125 ml/4 fl oz) water, boiling
1 lemon, cut into slices
strips of angelica
1 cup (250 ml/8 fl oz) milk
2 eggs
2 tbspns sugar
1 tspn vanilla essence
½ cup canned chestnut purée
1 tbspn water
1 tbspn lemon juice
1 tspn gelatine
300 ml crtn thickened cream
approx. 24 sponge fingers

SERVES 4–6

Lightly grease the base and sides of a 1 l (1 qt) microwave-safe charlotte russe mould, or any microwave-safe straight-sided jelly mould.

Place jelly crystals in a small microwave-safe bowl. Pour in ½ cup boiling water and stir until jelly is dissolved. Pour a very thin layer of jelly into mould and chill until set.

Place lemon slices and strips of angelica in a decorative pattern on top of the jelly and carefully pour in remaining jelly, ensuring that fruit pattern is undisturbed. Chill until set.

Place the milk in a 1–2 l (1–2 qt) microwave-safe jug. Beat in the eggs, sugar and vanilla essence. Cook on HIGH (100%) for 1 minute, whisk lightly, then reduce power and continue cooking on MEDIUM (50%) for 3–4 minutes. Whisk occasionally during cooking until the custard cooks and lightly coats the back of a spoon. Whisk in the chestnut purée until well blended.

Place the water, lemon juice and gelatine in a small microwave-safe bowl. Heat on HIGH for 30 seconds until gelatine dissolves. Stir into the custard mixture. Chill until custard sets around the edges of dish.

Meanwhile, whip the cream until stiff and place 2 tablespoons of cream into a piping bag fitted with a star-shaped nozzle. Arrange sponge fingers around the insides of the charlotte mould, sugared sides outwards.

Fold the whipped cream into the custard mixture, then pour custard into charlotte mould and chill until set.

To serve, trim the sponge fingers, if necessary, to the same height as the custard. Quickly dip mould into hot water and invert onto a serving dish. Decorate with the reserved whipped cream. (See photo pages 24–25.)

Rich Shortcrust Pastry

1½ cups (185 g/6 oz) plain flour
1 tbspn (15 g/½ oz) icing sugar
⅓ cup (90 g/3 oz) butter
1 egg yolk
1 tspn water
1 tspn lemon juice

Sift flour and icing sugar into a bowl. Rub in butter evenly. Beat together the egg yolk, water and lemon juice. Sprinkle over flour mixture, stir first with a fork and then with the hand to form into a dough, kneading lightly until smooth.

Roll out pastry between two sheets of baking paper to fit a 20–23 cm (8–9 in) microwave-safe pie plate. Prick sides and base of pastry shell with a fork. Cover the base of the pastry with one or two circles of absorbent kitchen paper and cook on HIGH (100%) for 4–5 minutes. Let pastry stand while preparing filling.

Banana Cream Pie

3 tbspns (60 g/2¼ oz) butter
170 g (5½ oz) ginger biscuits, crushed
3 bananas
finely grated rind and juice of 1 large lemon
410 g (13 oz) can sweetened condensed milk
2 tspns gelatine
2 tbspns cocoa
⅓ cup (60 g/2 oz) cooking chocolate chips
1–2 tbspns milk (if needed)

SERVES 6–8

Melt butter in a 20–23 cm (8–9 in) microwave-safe pie or flan dish on HIGH (100%) for 1 minute. Stir in crushed biscuits. Press the mixture into the base and sides of the dish. Chill while filling is being prepared.

Thinly slice two of the bananas into a medium-sized microwave-safe dish and sprinkle with all but 1 tablespoon of the lemon juice and rind. Add two-thirds of the condensed milk and all the gelatine. Cook on DEFROST (30%) for 10 minutes, stirring well after 3 and 6 minutes. Spread banana mixture over biscuit base. Return to refrigerator while topping is being made.

Combine remaining condensed milk with the cocoa in a medium-sized microwave-safe bowl. Cook on HIGH for 1 minute. Stir in chocolate chips, until chocolate melts. If mixture gets too thick, add the milk a little at a time to make a soft icing. Spread chocolate icing over banana mixture in flan case. Chill until set.

Just before serving, decorate with slices of remaining banana tossed in remaining lemon juice. Serve cold.

Lemon Meringue Pie

CRUST
⅓ cup (90 g/3 oz) butter or margarine
1¼ cups (45 g/1½ oz) cornflake crumbs
2 tbspns sugar

FILLING
juice and grated rind of 2 lemons
⅔ cup (180 ml/6 fl oz) water
½ cup (125 g/4 oz) sugar
2 tbspns plain flour
3 egg yolks

MERINGUE
3 egg whites
½ cup (125 g/4 oz) sugar

SERVES 6–8

Melt: butter in a 23 cm (9 in) microwave-safe pie plate on HIGH (100%) for 1½ minutes. Add crumbs and sugar and stir to combine thoroughly. With the back of a spoon, press mixture against the base and sides of plate, making an even crust. Cook about 2½ minutes on HIGH or until firm, turning plate at least once during cooking. Cool.

To prepare filling: Combine a little grated lemon rind with lemon juice and add other ingredients in a medium-sized microwave-safe glass bowl. Mix with a small wire whisk. Cook, uncovered, on HIGH for 3 minutes or until thickened, beating with a small whisk at regular intervals, particularly as mixture begins to thicken. When filling is cool, pour into crumb crust.

To prepare meringue: Beat egg whites until stiff but not dry. Gradually beat in sugar, about 2 tablespoons at a time, and continue to beat until sugar is almost dissolved and mixture is stiff and glossy.

Pile meringue onto filling in crumb case and spread to edges of pie so that meringue touches the edge of the crust. Cook 3 minutes on HIGH, turning plate each time you notice meringue cooking (and swelling) unevenly.

Chill before serving or crumb crust will not set. (See photo pages 164–165.)

VARIATION A precooked pastry shell may be used in place of the crumb crust.

Maple Pumpkin Pie

PASTRY

2½ cups (315 g/10 oz) plain flour
¼ cup (30 g/1 oz) toasted coconut
1 tbspn caster sugar
155 g (5 oz) butter, cubed
¼–⅓ cup (60–90 ml/2–3 fl oz) water

FILLING

750 g (1½ lb) pumpkin, seeded, peeled and cubed
1 cup (250 ml/8 fl oz) milk
2 eggs
½ cup (185 ml/6 fl oz) maple or golden syrup
¼ cup (30 g/1 oz) plain flour
1 tspn cinnamon
½ tspn ground ginger
½ tspn nutmeg

TOPPING

extra nutmeg

SERVES 6–8

Process flour, coconut and caster sugar with butter until mixture resembles breadcrumbs. Mix in water, then knead lightly. Wrap and chill for 15 minutes.

Place pumpkin into a microwave-safe bowl and cook on HIGH (100%) for 10–12 minutes or until tender. Blend or process until smooth. Mix in milk, eggs, maple or golden syrup, flour and spices until well combined.

Roll out pastry to cover a 25 cm (10 in) microwave-safe pie dish. Prick pastry with a fork. Cook on HIGH for 4 minutes.

Pour the pumpkin filling into the pastry. Sprinkle top of pie with extra nutmeg. Cook on MEDIUM HIGH (70%) for 10–12 minutes or until set.

Serve hot or cold.

Pavlova

A microwaved pavlova doesn't have the same crisp crust as the conventionally baked pavlova. However, the time saving is remarkable. For those who prefer a firmer surface on their pavlova, one minute under a heated grill (with moderate rather than full heat) will help to achieve it.

4 × 60 g egg whites
¾ cup (165 g/5½ oz) sugar
1 tspn vinegar
1 tspn vanilla essence
whipped cream
fresh or canned fruit

SERVES 6–8

Beat egg whites until stiff but not dry. Add sugar gradually, beating after each addition. Carefully fold in vinegar and vanilla and turn mixture out onto a microwave-safe tray lined with baking paper. Form into a circle approximately 23 cm (9 in) in diameter, drawing up the sides of the mixture a little to leave a recess in the centre after cooking. Cook on HIGH (100%) for 2–2½ minutes. Leave undisturbed in the microwave for 10–15 minutes with the door open.

Place on serving plate and decorate with whipped cream and fruit.

Strawberries, kiwi fruit and passionfruit are ideal toppings as their pleasant tartness is a very acceptable contrast to the sweet pavlova. For chocolate-lovers, any fruit topping will be enhanced with the addition of melted chocolate drizzled over the dessert and refrigerated briefly before serving. (See photo pages 82–83.)

Scones, Cakes, Biscuits and Sweets

SCONES AND BREADS

Yeast breads are a little disappointing when cooked in a microwave oven. Of course a combination oven (or convection-microwave) will handle the mixture with no problems. Scone or damper-type mixtures are acceptable, though not of the standard of those cooked in a conventional oven. A browning dish is really essential if you plan to make scones. They don't look very exciting at first sight, but when halved and topped with your favourite conserve and cream, you may not notice the difference!

Many types of cake cook well by microwave but you must not expect to obtain the same results with all your favourite recipes as you do when they are cooked conventionally. As a general rule, the best results are from quickly mixed ingredients rather than the traditional creamed butter and sugar varieties. Melted shortening and brief stirring of ingredients seem to mark the success of many mixtures. However, the addition of moisture-retaining ingredients such as grated apple, carrot and zucchini in combination with oil in place of butter or margarine, produces some really good, moist cakes. Cakes with sour cream as an ingredient also seem to fare well.

Many cakes rise more than when cooked conventionally, so it's wise to use a cake pan a little larger than you would normally use.

A QUESTION OF TURN-OUT

To grease or not to grease is a point in question. Some special microwave pans release cakes with

● *Previous pages, top shelf from left:* Banana Maple Cake (page 196); Festive Chocolate Gateau (page 204); Black Forest Cake (page 204); Spiced Walnut Loaf (page 198); *bottom shelf from left:* Lamingtons (page 200); Pineapple Coconut Sponge (page 201); Cherry Cake (page 203); Gingerbread Ring (page 196)

ease but many need greasing. The ideal pan for most cakes with a relatively light mixture is ring-shaped. This allows more even penetration of microwaves and, naturally, more even cooking. If you do not have one of these, substitute a round, microwave-safe dish or casserole and place a straight-sided glass in the centre to take the place of the tube in the special microwave pan. You may like to line the pan with special baking paper to ensure easier turning out — cutting out the centre of the paper for the 'tube'.

ADD AN INTERESTING TEXTURE

Another method for assisting the turning-out of cakes is to grease the pan and sprinkle with fairly finely chopped nuts or toasted breadcrumbs. Use medium rather than very fine crumbs. This will help to give a little colour and texture as well as flavour to the cake.

Most cakes are cooked on HIGH (100%) power, others give better results when started on 100% and then reduced to MEDIUM HIGH (70%). Some recipes for heavy fruit cakes cook for approximately half their cooking time on MEDIUM (50%) and the remainder on DEFROST (30%) power.

ALUMINIUM FOIL AS A SHIELD

When cooking the heavy fruit cakes referred to above, it is wise to shield the edges of the cake to prevent them overcooking. Take a strip of aluminium foil about 8 cm (3 in) wide and long enough to encircle the pan and form a collar around the container, extending 1–2 cm (½–¾ in) above the pan. Turn this section over to hold the foil in place — or tie it in place with string. Foil must never touch the walls of the oven. Leave the foil in place for approximately half of the cooking time. Cakes of this type are usually cooked for half of their time on MEDIUM (50%) and the remainder on DEFROST (30%).

ELEVATING THE PAN

When baking cakes, always elevate the pan — use a microwave rack specially designed for this purpose, or even an upturned cereal bowl or something similar. This allows the mixture to be exposed to more microwave action than when closer to the oven floor. If you notice a cake rising unevenly, give the pan a quarter turn or reposition it in the oven.

THE COSMETIC TOUCH

You will very likely be disappointed with the pale colour of a favourite cake when first cooked by microwave. The addition of a few drops of yellow food colouring or parisian essence will improve the cake's appearance. For a 2-cups-of-flour (250 g/8 oz) mixture add about 4–6 drops of colouring or 4 drops of essence for your first venture and alter the quantities for future mixtures to suit your taste.

IS THE CAKE REALLY COOKED?

New microwave cooks are often uncertain about whether or not the cake is cooked. This is mainly because the lack of dry heat in the oven leaves the surface of the cake more moist than if cooked in a conventional oven. However, when tested with a wooden cocktail stick the centre of the cake may in fact be cooked. Always take the cake from the oven at this stage and cover loosely with plastic wrap or a tea-towel for 4–5 minutes. Uncover and leave for several minutes before turning out. A transparent cake pan sometimes gives a better idea of whether or not a cake is cooked. Hold it up and look underneath. If you see obviously uncooked mixture in the base, put the cake back for a further minute or two in the oven.

If you don't plan to ice the cake, its appearance will be improved by topping it either before or after cooking with grated chocolate, toasted coconut, a sprinkling of spices or chopped nuts.

BISCUITS AND SLICES

Biscuits and slices cook well by microwave; however, fairly dry mixtures are the most successful. Cook only about 6 biscuits at a time, well spaced around the oven tray, and be on the lookout for the appearance of brown spots on the biscuits — they represent overcooking. A high concentration of sugar and the presence of chocolate pieces and dried fruits help generate excessive heat.

When cooking slices, shield the corners of the baking pan with strips of foil to prevent these areas from overcooking. Remove foil after half the cooking time. Lining the pan with baking paper will assist in the removal of the slices after cooking. When using slice recipes with packaged cereals and coconut among the ingredients, always press the dough down firmly before cooking, otherwise they tend to crumble when cut.

CONFECTIONERY

Some kinds of confectionery can be cooked with great success in the microwave oven. Those items that require the melting of chocolate are handled with ease though it must be remembered that chocolate may be quite soft but still retain its shape when heated by microwave. Regular stirring will save it from overheating and spoiling. (It is important to note that it can be quite dangerous to attempt to cook certain confectionery items such as toffee which are cooked at exceedingly high temperatures. Glass or ceramic oven trays may shatter in these conditions, and cooking containers become extremely hot to handle.)

When handling any confectionery items in the making, always remember to handle cooking containers with care.

Scones

Scone dough, like other bread mixtures, does not brown when cooked by microwave. Solve the problem by using a browning dish. The scones will not look like conventionally cooked scones, but when broken apart and spread with jam and cream, who will notice! The use of a browning dish gives a crisp crust to plain scones, though the ingredients in pumpkin scones results in a softer crust, whether cooked conventionally or by microwave.

2½ cups (310 g/10 oz) self-raising flour
½ tspn salt
3 tbspns (60 g/2oz) butter
1½ cups (375 ml/12 fl oz) milk
melted butter

MAKES 12

Sift flour and salt, rub in butter and mix to a soft dough with milk. Do not handle dough any more than is necessary to form a reasonably smooth mixture. Press out or roll on a floured surface to a thickness of about 2 cm (¾ in). Cut into 12 rounds and glaze tops with melted butter.

Preheat a microwave-safe browning dish on HIGH for 6 minutes. Quickly add six scones, buttered side down, evenly spaced around the dish and cook on HIGH (100%) for 2 minutes. Quickly brush tops of scones with melted butter and invert. Cook on HIGH for ½–1 minute. Wipe out browning dish with crumpled kitchen paper towel and reheat for 4 minutes before cooking second batch of scones.

Serve while still warm. (See photo page 199.)

Pumpkin Scones

2 tbspns (40 g/1½ oz) butter or margarine
½ cup (125 g/4 oz) caster sugar
1 egg
1 cup cooked, mashed pumpkin
½ cup (125 ml/4 fl oz) milk
3 cups (375 g/12 oz) self-raising flour
½ tspn salt
2 tspns cream of tartar
¾ cup (125 g/4 oz) mixed dried fruit

MAKES 15-20

Cream butter and sugar, add egg and beat to combine. Stir in pumpkin evenly. Add milk then flour sifted with salt and cream of tartar. Fold in fruit. Turn onto a floured surface and knead lightly. Press out to about 2 cm (¾ in) thickness. Cut into rounds.

Heat a microwave-safe browning dish for 5–6 minutes. Brush tops of six scones with melted butter and invert onto hot browning dish. Cook on HIGH (100%) for 2 minutes. Quickly brush tops with melted butter and turn over. Cook a further 30–60 seconds and remove. Repeat with remaining scones.

Pumpkin scones are usually served buttered. However, a spread of redcurrant jelly and a dab of whipped cream goes down well.

Herb Scone Ring

2½ cups (310 g/10 oz) self-raising flour
½ tspn salt (or to taste)
3 tbspns (60 g/2 oz) butter
1–1½ cups (250–375 ml/8–12 fl oz) milk
freshly ground pepper to taste
2 tbspns chopped fresh herbs, including chives
if possible
1 tbspn (20 g/¾ oz) melted butter

SERVES 6-8

Grease a 20 cm (8 in) microwave-safe ring mould. Sift flour with salt into a bowl. Rub in butter and mix to a soft dough with milk, pepper and herbs. With floured hands, roll portions of dough into balls and spread evenly around the ring mould. Glaze with melted butter. Cook on MEDIUM (50%) for 10–12 minutes. Scone ring is cooked when tapping the surface gives a hollow sound. Let stand for 2–3 minutes. (See photo page 199.)

Bacon and Cheese Muffins

1 cup (125 g/4 oz) self-raising flour
1 tbspn sugar
1½ tspns baking powder
½ tspn paprika
½ cup (60 g/2 oz) grated Cheddar cheese
2 bacon rashers, chopped and cooked until crisp
¼ green capsicum, finely chopped
3 spring onions, chopped
½ cup (125 ml/4 fl oz) milk
⅓ cup (90 ml/3 fl oz) cooking oil
1 egg

MAKES APPROXIMATELY 12 MUFFINS

*P*lace all ingredients in a large mixing bowl. Mix together quickly with a wooden spoon until mixture is well combined.

Place spoonfuls of the mixture into a well-greased muffin pan or paper patty cases set around outside of turntable. Cook six muffins at a time. Cook on HIGH (100%) for 2½–3 minutes, until well risen and spongy to touch. Cook remaining batter in the same way. Serve buttered.

Store left-over icing in a covered microwave-safe cup or small basin in refrigerator. When required, heat on MEDIUM (50%) for a few seconds — take care not to overdo it — the high sugar content ensures speedy melting.

Gingerbread Ring

When cooking cakes, use either a ring dish, which helps to cook the cake evenly as it has no centre to cook, or use a round container that has a collar of aluminium foil around it. This helps to slow down the cooking, thus allowing the centre to cook. (See Aluminium Foil as a Shield, page 193.)

2 tspns cinnamon
2¼ cups (280 g/9 oz) self-raising flour, sifted
1½ tspns baking powder
¼ tspn ground cloves
1 tbspn chopped ginger
½ cup (125 g/4 oz) butter or margarine
½ cup (90 g/3 oz) firmly packed brown sugar
½ cup (125 g/4 oz) caster sugar
2 eggs
1 cup (250 ml/8 fl oz) buttermilk
1 cup (185 g/6 oz) raisins

1 tbspn grated orange rind
⅓ cup (60 g/2 oz) glacé ginger, chopped
1 tbspn icing sugar, sifted

SERVES 4

*G*rease an 8 cup (2 1/2 qt) microwave-safe ring dish and sprinkle with half the cinnamon. Sift flour with baking powder, remainder of cinnamon, cloves and ginger.

Cream the butter or margarine and sugars until light and fluffy. Add the flour mixture, eggs, buttermilk, raisins and orange rind. Pour into the prepared dish and cook on MEDIUM HIGH (70%) for 13–15 minutes or until cooked. Allow to stand for 20 minutes, then turn out.

Decorate with glacé ginger and dust with icing sugar. (See photo pages 190–191.)

Banana Maple Cake

Like apples, using bananas in microwave cake mixtures adds moisture which doesn't evaporate, making the cake remain moist and well textured.

2 eggs
⅓ cup (60 g/2 oz) brown sugar
100 g (3½ oz) butter or margarine, cubed
2 ripe bananas
⅓ cup (90 ml/3 fl oz) maple-flavoured syrup
¼ tspn bicarbonate of soda
1½ cups (185 g/6 oz) self-raising flour
1 tspn parisian essence
GLAZE
1 cup (155 g/5 oz) icing sugar
1 tspn cocoa
¼ cup (60 ml/2 fl oz) maple-flavoured syrup
1–2 tspns water
DECORATION
chopped walnuts (optional)

SERVES 4

*U*sing the chopping blade of a food processor or electric mixer, process eggs and sugar for 1 minute. With the motor still running, add the butter or margarine. Peel the bananas and drop them into the feed tube with the motor still running. Process until completely smooth. Add the syrup, bicarbonate of soda and flour in one pour (this is easier if flour is measured onto a sheet of paper). As soon as the flour is added, turn the motor off and scrape down the sides of the bowl. Pulse once or twice to complete mixing.

Pour batter into a 23 cm (9 in) microwave-safe ring dish. Elevate the dish from the oven floor and cook on MEDIUM (50%) for 8–9 minutes or until cooked. When cooked, stand for 5 minutes, loosely covered, then turn out and allow to cool thoroughly.

To prepare glaze: Using chopping blade of a food processor or electric mixer, process icing sugar and cocoa until mixed. With the motor running, gradually add maple syrup, stopping when the glaze reaches a flowing consistency. If necessary, add water. Pour over the top of the cake, allowing it to flow down the sides.

Decorate top with chopped walnuts if desired. (See photo pages 190–191.)

Date and Apple Dessert Cake

1 large cooking apple, coarsely grated
1¼ cups (200 g/6½ oz) finely chopped pitted dates
½ cup (125 g/4 oz) butter or margarine, chopped
1 cup (250 ml/8 fl oz) very hot water
1 tspn bicarbonate of soda
1 cup (220 g/7 oz) caster sugar
1 large egg
1 tspn vanilla essence
1½ cups (185 g/6 oz) plain flour
1 tspn baking powder
¼ tspn salt (optional)

SERVES 4

Place grated apple, dates, butter or margarine and water in a microwave-safe large mixing bowl and heat on HIGH (100%) for 1 minute. Quickly stir the soda and sugar through and set aside until well cooled but not cold.

Break in the egg, add vanilla essence and whisk well. Sift the flour, baking powder and salt over the mixture and mix well. Do not overmix.

Turn into a greased, large microwave-safe ring pan. Place on a rack in the microwave and cook for 7–8 minutes on MEDIUM HIGH (70%). Increase to HIGH and cook a further 3–4 minutes. Allow to stand for 10 minutes, then turn onto a cake rack to cool.

VARIATIONS

• Serve warm as a dessert with custard.
• Scatter ½ cup (60 g/2 oz) chopped nuts over base of greased microwave-safe ring pan before adding the mixture.
• Replace vanilla with 1–2 tspns grated lemon or orange rind, or add 1 tspn mixed spice.

Boiled Fruit Cake

1¼ cups (315 ml/10 fl oz) water
1¼ cups (185 g/6 oz) butter or margarine
1 cup (185 g/6 oz) dark-brown sugar
500 g (1 lb) mixed fruit
1 tspn cinnamon
¼ tspn allspice
½ tspn ground cloves
2¼ cups (280 g/9 oz) plain flour
2 tspns baking powder
½ tspn bicarbonate soda
2 eggs, beaten

SERVES 4

In a large microwave-safe glass bowl or casserole place water, butter or margarine, brown sugar, mixed fruit and spices. Stir to mix well. Cook on HIGH (100%) for 6–8 minutes or until bubbling. Stir several times during cooking. Allow to cool for about 10–15 minutes.

Sift the dry ingredients together and quickly stir through batter. Stir in the eggs and mix well. Pour into a lightly greased 25 cm (10 in) microwave-safe ring dish. Cook elevated (see Elevating the Pan, page 194) on MEDIUM (50%) 13–16 minutes or until tested with a toothpick or skewer. Allow to stand, covered with a piece of paper towel, for about 10 minutes.

Turn out and allow to cool, covered loosely with plastic wrap or a clean tea-towel.

Spiced Walnut Loaf

2 cups (250 g/8 oz) plain flour
2 tspns baking powder
½ tspn bicarbonate of soda
½ tspn nutmeg
½ tspn cinnamon
2 eggs
½ cup (125 ml/4 fl oz) milk
1 cup (220 g/7 oz) raw sugar
1 cup cooked and mashed pumpkin
3 tbspns (60 g/2 oz) butter, melted
1 cup (125 g/4 oz) walnuts, roughly chopped
LEMON BUTTER ICING
1 cup (140 g/4½ oz) icing sugar, sifted
1 tbspn (20 g/¾ oz) butter
1 tbspn lemon juice
DECORATION
1 tbspn chopped mixed peel (optional)

Sift the flour, baking powder, bicarbonate of soda, nutmeg and cinnamon into a large mixing bowl. Make a well in the centre and add the eggs, milk, sugar, mashed pumpkin and melted butter. Mix well until all ingredients are thoroughly combined. Stir in the walnuts.

Pour mixture into a well-greased 25 × 11 cm (10 × 4 in) microwave-safe loaf pan. Shield the ends of the loaf pan with 3 cm (1¼ in) pieces of aluminium foil. Cook on MEDIUM (50%) for 5 minutes. Remove the aluminium foil and continue cooking on MEDIUM HIGH (70%) for 5–7 minutes until cooked through and spongy to touch.

Allow to cool in pan for 5 minutes before turning out onto a wire rack to completely cool.

To prepare icing: Place icing sugar in a microwave-safe bowl. Heat butter and lemon juice on MEDIUM (50%) only until butter melts. Stir into icing sugar until of spreading consistency. Ice cake quickly since icing begins to set as it cools.

Top with mixed peel if desired.(See photo pages 190–191.)

Fruit and Nut Teabread

Serve this delicious cake for afternoon tea.

CAKE
2 tbspns (45 g/1½ oz) butter or margarine
½ cup (90 g/3 oz) brown sugar
1 large egg, beaten
1 cup (155 g/5 oz) seedless raisins
½ cup (60 g/2 oz) almonds or walnuts, roughly chopped
1½ cups (185 g/6 oz) plain flour, sifted
¼ tspn vanilla essence
½ tspn cinnamon
1 tspn baking powder
¾ cup (185 ml/6 fl oz) boiling water
LEMON GLACÉ ICING
1 cup (140 g/4½ oz) icing sugar
1 tbspn lemon juice
DECORATION
chopped walnuts

SERVES 4

Place all ingredients for cake into a large mixing bowl, then beat with a wooden spoon for 2–3 minutes or with an electric mixer for 1–2 minutes.

Spoon mixture into a well-greased, large microwave-safe, round baking dish or ring. Cook for 4–6 minutes on HIGH (100%). The top should feel soft and slightly sticky, but if the teabread is left to stand for 5 minutes the top will become firm. Turn cake out onto a wire rack to cool.

To prepare icing: Sift icing sugar into a bowl, add lemon juice and stir well. The icing should have the consistency of thick treacle. If too thick add a few more drops of lemon juice. Heat icing in microwave on DEFROST (30%) for a few seconds and while still easy to spread, ice teabread.

Decorate with chopped walnuts.

● *Clockwise from top:* Sponge Cake (page 200); Fruit and Sherry Shortcake (page 206); Herb Scone Ring (page 195); Meringues (page 208); Scones (page 195); Fruit and Nut Teabread

Sponge Cake

This sponge makes no claim to superiority over a conventionally baked cake. Its appearance on removal from the microwave oven is not encouraging; however, with a careful coating of icing or a thick layer of whipped cream topped with strawberries it makes a very acceptable afternoon tea offering.

You will need a large container to hold the mixture — it rises considerably during cooking, but it sinks just as dramatically by the time cooking is completed. It is essential to line the container with microwave-safe plastic wrap. After standing, the over-hanging wrap is used to remove the cake from the dish. A large microwave-safe tube pan is a very good container for even cooking (though not so easily lined with the wrap) and provides a shape for easier cutting than a regular pan. The sponge should be eaten the day it is made.

⅓ cup (75 g/2½ oz) caster sugar
3 large eggs at room temperature
½ cup (60 g/2 oz) plain flour, sifted twice

SERVES 4

Line a 2.5 l (2½ qt) microwave-safe cake dish, either round or tube-shaped (a large gugelhopf dish is ideal) with microwave-safe plastic wrap.

Place sugar in a non-metal electric mixer bowl and warm for 2 minutes on DEFROST (30%). Add eggs and beat on electric mixer until the mixture bulks considerably (it almost fills the small bowl of the mixer) and has the consistency of thick whipped cream. Its colour at this stage is very pale.

Fold in flour with a large metal spoon, cutting and lifting the mixture over and over until combined. Spoon into prepared dish and cook uncovered on HIGH (100%) for 4–5 minutes. Remove from oven and stand 10 minutes. Lift from dish holding the plastic wrap and transfer to a cake cooler. When quite cold peel away the wrap and decorate with desired icing or whipped cream and fruit. (See photo page 199.)

VARIATION For a simple icing, melt 2 tablespoons (45 g/1½ oz) of butter in a microwave-safe bowl on HIGH. Add 1⅓ cups (220 g/7 oz) sifted icing sugar and 1½ tablespoons lime or lemon juice. Stir well and use to cover the cake. Decorate with mint leaves.

Lamingtons

Use a packet cake mix for the sponge base for lamingtons. The cake needs to be firm enough to be cut, handled and coated with icing. Home-made microwave cakes are a little too soft to hold the icing and do not seem to rise as much in a microwave-safe lamington pan.

1 pkt sponge cake mix
2 eggs
2 tbspns cooking oil
ICING
4 cups (500 g/1 lb) icing sugar, sifted
⅓ cup (45 g/1½ oz) cocoa
1 tbspn (20 g/¾ oz) butter
½ cup (125 ml/4 fl oz) boiling water, plus
approximately 2–3 tbspns
1½ cups (140 g/4½ oz) desiccated coconut

MAKES 18 CAKES

Make up cake mix according to the instructions on the packet. Use the two eggs and cooking oil at the beginning of the beating stage. (The extra egg helps beat more air into the mixture, while the addition of the cooking oil gives a better sponge texture.)

Beat cake mix, using an electric mixer on low speed, for 1 minute, then increase speed to high. Beat mixture until smooth, light and creamy.

Pour cake mix into a well-greased ovenproof lamington tray. Cook on HIGH (100%) for 7 minutes. Check cake after 5 minutes and, if necessary, cover corners with aluminium foil to prevent overcooking.

Allow cake to stand in cooking tray for 5 minutes before turning out to cool. When cool, cut into squares.

Sift icing sugar into a large mixing bowl.

Place cocoa and butter into a small microwave-safe bowl. Pour over ¼ cup of boiling water and stir until butter has melted and cocoa is well blended. Add cocoa mixture to icing sugar and stir gently, adding sufficient boiling water to make a smooth icing.

Pierce squares of cake with a fork. Dip cake into chocolate icing, then toss it in the coconut. Leave for 1–2 hours before serving. (See photo pages 190–191.)

Pineapple Coconut Sponge

CAKE
1 3/4 cups (220 g/7 oz) self-raising flour, sifted
1 1/4 cups (250 g/8 oz) caster sugar
1 tspn baking powder
3 eggs
3/4 cup (185 ml/6 fl oz) milk
425 g (13 1/2 oz) can crushed pineapple, drained
1/3 cup (90 ml/3 fl oz) vegetable oil
1 tspn vanilla essence
1 cup (60 g/2 oz) shredded coconut

TOPPING
1 cup (60 g/2 oz) shredded coconut

FROSTING
2 tbspns (45 g/1 1/2 oz) butter or margarine, softened
3 cups (500 g/1 lb) icing sugar, sifted
1–2 tbspns coconut liqueur or white rum or milk
1 tspn vanilla essence

DECORATION
strips of orange rind
orange segments

MAKES TWO 20 CM (8 IN) CAKES

Line the base and sides of two 20 cm (8 in) microwave-safe cake pans with greased greaseproof paper or baking paper.

Place flour, sugar, baking powder, eggs, milk, pineapple, oil and vanilla essence into a large mixing bowl. Beat well for 3–4 minutes until thoroughly combined. Gently stir in coconut.

Divide the cake mixture between the two prepared cake pans. Cook each cake separately on an elevated rack on MEDIUM (50%) for 6 minutes, then increase power to HIGH (100%) and cook for 3–4 minutes, until top springs back when lightly touched and no unbaked batter remains.

Allow to stand for 5 minutes. Repeat cooking procedure for remaining cake.

To prepare topping: Spread the shredded coconut onto an microwave-safe plate. Cook on HIGH for 2–3 minutes, stirring two or three times during cooking, until lightly brown and toasted.

To prepare frosting: Combine softened butter, icing sugar, coconut liqueur, or rum or milk, and vanilla essence in a large mixing bowl until smooth and of a spreading consistency.

Ice top of cooled cakes with frosting. Finish each with a topping of toasted coconut decorated with orange rind and segments. (See photo pages 190–191.)

NOTE Take care when removing lining paper from microwaved cakes. Pull back paper, holding it close to the base of the cake to prevent mixture sticking.

German Upside–down Cake

This is a real family favourite. When allowed to cool, the liquid from the base seeps into the sponge, giving a delicious fudge-like texture.

BASE

2 tbspns (45 g/1½ oz) butter or margarine
½ cup (90 g/3 oz) brown sugar
½ cup (60 g/2 oz) chopped pecan nuts or walnuts
½ cup (20 g/¾ oz) shredded coconut
¼ cup (60 ml/2 fl oz) milk

CAKE

100 g (3½ oz) chocolate
2 tbspns (45 g/1½ oz) butter or margarine
1¼ cups (155 g/5 oz) plain flour
1¼ cups (250 g/8 oz) sugar
¼ tspn bicarbonate of soda
½ tspn baking powder
1 tspn vanilla essence
2 eggs
¾ cup (185 ml/6 fl oz) natural yoghurt

SERVES 6

*P*lace the butter or margarine and sugar for base in a medium-sized microwave-safe bowl and cook on HIGH (100%) for 2–2½ minutes, until bubbly. Stir well, then stir in the pecans or walnuts, coconut and milk. Pour into a 20 cm (8 in) microwave-safe ring dish and set aside.

To prepare cake: Melt the chocolate and butter, or margarine, together in a large microwave-safe bowl, on MEDIUM (50%) for 3 minutes. Stir in remaining cake ingredients, then, using an electric mixer, beat batter for 2 minutes until smooth.

Spoon or pour mixture over base in ring dish. Cook on HIGH for 7–9 minutes, until cooked through.

Allow to stand for 5 minutes before turning out to serve. Serve with whipped cream, chopped nuts and cocoa.

Cherry Cake

1⅔ cups (200 g/6½ oz) plain flour
1 cup (185 g/6 oz) dark-brown sugar
¼ cup (30 g/1 oz) cocoa, sifted
1 tspn bicarbonate soda
⅓ cup (45 g/1½ oz) chopped pecans or walnuts
¾ cup (125 g/4 oz) maraschino cherries, drained and chopped (reserve syrup)

⅓ cup (90 ml/3 fl oz) vegetable oil
1 tspn vinegar
½ tspn vanilla essence

ICING

¼ cup (60 g/2 oz) sugar
2 tbspns liquid glucose (or Karo light corn syrup)
1 tbspn water
1 egg white
½ tspn vanilla essence
few drops red food colouring
¼ tspn cherry liqueur (optional)

SERVES 8

*I*n a bowl, mix the flour, sugar, cocoa, soda and pecans or walnuts with a fork. Pour reserved cherry syrup into a measuring cup and add enough water to measure 1 cup. Stir into flour mixture with the remaining cake ingredients. Pour into a lightly greased 21–23 cm (8–9 in) microwave-safe cake dish. Cook elevated on MEDIUM (50%) for 14–16 minutes or until the sides come away (centre may appear to be a little moist). Cover the cake with a piece of paper towel and allow to stand for about 6–8 minutes. Turn out the cake, cover loosely with plastic wrap or a clean tea-towel and allow to cool completely.

To prepare icing: Combine sugar, glucose and water in a microwave-safe bowl. Cook on HIGH (100%) for 1–2 minutes, or until the mixture comes to the boil. Beat egg white in a separate bowl until soft peaks form. Pour hot syrup in a thin stream slowly over the egg white, beating constantly on medium speed on an electric mixer. Add the remaining ingredients and beat on high speed until stiff peaks form. Spread icing on top of cake. (See photo pages 190–191.)

● German Upside-down Cake

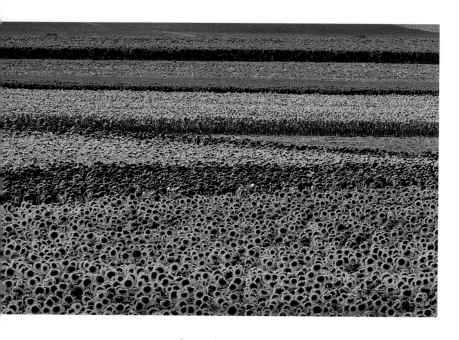

Black Forest Cake

CAKE
⅓ cup (90 g/3 oz) butter
150 g (5 oz) cooking or plain chocolate
2 cups (250 g/8 oz) plain flour
2 cups (440 g/14 oz) sugar
¼ tspn bicarbonate of soda
¾ tspn baking powder
1½ tspns vanilla essence
3 eggs
1¼ cups (310 ml/10 fl oz) buttermilk or ordinary milk
CREAM
300 ml carton thickened cream
2 tbspns kirsch
CHERRIES
425 g (13½ oz) can black cherries plus juice
2 tspns arrowroot
TOPPING
150 g (5 oz) plain chocolate
10–12 fresh cherries on stems
sifted cocoa

SERVES 6–8

Melt the butter and chocolate in a large microwave-safe mixing bowl on MEDIUM (50%) for 3–4 minutes. Stir well until chocolate is thoroughly melted. Add remaining cake ingredients and beat well with a fork or electric beater on low speed until batter is smooth.

Pour half of cake mixture into a 20–22 cm (8–9 in) well-greased microwave-safe cake pan. Bake on an elevated cooking rack or upturned saucer on HIGH (100%) for 5–6 minutes. Allow to stand in cake pan for 5 minutes before turning out onto a wire rack to cool. Cook remaining cake mixture in same way.

Whisk the cream until stiff and it forms soft peaks. Whisk in the kirsch.

Drain the cherries. Set the fruit aside and make liquid up to ½ cup with water. Stir in the arrowroot. Pour into a small microwave-safe bowl. Heat on HIGH for 2 minutes, stirring well after 1 minute, until liquid comes to the boil and thickens. Stir in the cherries and set aside to cool.

Grate the chocolate on a cheese grater. Put in refrigerator to keep cool.

When cakes and cherries are cool, slice both cakes in half horizontally. Place one layer of cake onto a serving plate. Spread cake with one-third of the cherry mixture, then 2–3 tablespoons of the whipped cream.

Cover with the second layer of cake. Repeat cherry, cream and cake layers twice more. Place remaining layer of cake on top. Cover sides and top with remaining cream. Decorate sides and top with grated chocolate. Decorate top with fresh cherries and a dusting of cocoa. (See photo pages 190–191.)

Festive Chocolate Gateau

CAKE
⅓ cup (90 g/3 oz) margarine or butter
80 g (2½ oz) cooking chocolate
2 cups (250 g/8 oz) plain flour, sifted
1 cup (220 g/7 oz) caster sugar
1 tspn baking powder
½ tspn bicarbonate of soda
⅓ cup (90 ml/3 fl oz) water, boiling
⅓ cup (90 ml/3 fl oz) natural yoghurt or sour cream
3 eggs, beaten
FILLING
100 g (3½ oz) cooking chocolate
2 tspns butter
¼ cup (30 g/1 oz) icing sugar
2 tbspns evaporated milk
1 tspn vanilla essence
ICING
200 g (6½ oz) cooking chocolate
¼ cup (30 g/1 oz) cocoa
DECORATION
chocolate curls (see recipe on page 168)

SERVES 6

Heat margarine or butter and cooking chocolate in a small microwave-safe bowl on DEFROST (30%) for 2–3 minutes or until melted, stirring several times. Meanwhile sift flour into a large mixing bowl, add remaining ingredients, plus melted chocolate mixture. Beat with an electric mixer for 3–4 minutes, until well combined.

Pour mixture into a deep well-greased 23 cm (9 in) microwave-safe cake pan. Cook on MEDIUM HIGH (70%) for 10–12 minutes, shielding edges if necessary after 6–8 minutes if edges appear to be overcooking or drying out. Test to see if cake is cooked by inserting a wooden cocktail stick into the centre. It should come out clean. Allow cake to stand in pan for 5–10 minutes before turning out to cool on a wire rack.

When cool, slice horizontally in half.

To prepare filling: Heat chocolate and butter in a medium-sized microwave-safe bowl on DEFROST for 3–4 minutes or until melted. Beat in remaining ingredients until smooth. Chill for 10 minutes, until thick enough to spread.

Use sandwich layers of cake together.

To prepare icing: Place chocolate and cocoa into a small bowl. Heat on DEFROST for 5 minutes stirring several times. If chocolate has not melted thoroughly replace in microwave and continue heating on DEFROST for 30 seconds. Stir well before using.

To assemble: Stand sandwiched cake on serving plate. Spread icing on top of cake and allow to drizzle down sides. Decorate top with chocolate curls. (See photo pages 190–191.)

Christmas Cake

Where possible, cook cakes in plastic containers. Cake mixtures tend to stick to china and glass dishes. One or two plastic cake pans made especially for microwave use will give the best possible results and represent a good investment. If buying two, make one a ring pan.

4½ cups (750 g/1½ lb) mixed dried fruit
¼ cup (60 ml/2 fl oz) brandy
½ cup (125 g/4 oz) butter
1 cup (155 g/5 oz) brown sugar
3 eggs
1 tspn vanilla essence
1 tbspn raspberry jam
1¼ cups (155 g/5 oz) plain flour
2 tspns cinnamon
1 tspn nutmeg
1 tspn mixed spice
1 tspn parisian essence
2 tbspns extra brandy
sifted icing sugar
morello cherries

SERVES 4

*G*rease and line, with a double thickness of baking paper, an 18 cm (7 in), round microwave-safe cake pan at least 7.5 cm (3 in) deep with the paper extending 5 cm (2 in) above the edge of the pan. To ensure the cake doesn't overcook around the outside, while the centre is still not cooked sufficiently, place a collar of aluminium foil around the outside of the dish extending 2 cm (¾ in) above the rim. Hold in place securely with adhesive tape. Soak dried fruit in brandy and set aside, stirring from time to time.

Cream butter and sugar, add eggs one at a time, beating after each addition. Stir in vanilla essence and raspberry jam. Sift dry ingredients and add alternately with fruit, soaked in brandy and parisian essence. Turn mixture into prepared dish and level the surface.

Cook on MEDIUM (50%) for 15 minutes. Remove foil. Reduce to LOW (10%) and cook a further 20 minutes. Fold paper collars down over the cake and cover with a sheet of aluminium foil. Stand for 15 minutes. With a skewer, pierce the cake surface in half a dozen places and spoon over the extra brandy. Re-cover with aluminium foil and then wrap in several layers of newspaper. If the cake pan is required, remove cake and wrap well until ready for cutting.

Serve dusted with icing sugar and decorated with morello cherries. (See photo pages 82–83.)

Fruit and Sherry Shortcake

1 cup (175 g/5½ oz) sultanas
¼ cup (45 g/1½ oz) chopped dates
¼ cup (60 ml/2 fl oz) sherry
⅓ cup (90 g/3 oz) butter
¼ cup (60 g/2 oz) raw sugar
1 egg
2 cups (250 g/8 oz) self-raising flour, sifted
2–3 tbspns milk
1½ cups stewed apples
1 tbspn mixed peel
1 tspn mixed spice
½ tspn ground ginger
¼ cup (30 g/1 oz) chopped walnuts
1 tbspn icing sugar, sifted
whipped cream or ice cream

SERVES 6

Put the sultanas, dates and sherry into a small microwave-safe bowl. Stand for 30 minutes. Meanwhile, cream the butter and sugar until light and fluffy. Beat in the egg, then gradually blend in the flour to form a stiff dough. Add milk and mix well.

Press two-thirds of this shortcake mixture into the base of a greased 20–23 cm (8–9 in) shallow microwave-safe cake pan.

Drain the excess syrup off the stewed apples and mix with sultanas, dates, sherry and peel. Spread over the shortcake. Lightly sprinkle with the mixed spice and ginger, then the walnuts. Crumble the remaining shortcake mix over the top.

Cook on MEDIUM HIGH (70%) for 10 minutes until shortcake is cooked and not doughy to touch. Dust top with icing sugar.

Serve hot with whipped cream or ice cream. (See photo page 199.)

Anzac Biscuits

½ cup (125 g/4 oz) butter or margarine
1 tbspn golden syrup
1 tspn bicarbonate of soda
2 tbspns water, boiling
1 cup (90 g/3 oz) quick-cook oats
1 cup (95 g/3 oz) desiccated coconut
1 cup (125 g/4 oz) plain flour, sifted
1 cup (220 g/7 oz) sugar

MAKES APPROXIMATELY 50 BISCUITS

Place butter or margarine and golden syrup into a small microwave-safe bowl. Heat on HIGH (100%) for 2 minutes, until butter melts. Meanwhile, blend bicarbonate of soda with the boiling water, stir into the melted butter mixture.

Mix all remaining ingredients in a large mixing bowl. Pour the melted butter mixture into a well made in the centre of the flour and mix to form a moist but stiff consistency, using a wooden spoon.

Cover a large round microwave-safe glass plate with baking paper. Drop teaspoons of the biscuit mixture onto it, placing the spoonfuls approximately 4 cm (1½ in) apart around the edge of the plate.

Put plate into microwave, cook on HIGH for 3–3½ minutes, until the biscuits are almost completely brown. The edges may still look pale.

Allow biscuits to cool in the oven for 2–3 minutes to firm up before removing to a wire rack to cool completely.

Repeat cooking procedure until all the mixture is used up.

Chocolate Nut Cookies

2 tbspns dark cooking-chocolate chips
2 tbspns (45 g/1½ oz) butter or margarine
½ cup (125 g/4 oz) raw sugar
1 egg, lightly beaten
1¼ cups (155 g/5 oz) self-raising flour, sifted
¼ cup (30 g/1 oz) finely chopped nuts
½ cup (60 g/2 oz) icing sugar, sifted

MAKES APPROXIMATELY 20 COOKIES

Melt chocolate and butter or margarine together in a medium-sized bowl in the microwave on HIGH (100%) for 1 minute. Beat well until smooth. Beat in sugar and egg, then stir in sifted flour and nuts. Knead mixture to form a smooth dough. Chill for 15 minutes.

Divide mixture into approximately 20 small balls. Toss each in a little icing sugar. Flatten slightly and arrange 10 of the balls around the outer edge of a microwave-safe baking tray or large plate, covered with a sheet of baking paper. Cook on MEDIUM (50%) for 4 minutes. Leave to stand on plate for 5 minutes before transferring to a wire rack to cool. Repeat process with remaining 10 uncooked biscuits. Sift a little icing sugar over cookies before serving.

● *Clockwise from top:* Chocolate Nut Cookies; Almond and Cherry Crisps (page 208); Anzac Biscuits

Almond and Cherry Crisps

½ cup (125 g/4 oz) peanut butter
3 tbspns (60 g/2 oz) butter or margarine
¾ cup (170 g/5½ oz) raw sugar
1 egg
½ tspn almond essence
1½ cups (185 g/6 oz) plain flour, sifted
½ tspn baking powder
6 glacé cherries, halved
12 blanched almonds

MAKES APPROXIMATELY 24 BISCUITS

Place peanut butter and butter or margarine into a large microwave-safe mixing bowl. Soften on HIGH (100%) for 15 seconds. Add the sugar and cream the mixture until light and fluffy. Stir in the egg and almond essence. Continue mixing until well combined. Stir in flour sifted with baking powder to form a stiff dough.

Roll teaspoonsful of the mixture into small balls. Place six balls, spread well apart, on a large well-greased (or baking-paper covered) microwave-safe plate or baking sheet. Flatten each lightly with the heel of your hand and place half a glacé cherry or blanched almond in the centre of each.

Cook on HIGH for 1½–2 minutes, until cooked through and set. Allow to stand for 1–2 minutes to crisp a little before removing to a wire rack to complete cooling.

Repeat cooking procedure until all the mixture is used up. (See photo page 207.)

Meringues

1 egg white
approx. 3 cups (410 g/13 oz) icing sugar, sifted
(amount of icing sugar used will depend on the size of the egg white)
whipped cream
cocoa

MAKES 24 MERINGUES

Break egg white into a large microwave-safe bowl and whisk gently with a fork or balloon whisk only until light and frothy. Gradually add the icing sugar, a little at a time, working it in at first with a spoon or fork and then, as mixture becomes stiffer, by hand.

The mixture formed should be stiff, firm and dough-like, but still pliable.

Knead well on a surface dusted with icing sugar for 2–3 minutes until mixture forms a smooth ball. Mould into a long sausage shape and cut into 48 equal-sized pieces. Roll each piece of icing-sugar mixture between fingers and form into a small ball.

Place six balls, well apart, on a baking paper-lined microwave-safe baking tray or plate. Cook on HIGH (100%) for 1½ minutes.

Meringues will spread during cooking, so don't be tempted to cook more than six at a time. Also turn paper over or use a fresh piece of baking paper for each batch as the meringues will stick to the sugar residue left from the previous batch.

Cooked meringues should be well-risen, crisp and dry throughout. Remove from paper and allow to cool on a wire rack. Repeat procedure until all balls are cooked.

Serve sandwiched together with whipped cream and dusted with cocoa. (See photo page 199.)

VARIATIONS

Chocolate Drizzle Melt 3 tablespoons cooking chocolate chips in a small bowl on DEFROST (30%) for 2–3 minutes. Stir well until smooth. Pour melted chocolate into a piping bag and drizzle a little chocolate over some of the cold cooked meringues.

Sandwich one plain half and one chocolate half together with whipped cream.

Kahlua Cream Add 1 tablespoon Kahlua or Baileys Irish Cream liqueur to cream before whipping. Whip cream until stiff and use to sandwich plain meringue halves together.

Rainbow Meringues When kneading mixture into a smooth ball, divide into four equal-sized portions. Add a drop of pink, blue or green food

colouring to each of three of the portions, leaving one portion white. Continue kneading each portion separately until colour is even throughout and mixture is smooth. Cut each portion into 12 small pieces. Roll into balls and cook as above.

Peach Meringues Pipe or spoon whipped cream onto one meringue half. Top with a fresh peach half. Serve drizzled with melba sauce for a delicious dessert.

Caramel Slice

This delicious slice cooks well by microwave although the base is not as crisp as that of a slice cooked in a conventional oven.

BASE

½ cup (90 g/3 oz) brown sugar, firmly packed
1 cup (125 g/4 oz) self-raising flour, sifted
1 cup (90 g/3 oz) desiccated coconut
½ cup (125 g/4 oz) melted butter

TOPPING

1 × 410 g (13 oz) can sweetened condensed milk
2 tbspns golden syrup
¼ cup (60 g/2 oz) butter, melted
125 g (4 oz) dark cooking chocolate
3 tspns copha or butter, melted

MAKES 30–35 SLICES

Combine all base ingredients in a bowl and mix well. Press into a baking-paper-lined, shallow microwave-safe casserole approximately 23 cm (9 in) square. Cook on HIGH (100%) for 5–5½ minutes. The mixture should still feel a little soft but not damp. Cover lightly with a clean tea towel and stand until cool. If not firm after standing, cook a further minute on HIGH.

Combine condensed milk, golden syrup and butter in a medium-sized, microwave-safe bowl and heat on HIGH for approximately 7 minutes, stirring every minute for the first 3 or 4 minutes, then every 30 seconds until the mixture is a light caramel colour and appears to have curdled. (Beating well on these occasions soon returns the mixture to a smooth consistency.) Put 2 teaspoonsful of the mixture in a saucer and chill in refrigerator for a few minutes. When firm enough to cut with a knife without the mixture running together again, the caramel is ready. Pour caramel over base and spread evenly.

Melt chocolate, broken into pieces, with shortening for about 1 minute on HIGH, stirring every few seconds. When melted, pour over caramel. Chill if the day is warm or until firm enough to cut into slices.

Liqueur Fruit Slice

This dessert has a cake base with a subtle sweet cream. It can be made up to three days in advance and decorated on the day of serving.
For best results, cook cakes and puddings on MEDIUM (50%), elevated on a small rack. The elevation should be no higher than 5 cm (2 in). If you don't have a small microwave-safe rack or plastic cake cooler you can use an upturned saucer.
This helps give a lighter and more evenly cooked cake. Allow the cake to cool after cooking, loosely covered with plastic wrap, to prevent it from drying out. Substitute the liqueur with apricot, pineapple or orange juice if desired.

CAKE
3 tbspns (60 g/2 oz) butter or margarine
¼ cup (45 g/1½ oz) brown sugar
1 tspn lemon juice
1 egg, beaten
½ cup (60 g/2 oz) self-raising flour
1 tbspn orange liqueur
extra 2–3 tbspns orange liqueur
TOPPING
½ carton (155 ml/5 fl oz) sour cream
½ carton (155 ml/5 fl oz) thickened cream
¼ cup (45 g/1½ oz) brown sugar
2 tbspns lemon juice

DECORATION
selection of fresh or canned fruit
2 tbspns (60 g/2 oz) apricot jam

SERVES 6–8

Cream the butter or margarine, brown sugar and lemon juice until light and fluffy. Beat in egg, and fold in flour and 1 tablespoon liqueur. Spoon the batter into a greased 15 × 25 cm (6 × 10 in) microwave-safe baking dish.

Cook, elevated, on MEDIUM (50%) for 4–6 minutes or until slightly tacky on top. Pour over extra liqueur and allow to cool, loosely covered.

To prepare topping: Using an electric or hand beater, beat the sour cream, thickened cream, brown sugar and lemon juice until very thick. Spread evenly over the cooled cake.

Decorate with fruit of your choice. Heat the jam in a small bowl on HIGH (100%) for 20–30 seconds. Brush over the fruit and refrigerate at least 2 hours before serving.

● Liqueur Fruit Slice

Chocolate Fudge Brownies

When cooked by microwave, these brownies are more like a confection than the original slices. However, few could argue that there could be anything better to serve with after-dinner coffee than this fudge version.

185 g (6 oz) dark cooking chocolate
½ cup (125 g/4 oz) butter
¾ cup (155 g/5 oz) caster sugar
2 eggs
1 cup (125 g/4 oz) chopped pecans or walnuts
1 cup (125 g/4 oz) plain flour

MAKES 30–35 BROWNIES

Break chocolate into pieces and melt in a small microwave-safe bowl with chopped butter on HIGH (100%) for 1½ minutes, or until almost melted, stirring at 30 second intervals. Leave to stand for 1 or 2 minutes during which time the chocolate should have completely melted.

Stir in sugar and eggs, one at a time, beating well with a wooden spoon. Stir in nuts and flour and pour into a paper-lined 23 cm (9 in) square, shallow, microwave-safe casserole.

Cook on HIGH (100%) for 6–7 minutes or until the centre is just cooked.

Allow to cool completely before cutting.

Candied Citrus Peel

peel from 4 large oranges, lemons or 8 mandarins
½ cup (125 ml/4 fl oz) water
¾ cup (175 g/5½ oz) sugar

MAKES APPROXIMATELY 400 g (13 oz)

Remove peel from fruit, taking care to keep it in neat quarters. Wash thoroughly and remove any white pith that may be still attached. Put peel into a microwave-safe bowl and add water. Cover with a well-fitting lid or plastic wrap and cook on HIGH (100%) for 2 minutes. Reduce power and cook on DEFROST (30%) for 20 minutes, until peel is tender. Stir well. (A little more water may be added if it evaporates during cooking.)

Stir in the sugar and cook on HIGH for 3 minutes until boiling. Leave to stand in a cool place for 24 hours.

Cook peel in the syrup again on HIGH for 3 minutes, until it boils, then reduce the power and cook on DEFROST for 3 minutes. Leave to stand for a further 24 hours.

Cook on HIGH again for 3 minutes until the syrup boils and the peel has absorbed nearly all the syrup. Be careful not to allow the syrup to burn.

Drain the peel and spread on a wire cooling rack. Leave to dry out for 24 hours until the sugar coating candies.

White Christmas

250 g (8 oz) copha (white vegetable shortening)
2 cups (50 g/1½ oz) rice bubbles
1 cup (95 g/3¼ oz) desiccated coconut
1 cup (80 g/2¾ oz) skim milk powder
½ cup (75 g/2½ oz) icing sugar, sifted
½ cup (90 g/3 oz) raisins, roughly chopped
½ cup (90 g/3 oz) chopped glacé cherries
1 slice glacé pineapple, chopped
2 tspns vanilla essence

MAKES APPROXIMATELY 24 SQUARES

Place copha in a small microwave-safe bowl. Heat on MEDIUM (50%) for 5 minutes, until melted. While copha is melting, combine remaining ingredients in a large mixing bowl. Stir copha into mixture until well combined then press into a buttered foil-lined lamington tin. Chill until set. Cut into 2 cm (¾ in) squares.

Apricot Crunch

2 tbspns (45 g/1½ oz) butter or margarine
½ cup (125 g/4 oz) sugar
2 tbspns self-raising flour
1 egg
½ cup (60 g/2 oz) roughly chopped dried apricots
1 cup (45 g/1½ oz) bran flakes
½ cup (60 g/2 oz) roughly chopped pecans or walnuts
½ cup (60 g/2 oz) icing sugar, sifted

MAKES 24 BALLS

Place butter or margarine into a 2–3 l (2–3 qt) microwave-safe dish or casserole. Cook on HIGH (100%) for 45 seconds, stir in sugar, flour, egg and apricots. Cook on HIGH for 2 minutes until mixture bubbles. Stir well, then stir in bran flakes and nuts until all ingredients are thoroughly combined. Leave mixture to cool for a few minutes. Shape into 2 cm (¾ in) balls.

Place icing sugar into a plastic bag, add three or four balls to bag and gently toss to coat with sugar. Repeat until all balls are coated with sugar.

Chill for 2–3 hours before packing into boxes.

Date and Nut Brittle

1 cup (220 g/7 oz) sugar
½ cup (185 g/6 oz) clear honey
1 cup (155 g/5 oz) peanuts
½ cup (90 g/3 oz) roughly chopped stoned dates
1 tbspn (20 g/¾ oz) butter
1 tspn baking powder

MAKES APPROXIMATELY 500 g (1 lb)

Place the sugar and honey into a 3–4 l (3–4 qt) microwave-safe dish or casserole. Cook on MEDIUM (50%) for 6–8 minutes, stirring well after 4 minutes. On removal, ensure that the sugar is thoroughly dissolved. Stir in the nuts and dates. Cook on HIGH (100%) for 4–5 minutes until the syrup becomes a rich golden colour. Do not overcook.

Stir in the butter, then the baking powder until the mixture begins to foam and appears creamy. Quickly pour mixture into a 20 × 30 cm (8 × 12 in) lightly greased metal tray or baking sheet and leave to cool. When cool, break into pieces.

● *From left:* Coconut Ice; Date and Nut Brittle; Apricot Crunch

Home-made Chocolates

250 g (8 oz) dark, milk or white chocolate

PEPPERMINT FILLING
Mix ⅓ cup (90 g/3 oz) sweetened condensed milk with ¾ cup (90 g/3 oz) icing sugar, few drops of peppermint essence to taste and 2–3 drops green colouring.

APRICOT FILLING
Mix ⅓ cup (90 g/3 oz) sweetened condensed milk with ⅓ cup (60 g/2 oz) icing sugar and ½ cup (60 g/2 oz) finely chopped dried apricots.

CARAMEL FILLING
Combine ⅓ cup (90 g/3 oz) sweetened condensed milk with 1 tspn butter, 1 tbspn brown sugar, 2 tbspns golden syrup and 1–1¼ cups (125–155 g/4–5 oz) icing sugar.

MAKES APPROXIMATELY 40

Break chocolate into pieces or place chocolate bits into a medium-sized microwave-safe bowl. Melt on DEFROST (30%) for 3–4 minutes, stirring well after 2 minutes. Roll teaspoonfuls of filling mixture into small balls, or form into squares. Allow to set in refrigerator. Secure fillings to the end of a fork and dip into the melted (not hot) chocolate.

Place chocolates into small paper patty cases. Refrigerate until set. Use within 2–3 weeks.

Coconut Ice

It is important to use a large container for this recipe as the mixture bubbles up during cooking. Be careful also not to overcook the sugar syrup as the finished result will be too brittle.

⅔ cup (180 ml/6 fl oz) milk
2 cups (440 g/14 oz) sugar
2 cups (185 g/6 oz) desiccated coconut
red food colour

MAKES APPROXIMATELY 36 SQUARES

Combine the milk and sugar in a 3–4 l (3–4 qt) microwave-safe dish or casserole. Cook on HIGH (100%) for 5 minutes, stirring every minute until the mixture bubbles and reaches 100°C (200°F). Stir in the coconut. Pour half the mixture into a greased 18 cm (7 in) tin, allow to cool and place in refrigerator.

Mix a few drops of food colour into the remaining coconut mixture and cook on MEDIUM (50%) for 1 minute. Cool mixture slightly and pour over top of white coconut. Mark into 2.5 cm (1 in) squares and place in refrigerator to set.

When cold, cut into squares.

Sauces, Preserves and Beverages

One of the most delightful discoveries in microwave cooking is that many of the world's classic sauces can be cooked in a fraction of the time required for traditional methods. Mousseline, bearnaise and superb chocolate sauces, cooked by microwave, are indistinguishable from those cooked conventionally. Fruit sauces retain a wonderfully fresh fruit flavour which can never be achieved by stove-top cooking.

PRESERVES

The same basic rules for preparing preserves conventionally apply also when the microwave oven is used. Though the zeal for making up a batch of marmalade or pickles is not as evident today as it was in Grandma's day, more people are discovering that with a microwave oven the whole operation seems a less daunting task.

Flavours, particularly with fruit, seem to be enhanced when cooked for preserving in the microwave. Strawberry jam has been the outstanding success, with the flavour of the finished product being remarkably close to the wonderful fresh flavour of the uncooked fruit.

GET THE PRESERVING HABIT

Take the opportunity to turn small batches of fruit or vegetables into preserves when friends offer their oversupply from an abundant garden. You'll feel a great degree of satisfaction when you're spreading your own marmalade on the breakfast toast or offering the strawberry conserve with the cream to top the afternoon tea scones.

Remember that with some fruits you may need to have on hand a supply of commercial pectin — the setting agent that encourages gelling in jam making. Some fruits are naturally high in pectin — a lemon is the most common fruit used to help out the weaker characters in the fruit world. Check out our recipe for Strawberry Jam (page 222) and you'll see just how easy it is to whip up a vintage conserve.

BE PREPARED

Always keep back a few odd jars from the bottle collection just in case the urge to preserve overcomes you. Don't become too ambitious. Settle for a small operation if you're not a regular preserver. You will need to sterilise all jars and lids used for preserves. Boil the jars and lids completely immersed in water, in a large pan on top of the stove, for 15 minutes. Remove with tongs, drain and place in a conventional oven on very low heat with the door open just a little until both jars and lids are quite dry. Leave in the oven until you're ready to fill. It is very important that the jars be hot when the hot preserves are added (otherwise they could crack). Don't fill the jars so that the contents touch the lid. This is particularly important when making pickles and chutney which contain vinegar.

● *Clockwise from top left:* Quick Onion Sauce (page 219); Rich Plum Sauce (page 220); Apricot Honey Glaze (page 220); Tangy Citrus and Brandy Sauce (page 221); Pear and Ginger Sauce (page 220)

Bearnaise Sauce

For this sauce the eggs must be at room temperature. Do not leave the microwave. Watch and whisk often; at the first sign of any bubbles forming, whisk again. Whisk well again at the end of the cooking time. Remember the heat in the sauce will continue to cook the egg after removal from the oven.

⅓ cup (90 ml/3 fl oz) wine vinegar
1 bay leaf
6 peppercorns
1 tspn chopped fresh tarragon, or ¼ tspn dried tarragon
1 slice onion
2 tbspns (45 g/1½ oz) butter
2 egg yolks

MAKES 1 CUP (250 g/8 fl oz)

Place the vinegar, bay leaf, peppercorns, tarragon and slice of onion into a small microwave-safe jug or bowl. Heat on HIGH (100%) for 1 minute until the mixture boils. Continue to boil for a further minute until reduced slightly. Strain into a microwave-safe jug.

Add the butter and melt on HIGH for 1 minute. Stir in egg yolks and whisk mixture well with a fork or balloon whisk until well blended.

Cook on DEFROST (30%) for 1–2 minutes, whisking mixture well every 15 seconds until sauce thickens slightly. Whisk well and leave to stand for 5 minutes to thicken slightly.

● Béchamel Sauce

Béchamel Sauce

This sauce turns a simple vegetable or fish dish into a culinary delight.

1¼ cups (310 ml/10 fl oz) milk
1 thick slice onion
6 black peppercorns
1 bay leaf
1 bouquet garni
2 whole cloves
2 tbspns (45 g/1½ oz) butter
2 tbspns plain flour

Place milk, onion, spices and herbs in a 4 cup (1 litre) microwave-safe bowl or dish. Cover and heat on MEDIUM (50%) for 5–6 minutes until milk begins to bubble around the edges. Remove from oven and leave to stand for 15 minutes.

Heat butter separately in a 4 cup (1 litre) bowl on HIGH (100%) for 1 minute or until melted. Stir in flour and cook on HIGH for 1 minute, stirring after 30 seconds. Add strained milk, stir well and cook on MEDIUM HIGH (70%) for 3–4 minutes, stirring every minute until sauce boils and thickens.

Serve hot poured over green vegetables or mixed with leftover cooked meat as basis for other dishes.

Rich Tomato Sauce

2 rashers bacon, chopped
1 onion, chopped
6 medium tomatoes, peeled and chopped
(approx. 2 cups)
2 tbspns tomato paste
¾ cup (185 ml/6 fl oz) stock
½ cup (125 ml/4 fl oz) red wine (or stock)
pinch dried basil
pinch lemon pepper
2 tspns lemon juice
freshly ground black pepper to taste
2 tbspns plain flour

MAKES APPROXIMATELY 4 CUPS (1 l/1 qt)

*P*lace bacon and onion in a 1–2 l (1–2 qt) microwave-safe dish or casserole. Cover with a well-fitting lid or plastic wrap and cook on HIGH (100%) for 2 minutes. Stir in tomatoes, cover and cook for 1 minute. Stir in remaining ingredients except flour. Re-cover dish and cook on HIGH for 10 minutes, stirring well after 3 and 6 minutes, until tomatoes are softened to a pulp.

Blend flour with a little cold water and stir into tomato mixture. Continue cooking on HIGH for 2–3 minutes until sauce comes back to the boil and liquid thickens. Stir well. Adjust seasonings to taste if necessary.

Serve poured over hamburgers, fish or meat dishes. This sauce also goes particularly well served with pasta dishes.

Quick Onion Sauce

This sauce is a perfect accompaniment to barbecued meat or fish.

5 tbspns (100 g/3½ oz) butter
1 tbspn Dijon seeded mustard
4 spring onions, chopped
1 tspn Worcestershire sauce

SERVES 3–4

*P*lace all ingredients in a 1 l (1 qt) microwave-safe dish or jug. Cover with a well-fitting lid or plastic wrap and cook on HIGH (100%) for 2 minutes or until butter is melted and ingredients combined, stirring well after 1 minute.

Serve immediately. (See photo page 216.)

● Rich Tomato Sauce

White Parsley Sauce

1 tbspn (20 g/¾ oz) butter or margarine
2 tbspns plain flour
salt and pepper to taste
1 cup (250 ml/8 oz) milk
2 tbspns chopped fresh parsley

MAKES 1 CUP

*H*eat butter, uncovered, in a microwave-safe bowl on HIGH (100%) for 30 seconds or until melted. Stir in flour and seasonings and return to microwave. Cook, uncovered, on HIGH for a further 30 seconds, stirring once. Add milk gradually, stirring well with a whisk. Cook, uncovered, on HIGH for about 2 minutes or until smooth and bubbling, stirring every 30 seconds. (For a thinner sauce, add a little more milk.) Stir in parsley and serve immediately. (See photo page 112.)

Pear and Ginger Sauce

Here is an easy-to-make sauce, which is delicious hot or cold, served over ice-cream or fruit. It's also great with meat or poultry.

6 pears, peeled, halved and cored
¼ cup (45 g/1½ oz) brown sugar, well packed
1–2 tbspns preserved ginger, finely chopped
1 tbspn brandy
1 tbspn chopped toasted almonds

MAKES APPROXIMATELY 2½ CUPS (375 ml/12 fl oz)

Place pears, sugar and ginger in a medium-sized microwave-safe dish. Cover with a well-fitting lid or plastic wrap and cook on HIGH (100%) for 8–10 minutes, stirring several times during cooking. Allow to stand for 2 minutes. Mash pears well with a fork and stir in brandy and toasted almonds. Serve hot or cold. (See photo page 216.)

Orange Sauce

2 large oranges
1 tbspn cornflour
¼ cup (60 ml/2 fl oz) water
¼ cup (30 g/1 oz) brown sugar
1 tbspn Grand Marnier

SERVES 4–6

Squeeze oranges and strain juice. Blend cornflour with water and mix with orange juice and brown sugar in a microwave-safe jug. Cook on HIGH (100%) for 2 minutes, stirring every 30 seconds. Continue to cook on HIGH until sauce is thickened and bubbling. Stir in liqueur.

NOTE This sauce may also be served with pancakes — enough for 8 pancakes.

Cranberry Sauce

This sauce goes well with turkey, and also with ham or pork.

½ cup (125 g/4 oz) sugar
½ cup (125 ml/4 fl oz) water
250 g (8 oz) can or jar cranberries
1 tbspn sherry (optional)

MAKES 2 CUPS (500 ml/16 fl oz)

Place the sugar and water in a small microwave-safe bowl. Heat on HIGH (100%) for 1 minute to dissolve sugar. Stir in cranberries and heat, covered, on HIGH for 2 minutes, until cranberries are soft. Stir in sherry. Allow to cool before serving. (See photo pages 82–83.)

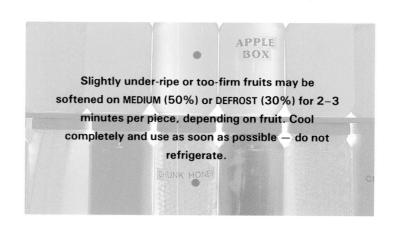

Slightly under-ripe or too-firm fruits may be softened on MEDIUM (50%) or DEFROST (30%) for 2–3 minutes per piece, depending on fruit. Cool completely and use as soon as possible — do not refrigerate.

Apricot Honey Glaze

This is a good glaze for roasts, meat or poultry.

¾ cup (185 ml/6 fl oz) thick apricot juice, or juice from 425 g (13½ oz) can apricots in natural juice
2 tbspns honey
1 tspn prepared mustard
½ tspn mixed spice
2 tbspns sherry
1 tbspn wine vinegar

Mix the apricot juice with the honey, prepared mustard, mixed spice, sherry and wine vinegar. Heat in a microwave-safe jug on HIGH (100%) until honey melts. Stir well to combine ingredients. Spoon glaze over meat several times during cooking period.

Serve meat hot or cold, garnished with apricot halves if canned apricot juice is used. (See photo page 216.)

Rich Plum Sauce

425 g (13½ oz) can plums
2 tbspns sugar
¼ cup (45 g/1½ oz) raisins
pinch each ground cloves and nutmeg
¼ cup (60 ml/2 fl oz) white vinegar
1 tbspn arrowroot
¼ cup (60 ml/2 fl oz) water

SERVES 4

Combine all ingredients except arrowroot and water in a 1 l (1 qt) microwave-safe bowl or jug. Cook on HIGH (100%) for 3–4 minutes until mixture comes to the boil.

Meanwhile, mix arrowroot with water and add to hot plum mixture. Cook on HIGH until sauce boils and thickens.

Serve warm with turkey or chicken. (See photo page 216.)

Tangy Citrus and Brandy Sauce

This sauce is excellent with turkey or duck.

3 tbspns meat juices, saved from the cooking pan
2 tbspns plain flour
finely grated rind and juice of 1 large grapefruit
1¼ cups (310 ml/10 fl oz) chicken stock, hot (made from the giblets of the meat, or use stock powder and water)
1 tspn soy sauce
2 tspns raw sugar
1½ tbspns brandy
freshly ground black pepper to taste

MAKES APPROXIMATELY 1½ CUPS (375 ml/12 fl oz)

*P*lace the meat juices in a medium-sized microwave-safe bowl. Add the flour and stir well until mixture forms a smooth paste. Add the grapefruit rind and juice, chicken stock and stir until well combined. Cook on HIGH (100%) for 3–4 minutes until liquid boils and thickens slightly, stirring once every minute. Stir in the soy sauce, sugar, brandy and black pepper.

Serve hot. (See photo page 216.)

Brandy Sauce

This is a great accompaniment to rich fruit puddings, particularly Christmas pudding.

2 tbspns cornflour
1½ cups (375 ml/12 fl oz) milk
½ tbspn (10 g/½ oz) butter
2 tbspns sugar
¼ cup (60 ml/2 fl oz) brandy

SERVES 6

*M*ix cornflour to a smooth paste in a 1 l (1 qt) microwave-safe jug with a little of the milk. Stir in remaining milk, butter and sugar. Cook on HIGH (100%) for 3–4 minutes until mixture boils and thickens, stirring well after 2 minutes to prevent lumps forming. Stir in brandy.

Serve hot. (See photo pages 82–83.)

Fudge Sauce

¼ cup (60 g/2 oz) butter
30 g (1 oz) cooking chocolate
1½ cups (345 g/11 oz) sugar
¾ cup (185 ml/6 fl oz) evaporated milk
1 tspn vanilla or brandy

MAKES 2½ CUPS (375 ml/12 fl oz)

*C*ombine butter and chocolate in a microwave-safe dish and cook on HIGH (100%) 1½–2 minutes, stirring after 1 minute. Add sugar, stirring well, then add evaporated milk. Cook on HIGH for 2 minutes, stirring once. Continue to cook 2–3 minutes. Add vanilla or brandy. Stir well. Store at room temperature.

Passionfruit and Pineapple Jam

Kiwi fruit or strawberries may be substituted for passionfruit in this recipe. These are all low-pectin fruits so all require the addition of pectin to aid setting.

410 g (13 oz) ripe passionfruit pulp
410 g (13 oz) pineapple, cut into small chunks
½ cup (125 ml/4 fl oz) water
3¼ cups (810 g/26 oz) sugar
½ tspn pectin

MAKES THREE 450 g JARS

*P*lace prepared fruit and water in a 3–4 l (3–4 qt) microwave-safe dish or bowl. Cover with a well-fitting lid or plastic wrap. Cook on HIGH (100%) for 5 minutes. Stir well.

Stir in sugar and pectin. Cook uncovered, on HIGH for 30–40 minutes, stirring well after 10 and 20 minutes, until setting point is reached.

Cool jam for 2–3 minutes before ladling into sterilised jars. Seal and label.

NOTE As passionfruit pips are light, they may rise to the surface after potting. Gently shake sealed jars of jam just as it sets to distribute pips and give a better appearance. (See photo page 223.)

Strawberry Jam

*Do not attempt to make large quantities of jam in the micro-
wave oven. Larger quantities require longer cooking time
which will destroy the remarkable fresh-fruit flavour of preserves cooked in the microwave. This recipe uses only one
punnet, or about two cups, of strawberries, but the wonderful fresh-strawberry flavour is quite unlike any result you'll
achieve with conventional cooking methods.*

*1 punnet (approx. 2 cups) strawberries
1½ cups (345 g/11 oz) sugar
3 tbspns lemon juice*

MAKES TWO SMALL JARS

Wash and hull strawberries, cutting in half extra-
large berries.

Place strawberries, sugar and lemon juice in a
large microwave-safe bowl. Cook, covered, on
HIGH (100%) for 5 minutes, then stir to dissolve
sugar. Cook, uncovered, on HIGH for a further 10
minutes, or until jam gels when tested, stirring
occasionally.

Pour hot jam into sterilised jars. When jam is
cool, seal and label.

Grapefruit, Lemon and Apple Marmalade

*1 large grapefruit
2 large lemons
4 large Granny Smith apples, peeled, cored and roughly
chopped
5 cups (1.25 l/1¼ qt) water, boiling
5 cups (1.25 kg/1¼ lb) sugar*

MAKES APPROXIMATELY 2 kg (4 lb)

Wash the citrus fruit and peel off the zest very
thinly, shred finely and set aside. Peel away the
pith and chop the flesh roughly. Place grapefruit
and lemon flesh and shredded zest, together with
prepared apples in a 3–4 l (3–4 qt) microwave-safe
casserole or dish. Cover and cook on HIGH (100%)
for 5 minutes.

Add the water, re-cover and bring back to the
boil. Uncover and cook on HIGH for 45 minutes.
Add the sugar and stir well until dissolved. Bring
back to the boil and boil rapidly on HIGH for
60 minutes until setting point, or a temperature
of 106°C (222°F) is reached. Stir approximately
every 10 minutes.

Leave to stand for 15 minutes before putting
into warmed, sterilised jars. Seal, cover and label.

Watermelon Conserve

*This unusual jam is an old traditional recipe, used in the days
when bottling and jam-making were the only ways to preserve fruit. Our modern version shows how it can be cooked
perfectly in the microwave.*

*500 g (1 lb) watermelon rind
1 tbspn bicarbonate of soda
500 g (1 lb) sugar
juice of ½ lemon
1–2 tspns finely chopped fresh ginger to taste*

MAKES TWO 400 g JARS

Cut the watermelon into strips. Remove the red
fleshy part and thinly peel off the outer green rind.

Prick the remaining white rind all over with a
fork and cut into 10 × 3 cm (4 × 1¼ in) strips.
Soak overnight in a solution of the bicarbonate of
soda and 1.5 l (1½ qt) cold water.

Thoroughly rinse and drain the fruit and leave
to soak for 1 hour in a bowl of cold water. Place
in a shallow microwave-safe dish and cover with
plastic wrap. Cook on HIGH (100%) for 20 minutes,
stirring and turning frequently, until flesh is tender
when pierced with a fork. Leave to stand, covered,
while syrup is prepared.

In a 3 l (3 qt) microwave-safe dish or casserole,
combine sugar and 3 cups (750 ml/24 fl oz) hot
water. Heat on HIGH for 8–10 minutes, until syrup
comes to the boil, stirring occasionally until sugar
dissolves. Gradually add cooked fruit. Cook on
HIGH for 3–4 minutes, until syrup comes back to the
boil; stir in lemon juice.

Place ginger in a small muslin bag and stir into
fruit and syrup. Cook on HIGH for 30 minutes, until
pieces of fruit are clear and syrup is thick. Remove
muslin bag.

Ladle an even amount of fruit and syrup into
sterilised jars. Seal and label. Store in refrigerator.
NOTE Smaller or larger quantities of jam can be
made by using equal quantities of sugar to fruit,
and 3 cups (750 ml/24 fl oz) of water for syrup to
each 500 g (1 lb) fruit. For example: 250 g (8 oz)
fruit, 250 g (8 oz) sugar and 1½ cups (375 ml/
12 fl oz) water.

● *Top shelf from left:* Strawberry Jam; Orange Whisky
Marmalade (page 225); Passionfruit and Pineapple Jam
(page 221); Grapefruit, Lemon and Apple Marmalade;
bottom shelf from left: Pickled Onions (page 226); Tangy
Tomato Chutney (page 226)

Apricot, Almond and Grand Marnier Preserve

This jam does not set firm, though it is delicious spread on bread and butter; it also makes a good topping for ice-cream.

410 g (13 oz) dried apricots
3 cups (750 ml/24 fl oz) water
juice of 1 large lemon
3 cups (750 g/1½ lb) sugar
1 cup (155 g/5 oz) blanched almonds
¼–⅓ cup (60–90 ml/2–3 fl oz) Grand Marnier (to taste)

MAKES THREE 500 g JARS

Place apricots and water in a 3 l (3 qt) microwave-safe casserole and cook on HIGH (100%) for 10 minutes. Add remaining ingredients, except Grand Marnier, and stir until sugar is dissolved. Continue cooking on HIGH for 35 minutes, until a temperature of 106–108°C is reached. Remove from microwave and stir in Grand Marnier. Pour into sterilised jars, seal and label ready for use.

Orange Whisky Marmalade

3 large oranges
1 lemon
1 l (1 qt) water, boiling
½ cup (125 ml/4 fl oz) whisky
2 cups (440 g/14 oz) white sugar
2 cups (440 g/14 oz) raw sugar
2 tbspns black treacle

MAKES THREE 410 g (13 oz) JARS

Coarsely grate the rind from the oranges and lemon on the large side of the grater. Place in a 3–4 l (3–4 qt) microwave-safe casserole or dish. Squeeze the juice from the fruit and mix with rind. Cut the orange and lemon skins into pieces and place in a muslin bag with the fruit pips. Tie securely and place this bag into dish with juice. Stir in the boiling water and whisky. Cook on HIGH (100%) for 20 minutes.

Stir juice mixture well, squeeze the muslin bag* tightly to release concentrated juices and remove from liquid. Stir in the sugars and black treacle. Continue cooking on HIGH for a further 40–45 minutes until jam reaches setting point, or 106°C

(222°F) when tested with a sugar thermometer.

Stir jam well and pour into sterilised jars. Seal and label.

*NOTE As the muslin bag is very hot, use rubber gloves or place the bag in a sieve and squeeze with a metal spoon.

Lemon Butter

½ cup (125 g/4 oz) unsalted butter
2 cups (500 g/1 lb) sugar
6 eggs, warmed to room temperature
finely grated rind and juice of 4 large lemons

MAKES APPROXIMATELY 1.5 kg (3 lb)

Melt the butter in a medium-sized microwave-safe bowl on HIGH (100%) for 2 minutes. Meanwhile, beat sugar, eggs and lemon rind and juice, preferably with an electric mixer, so that mixture is thoroughly combined. Gradually whisk in melted butter. Cook mixture in a 1.5–2 l (1–2 qt) microwave-safe dish on HIGH for 8 minutes, stirring every 2 minutes, until mixture thickens and coats the back of a spoon.

Pour lemon butter into warmed, sterilised jars, seal, cover and label.

Spiced Apple and Pear Chutney

4 apples, peeled, cored and chopped
4 pears, peeled, cored and roughly chopped
2 large onions, finely chopped
1 cup (185 g/6 oz) brown sugar
1 cup (170 g/5½ oz) sultanas
2 tspns coriander seeds
2 tspns ground allspice
¼ tspn ground cloves
1 cup (250 ml/8 fl oz) wine vinegar

MAKES 4–5½ 500 g (1 lb) JARS

Place all ingredients in a 3–4 l (3–4 qt) microwave-safe dish or casserole. Cover with a well-fitting lid or plastic wrap and cook on HIGH (100%) for 25 minutes, stirring every 5 minutes.

While chutney is cooking, wash four or five 500 g (1 lb) jars. Fill with boiling water and leave to stand. When chutney is cooked, empty water out of jars, fill each with chutney, cover tightly and label.

Store in a cool place. Chutney will keep for 6–8 weeks.

● Spiced Apple and Pear Chutney

Tangy Tomato Chutney

1 large onion, finely chopped
1 cup (250 ml/8 fl oz) malt vinegar
700 g (1¼ lb) ripe, firm red tomatoes, skinned
and chopped
1 large Granny Smith apple, peeled, cored and chopped
¼ cup (60 g/2 oz) raw sugar
pinch cayenne pepper
pinch dry mustard
2 tbspns lemon juice

MAKES APPROXIMATELY THREE 315 g (10 oz) JARS

*P*ut the onion and vinegar in a 3–4 l (3–4 qt) microwave-safe dish or bowl. Cover with a well-fitting lid or plastic wrap. Cook on HIGH (100%) for 5 minutes.

Stir in remaining ingredients. Cook, uncovered, on HIGH for 40 minutes, stirring occasionally until thick and pulpy.

Ladle into sterilised jars. Cover with plastic or non-metallic lids. Label and store for at least one month in a cool dark place before consuming. (See photo page 223.)

Fresh Mint Chutney

1 cup firmly packed fresh mint leaves, washed
1 onion, roughly chopped
1 fresh green chilli, chopped
1 tspn white sugar
¼ cup (60 ml/2 fl oz) malt vinegar

SERVES 8

*P*ut the mint into a blender or liquidiser. Process until fine, add onion and chilli. Blend again until mixture is fine, then gradually add sugar and vinegar. Process until all ingredients are well mixed. Refrigerate until required.

Tomato and Onion Sambal

1 large onion, finely chopped
4 tomatoes, finely chopped
¼ bunch fresh coriander leaves, finely chopped

MAKES APPROXIMATELY 2 CUPS (500 ml/16 fl oz)

*M*ix all ingredients together in a serving dish and chill until required.

Alternatively these three ingredients may be chopped all together in a food processor until final texture is smooth. (See photo page 162.)

Pickled Onions

18–20 small pickling onions, skinned
salted water
6 cups (1.5 l/1½ qt) malt vinegar
1 tbspn each peppercorns, mustard seeds and whole cloves
2 tspns each allspice, cinnamon and ground ginger
1 tspn whole small dried chillies

MAKES THREE JARS

*U*sing a sharp knife, cut a cross in the base of each onion. Soak in a large bowl of salted water for 30 minutes.

Combine all remaining ingredients in a large microwave-safe dish or bowl. Cover with a well-fitting lid or plastic wrap. Heat on MEDIUM (50%) for 8 minutes and remove from oven. Allow to stand for 2–3 hours, until cold, without removing cover.

Drain the onions well and place in sterilised jars. Strain the vinegar into each jar until all onions are covered with flavoured vinegar.

Seal jars and store for 2 weeks before use. (See photo page 223.)

Corn Relish

1½ tbspns cornflour
½ cup (125 g/4 oz) raw sugar
½ tspn dry mustard
cayenne pepper to taste
¼ cup (60 ml/2 fl oz) white vinegar
310 g (10 oz) can sweet corn kernels, drained
310 g (10 oz) can creamed sweet corn
1 onion, thinly sliced
½ red and ½ green capsicum, seeded and finely sliced

MAKES THREE 250 g (8 oz) JARS

Combine the cornflour, sugar, seasonings and vinegar in a 3 l (3 qt) microwave-safe dish. Cover with plastic wrap. Cook on HIGH (100%) for 2 minutes, until the sugar has dissolved and the mixture has thickened.

Carefully peel back the plastic wrap and beat mixture well. Stir in the corn, onion and capsicum. Re-cover dish with wrap and cook for a further 2 minutes. Allow dish to stand until mixture is cool. Stir well.

Spoon mixture into sterilised jars. Cover securely with plastic wrap, held into place with an elastic band or string, and chill until required.

Serve with cold meats and sandwiches.

● Corn Relish

Pumpkin and Yoghurt Raita

*½ butternut pumpkin, peeled and cut into 1–2 cm
(¼–½ in) cubes
1 tbspn cooking oil
1 tspn brown mustard seeds
½ tspn turmeric
pinch cumin
½ (125 g/4 oz) cup natural yoghurt
¼ bunch fresh coriander, finely chopped*
GARNISH
2 green chillis, finely chopped

SERVES 8

Place pumpkin in a medium-sized microwave-safe dish or bowl. Cover with a well-fitting lid or plastic wrap. Cook on HIGH (100%) for 4–5 minutes, until tender.

Heat oil on HIGH in another microwave-safe dish for 1 minute. Add mustard seeds and cook for 1 minute. Stir in cooked pumpkin, turmeric and cumin. Cook on HIGH for 2–3 minutes. Remove from oven and stir in remaining ingredients.

Serve cold, garnished with fresh chopped chillis. (See photo page 162.)

Tropical Fruit Whizz

*2 cups (500 ml/16 fl oz) skim milk
honey to taste
1 orange, peeled and quartered
1 banana, peeled
⅓ cup (90 ml/3 fl oz) pineapple juice
1 egg
½ tbspn skim milk powder
pinch grated nutmeg*

SERVES 2

Pour milk into a 1 l (1 qt) microwave-safe bowl. Stir in honey and heat on HIGH (100%) for 3 minutes, until it steams. Stir well to ensure honey is dissolved. Meanwhile, place remaining ingredients, except nutmeg, into a liquidiser or blender. Blend until smooth, then gradually blend in flavoured milk.

Pour into two glasses through a sieve. Serve warm or chilled, topped with a pinch of grated nutmeg.

● Mulled Claret

Tomato Pick-me-up

This is a delicious low-kilojoule drink for cool days. Drink it just before lunch to blunt a too hearty appetite.

*½–1 tspn Vegemite
1 cup (250 ml/8 fl oz) tomato juice
freshly ground pepper to taste*

SERVES 1

Put Vegemite in a microwave-safe mug, add 1 tablespoon of canned or home-prepared tomato juice and heat in oven for 30 seconds on HIGH (100%). Stir to dissolve Vegemite. Top with remaining tomato juice and heat 1½ minutes on HIGH or until sufficiently hot. Season with pepper to taste.

Spicy Hot Chocolate

*2 tspns cocoa
½ tspn ground cinnamon
2 tspns sugar
2 cups (500 ml/16 fl oz) milk
4 marshmallows*

SERVES 2–4

Blend cocoa, cinnamon and sugar in a 1 l (1 qt) microwave-safe jug. Gradually stir in the milk, until all ingredients are combined.

Heat jug, uncovered, on MEDIUM (50%) for 4–6 minutes, until milk just begins to bubble around edges of jug. Stir well.

Pour hot chocolate into mugs and top each with a marshmallow.

Mulled Claret

*2 l (2 qt) claret
1 cup (250 g/8 oz) sugar
juice of 1 lemon
4 cinnamon sticks
10 cloves
10 whole allspice
2 sliced oranges*

MAKES ABOUT 8 CUPS (2 1/2 qt)

Combine all ingredients in a large microwave-safe bowl and heat on HIGH (100%) for about 15 minutes or until hot, stirring occasionally. Strain if desired and serve hot. Return bowl to microwave oven for reheating as required, or heat individual serves.

229

Reheating and Defrosting in the Microwave

It is estimated that a very large percentage (up to 80 per cent) of microwave oven buyers, purchase their oven with defrosting and reheating food as their main objectives. It is unfortunate, therefore, that these seem to be the areas where most dissatisfaction lies.

Because of a lack of understanding and a failure to use correct power levels for these two processes, food is being spoilt and the microwave oven is being unfairly blamed. Generally speaking, if more thought were given to the methods used for reheating foods conventionally, perhaps the microwave owner would realise that fast reheating is rarely the way to go. Microwave reheating will certainly be quicker and more satisfactory than conventional methods, but it is still necessary to understand what happens to food when it is exposed to the excessive heat generated in certain foods when heated too quickly.

REHEATING

We all know that meat, poultry and fish especially are ruined when overcooked or cooked on too high a power level. Since reheated food has already been cooked once, it should be obvious that to present it at the table for the second time around will need special care to bring it to the right temperature without actually extending the cooking process too much.

START AT ROOM TEMPERATURE

If possible, food that has been refrigerated should be allowed to stand at room temperature for 10 minutes before reheating. This will help to achieve even reheating without drying out the food.

MOISTURE RETENTION

It is vital to preserve the desired moistness in all reheated food. This can be done in several ways. For a dinner on a plate, a covering of sauce or gravy will help where cut meats are involved (meats that are to be reheated should be sliced thinly). If no sauce is available, sprinkle over a tablespoon of stock before covering the plate with microwave-safe plastic wrap. Vegetables on the plate should ideally be of similar density and cut into pieces of similar size. Reheat on MEDIUM HIGH (70%) or REHEAT (80%) for 1½–3 minutes, depending on the type and size of food pieces and size of the serving.

CASSEROLES

Casseroles should receive special attention. It is very easy to turn originally tender, juicy meat into tough little nuggets with overcooking, and even easier to achieve this result when reheating the second time around. Keep the reheating for these dishes at MEDIUM (50%) or even a little less. At this power level you will achieve reheating without recooking.

NON-STIRRED DISHES

Foods that cannot be stirred or moved about in their container to encourage even reheating should be heated on DEFROST (30%). This would apply to dishes such as lasagne.

HIGH FAT AND SUGAR FOODS

Foods high in fats or sugar attract microwaves more quickly than any other foods. Undoubtedly, you have at some stage had the unpleasant experience of biting into a reheated pie or sausage roll to find the pastry barely warm and the meat filling hot enough to scorch the tongue! A quickly heated Danish pastry could give the same unpleasant shock. Reheat this type of pastry on MEDIUM HIGH (70%) and allow it to stand for a short time for the heat to equalise, with the pastry pleasantly warm and the filling no longer at scorching temperature.

DEFROSTING

The microwave oven enables us to defrost and cook food quickly, without any flavour loss, rather than thawing foods and meals hours in advance. This is a boon to working men and women who have to prepare an evening meal, singles, families with conflicting timetables, and for fussy eaters who have to have something different from the rest of the family.

Yet little is known about correct microwave technique for successful defrosting. How long does it take to defrost one chop or six? One slice of bread or the whole loaf? Simple, you may think. But how many times have you tried defrosting a piece of bread without heating it? Without care the finished result can be dry and as solid as a brick. Meat and fish can often be overcooked at the edges, yet still frozen in the centre.

THE DEFROST SETTING

A microwave with a DEFROST (30%) setting is obviously desirable — especially for those who serve food from freezer-to-oven frequently. But dishes such as casseroles or those that can be stirred can be thawed successfully on higher settings provided they are frequently stirred or the lumps broken up and moved to the middle of the dish.

Pies, puddings and large items such as joints of meat and whole poultry are best thawed on DEFROST (30%) which provides a more even thawing process. Thirty per cent power means microwaves are active for just 30 per cent of the time. The remainder is 'rest' time, to allow heat to penetrate and ice crystals to melt slowly, thereby preventing the food from cooking.

If you have an older oven which has only a HIGH setting, switch it to ON for 25 seconds and OFF for 45 seconds. When defrosting delicate foods or large items such as whole chicken or duck, switch ON for 1 minute per 500 g (1 lb) then let it rest for 10 minutes. Repeat this process for as long as necessary.

Poultry must always be defrosted very carefully to ensure that it is **thoroughly thawed** before the cooking process begins. (Even when the flesh is thawed, ice crystals can still remain in the bone cavity. These disappear with a thorough wash under cold running water.) If food, particularly poultry, is not thoroughly thawed, there is a possibility that during eventual cooking, some sections of the food may not reach the temperature at which certain bacteria, such as salmonella, are destroyed, therefore providing a health hazard.

QUICK TIPS FOR DEFROSTING SUCCESS
• Allow minimum defrost times — extra time can always be added if the food is not sufficiently thawed. Excess heating ruins the food.
• Always take special care with poultry. It must be **thoroughly** thawed before cooking.
• Pierce any skins or membranes before thawing to prevent bursting. During thawing (as well as during cooking) by microwave there can be a build-up of steam pressure in parts of certain foods such as chicken livers, brains, some seafood and fruit and vegetables. Piercing the skins or membranes with a fork or the tip of a sharp knife will prevent their splitting or bursting.
• Turn food over at least once during defrosting.
• If your microwave does not have a turntable, rotate the dish every 2–3 minutes during the defrost cycle for even thawing.
• Blocks of frozen food should be broken up with a fork during defrosting so that the microwave energy can work more efficiently.
• Separate blocks of frozen meat, like hamburgers, sausages and steaks as they thaw, to prevent cooking.
• Remove giblets from the cavity of poultry as it thaws. This speeds up the defrost cycle by allowing more air to circulate.
• Remove all thawed juice and drips from frozen foods during defrosting to prevent cooking.
• Open all cartons and remove any lids and wrappings before defrosting.
• If any parts of the food start to thaw out too fast or become warm, shield or protect these areas with small pieces of foil, if necessary attached with wooden cocktail sticks.
• Always observe a standing time at the end of the defrost cycle. Food will always continue to thaw with the heat produced by conduction.
• Home-frozen food tends to take longer to thaw out than commercially frozen food because of the size of the ice crystals formed. (Home freezers cannot freeze food as fast or to as low a temperature as commercial ones — therefore large ice crystals are formed that take longer to thaw.)
• When freezing a meal on a plate for a plan-ahead menu, do not overlap foods. Place the thicker, denser items to the edges of the plate rather than the centre.
• Remember that covering dishes helps to speed up defrosting.
• Most foods should be microwave-defrosted for a short time, then if possible allowed to defrost naturally. The best results are achieved if the food is still slightly icy when left to stand.
• Last but not least: defrosting times vary depending on the frozen temperature of the food, the wattage of the defrost cycle and the shape of the food. Always try the shortest times first and record your notes for future reference.

FOOD DEFROSTING GUIDE		
FOOD	**APPROXIMATE WEIGHT**	**DEFROSTING TIME IN MINUTES ON DEFROST (30%)**
Beef roasts	per kg (2 lb)	18–20
Lamb legs	per kg (2 lb)	15–18
Meatloaf	per kg (2 lb)	18–20
Pork loin	per kg (2 lb)	12–15
Minced meat	per 500 g (1 lb)	6–8
Steaks — thick	per 500 g (1 lb)	7–9
Chops — thick	per 500 g (1 lb)	7–9
Sausages	per 500 g (1 lb)	4–8
Meat casserole	per kg (2 lb)	15–18
Poultry — whole	per kg (2 lb)	8–10
Poultry — pieces	per kg (2 lb)	8–10
Fish — whole	per kg (2 lb)	12–15
Fish — fillets	per 500 g (1 lb)	4–5
Prawns — block	per 500 g (1 lb)	8–10
Quiche	20 cm (8 in)	5–8 on MEDIUM (50%) then 5–8 on HIGH (100%)
Cheesecake	20 cm (8 in)	3–5 on MEDIUM (50%)
Butter cake	20 cm (8 in)	3–5 on MEDIUM (50%)

NOTE All thawing times are approximate, taking into account a number of conditions — oven wattage, texture and thickness of food and methods of packaging for the freezer. Check thawing progress regularly, removing or covering with foil portions already defrosted. For large or dense food portions, even thawing will be assisted by allowing one or more periods of 10 to 15 minutes standing time part way through the recommended defrosting time.

Glossary of Terms

ARCING This occurs if microwaves hit some metal objects in the oven while it is in operation — discharging static electricity and creating small sparks. Metal containers, crushed aluminium foil and foil touching the metal walls of the oven are all possible causes. Arcing can damage the oven walls and in time the magnetron.

ARRANGEMENT Placing food in the oven to ensure it receives the maximum amount of microwave energy; for example, placing thicker sections of food at the outside edge of containers to promote even cooking.

AUTO-DEFROST Many ovens are programmed to switch on and off automatically during defrosting to ensure that food thaws slowly and gently. Follow the directions in your oven manual for this operation.

AUTO-SENSOR A device built into the microwave oven which automatically 'senses' the heat/humidity of foods to determine the correct length of cooking time. If your oven has an auto-sensor check your manual to see how it operates.

AUTO-START A special program allowing the power to turn on at a preset time.

AUTO-WEIGHT DEFROST Some ovens have an automatic program that defrosts frozen foods at the correct power level in proportion to the weight of the food.

BROWNING This refers to the colour of food after cooking. Because of the speed of microwave cooking, food does not brown naturally unless it has been in the oven for longer than 20 minutes; for example, roasting large meat cuts. A 'brown' look can be achieved by using special techniques and equipment.

BROWNING DISH This specially designed dish for microwave ovens browns meat, poultry and fish. It has a special metal oxide coating in its base which absorbs energy and reaches a temperature that will sear and brown food. Though expensive they are a worthwhile investment for any microwave owner.

BULB BASTER This very useful kitchen aid is available in most good kitchenware departments. A bulb baster is an oversized syringe invaluable for efficient extraction of unwanted liquid from cooking containers. It is particularly helpful during microwave cooking of meat where a build-up of juices in the bottom of a roasting dish can result in an undesirable braised effect. Expel the extracted juices from the bulb baster into a tall, narrow (rather than broad) container such as a jug or mug. Later the meat juices may be separated from any fat on the surface by using the bulb baster to syphon off the fat, leaving only the juices. If preferred, put the end of the bulb baster close to the bottom of the meat juices and syphon the juice until only the fat is left in the container. The bulb baster has uses in many other cooking operations. It is very convenient and much safer to be able to syphon hot liquids, particularly fats, from any container without having to remove food first, so the container can be tilted to pour off liquids.

CARRY-OVER COOKING Cooking that continues in food after it leaves the oven. It is important to remember when cooking by microwave.

DENSITY Refers to the porosity and/or thickness of food. Microwaves penetrate more slowly in less porous food resulting in longer cooking times. Porous food will cook more quickly.

ELECTROMAGNETIC WAVES These are converted into energy during microwave cooking. Also used in television, radio and radar.

MAGNETRON The most important element in the oven because it sends the microwaves into the oven cavity.

OVEN BAGS These bags, suitable for use in conventional and microwave ovens, have made it possible to achieve better microwave results with some of the less tender meat cuts. The moist, steamy atmosphere in an oven bag is particularly suitable for corned meats and meats recommended for pot roasting on conventional stoves. Oven bags should be dusted with flour inside before use and after food is added tied with the plastic strip supplied with the bag. Tie the bag loosely to allow steam to escape, or tie securely and make several holes near the top of the bag for this purpose. When liquid is added it is essential to position the bag so that the tied end is high enough to prevent the liquid from escaping. Foods other than meat may be cooked in oven bags.

PIERCING Making small holes in plastic bags or containers to allow steam to escape during cooking to prevent skins of vegetables or surface of egg yolks from splitting.

POWER LEVEL Settings marked on the front of the oven to indicate cooking functions — HIGH, DEFROST, etc.

POWER OUTPUT The wattage output of the oven. This ranges between 400 and 700 watts. Cooking times may have to be adjusted to get correct results for recipes in ovens of differing power output. The recipes in this book were tested using a 650 watt model oven.

REARRANGING This refers to moving food around in the oven to ensure even cooking.

SHIELDING Thinner parts of food that cook first risk being overcooked. Shielding is protecting these parts with small pieces of foil. Foil must not touch the oven walls.

STANDING TIME The time allowed after the food has finished its cooking time in the oven. Food is covered and allowed to stand to complete cooking. During this time it is being cooked by heat conduction, not by microwaves.

STIRRER FAN Some ovens are equipped with a fan which distributes the microwaves around the inside of the oven, causing more even and quicker cooking.

STIRRING Moving food around several times during cooking so that food in the centre of the container which cooks more slowly is moved towards the outside for more even cooking. Unlike conventional ways of cooking sauces, for example, constant stirring is not necessary.

THERMOMETER Some ovens have a built-in temperature probe or thermometer. Only thermometers made specifically for microwave ovens may be used. A conventional meat thermometer must be removed when the oven is in operation.

TOUCH CONTROL The computerised panel of controls on the front of an oven. Simple touch pads are used instead of knobs and dials.

TURNING If your oven does not have a turntable, it may be necessary to turn the dish inside the oven at intervals to ensure even cooking.

TWO-STAGE COOKING Two different stages of cooking for the one food. For instance a pudding may need to be microwaved on HIGH for several minutes and then on LOW or DEFROST for 20 minutes.

VARIABLE POWER This is a system of power settings that provides greater control of cooking to suit various types of food; for example, LOW for defrosting, HIGH for cooking vegetables.

VOLUME The amount of food in the oven. As the volume doubles, the cooking time, generally, is increased by one and a half times.

Index

Figures in italics indicate
illustrations

Acknowledgements

Weldon Russell would like to thank the following people for their help in the production of this book:

For the photographs on pages: 29, 37, 42–43, 49, 56, 62, 79, 82–83 (also on cover), 91, 94, 113, 121, 129, 140, 153, 164–165, 171 (also on half-title), 174, 179, 190–191, 199, 202, 207, 212, 216, 223, 224, 228.

Photographer, Rowan Fotheringham; food and styling, Carolyn Fienberg, assisted by Jo Forrest. Props courtesy of Bohemia Crystal Pty Ltd; Country Furniture Antiques; Gallery Nomad; Krosno Glass; Nazar Rug Galleries Pty Ltd; Oneida Silverware; I. Redelman & Son; Wedgwood.

Food for these photographs cooked in a Sharp Mid-size Autocook Microwave, Model R-4A11, courtesy Sharp Corporation of Australia.

For recipes and other photographs (R = recipe, P = photograph): *Elizabeth Affleck* for the following recipes: Banana Maple Cake (R), Boiled Fruit Cake (R), Cherry Cake (R), Golden Nuggets Filled with Spiced Vegetables (R), Lentil and Mushroom Pie (R), Mushroom Moussaka (R), Stir-fry Chinese Vegetables (R), Swiss Potato Casserole (R). *Andi-Co Australia Pty Ltd* for Escargots with Garlic Butter (R & P). *Australian Dairy Corporation* for Baked Lemon Cheesecake (R & P), Banana-Yoghurt Cheesecake (R & P), Choc-Mallow Swirl (R & P), Gingered Pumpkin Cheesecake (R & P). *Australian Pork Corporation* for Pork Roll-ups (R & P). *Rachel Blackmore* for Basic Steamed Pudding (R). *Brookvale TAFE* for Meatballs in Cream Sauce (R), Tagliatelle with Ham and Ricotta Sauce (R). *Canned Food Information Service* for Almond Pears Hélène (R), Passionfruit Crèmes (R), Plum Soufflé Omelette (R), Tuna Terrine (R), Tunabalaya (R), Veal and Pork Terrine (R & P). *Department of Agriculture,*

NSW for Artichokes with French Dressing (R), Kumara with Sherried Orange Sauce (R), Stuffed Kohlrabi (R), Sweet Potato Dauphinoise (R). *Fish Marketing Authority* for Potato-topped Fish Casserole (R), Kingfish with Herb and Lemon Butter (R), Lemon Mustard Jewfish (R), Ricotta-stuffed Trout (R), Scallops in Wine (R), Spiced Perch (R), Tropical Coconut Redfish (R). *GLAD Products of Australia* for Colonial Roast Lamb (R & P), Corn Relish (R & P), Dijon Trout (R & P), Mexican-style Beef (R & P), Muscat Quails (R & P). *Bernard King* for Beef Madeira (R), Fish Curry (R), Gingerbread Ring (R), Hearty Beef Casserole (R), Veal and Pineapple Casserole (R). *Kraft Foods Ltd (Consumer Relations Department)* for Seafood Ramekins (R). *Mushroom Growers Association* for Carrot and Mushroom Ring (R), Mushroom Quiche (R), Mushroom Soup (R). *National Panasonic* for Almond and Cherry Crisps (R), Beef and Cheese Roll-up (R), Cheese Fondue (R & P), Chicken Satay (R), Coquille St Jacques (R), Curried Pumpkin Soup (R), Fettucine with Pesto Sauce (R), Fruit in Rum Syrup (R & P), Greek-style Mushrooms (P), Cheese and Ham Croissant (R), Oyster Soup (R & P), Ham, Cheese and Chive Stuffed Potatoes (R), Roast Chicken Dinner (R), Pasta Marinara (R), Spiced Walnut Loaf (R), Veal and Pineapple Casserole (P), Watermelon Conserve (R). *Philips Consumer Products* for Pastitso (R). *Rowntree Lifesavers* for Festive Chocolate Gateau (R). *Sunrice Australia* for Perch Fillets with Saffron Rice (R & P), Pilau Rice (R), Pineapple Honey Prawns (R & P), Rice and Vegetable Loaf (R), Strawberry Cream Rice (R). *Sydney Market Authority* for Golden Nuggets Filled with Spiced Vegetables (P). *White Wings* for Broccoli with Piquant Topping (R). *Hilary Wright* for Souffléd Tomatoes (R), Stuffed Mushrooms (R).